Veröffentlichungen des Instituts
für Deutsches, Europäisches und Internationales Medizinrecht,
Gesundheitsrecht und Bioethik
der Universitäten Heidelberg und Mannheim **26**

Herausgegeben von
Görg Haverkate, Thomas Hillenkamp, Lothar Kuhlen, Adolf Laufs,
Eibe Riedel, Jochen Taupitz (Geschäftsführender Direktor)

Eibe Riedel
(Hrsg.)

Social Security as a Human Right

Drafting a General Comment on Article 9 ICESCR - Some Challenges

Springer

Bandherausgeber
Prof. Dr. Eibe Riedel
Universität Mannheim
Lehrstuhl für Deutsches und Ausländisches Öffentliches Recht,
Völkerrecht und Europarecht
Schloss Westflügel
68131 Mannheim
Deutschland
riedel@uni-mannheim.de

ISSN 1617-1497

ISBN-10 3-540-31467-9 Springer Berlin Heidelberg New York
ISBN-13 978-3-540-31467-7 Springer Berlin Heidelberg New York

Bibliografische Information der Deutschen Nationalbibliothek
Die Deutsche Nationalbibliothek verzeichnet diese Publikation in der Deutschen Nationalbibliografie; detaillierte bibliografische Daten sind im Internet über http://dnb.d-nb.de abrufbar.

Springer ist ein Unternehmen von Springer Science+Business Media

springer.de

Production: LE-TEX Jelonek, Schmidt & Vöckler GbR, Leipzig
Cover-design: Erich Kirchner, Heidelberg

SPIN 11660866 64/3100YL - 5 4 3 2 1 0 Gedruckt auf säurefreiem Papier

I am indebted to the following organisations who supported the workshop that led to this volume.

The German Institute for Human Rights

Friedrich Ebert Foundation

Centre on Housing Rights and Evictions

University of Mannheim

Eibe Riedel

Preface

This book emerged from presentations made at the International Expert Workshop on Right to Social Security in Berlin, Germany, 6-7 April 2005. Hosted by the German Institute for Human Rights in cooperation with the Friedrich Ebert Foundation, University of Mannheim and the Centre on Housing Rights and Evictions (COHRE), the workshop brought together academics and practitioners from the fields of social security and human rights and offered a unique opportunity for an inter-disciplinary dialogue on the content and scope of the right to social security.

Discussions were particularly focused on the right to social security in Article 9 of the International Covenant on Economic, Social and Cultural Rights. It is the shortest provision in the Covenant and one that has attracted less than its fair share of attention in scholarly literature and amongst the deliberations of the Committee on Economic, Social and Cultural Rights. But experience has demonstrated that the quality of the State reporting to the Committee improves greatly after the adoption of a General Comment, and with the recent decision by the Committee to adopt a comment on the subject, it seems desirable to help close the gap with some considered reflections on the topic.

The opening chapters of the book by *Reynaud*, *Riedel* and *Langford* map out the practical and legal challenges in recognising and implementing the right and the value-added in taking a rights-based approach to social security. This legal analysis is complemented by *Liebenberg*, who explores the innovative judicial enforcement of the right to social security in South Africa, and *Kulke*, *López-Morales* and *Nußberger* who chart the contribution that the ILO framework on social security could make to our conceptual understanding of the right. The remaining chapters take up various practical and conceptual challenges. *Mueller* and *Bakvis* analyse the push for privatisation of social security schemes, *Sinha* considers the rights of women to social security in India, *Bolderson* takes up the rights of asylum seekers to equal access to social security in the United Kingdom while *McGillivray* analyses the nature and reasonableness of cutbacks to social security schemes. The book concludes with an overview of the rich and lively workshop discussion by *Bierweiler*.

I am indebted to the German Institute for Human Rights, and in particular to Heiner Bielefeldt, Frauke Seidensticker and Valentin Aichele, for coordinating the workshop. I am most grateful for the generous support of the Friedrich-Ebert Foundation and to Erfried Adam for his personal involvement and encouragement. Special thanks must go to Malcolm Langford of COHRE for his competent and energetic assistance in the planning and organisation of the workshop and in the editing of this volume.

At the University of Mannheim, my warmest gratitude is extended to Alexia Bierweiler (Senior Research Assistant), who worked untiringly and diligently in editing and preparing this volume. She was ably assisted by Lukas Metzger, Dr. Dirk Hanschel, Jan Arend, Dr. Sebastian Graf Kielmansegg and Christel Selzer. I also wish to thank the Springer Verlag, Heidelberg, and Ms. Brigitte Reschke for her supervision of the publication.

Mannheim, September 2006 Eibe Riedel

Table of Contents

The Right to Social Security – Current Challenges in International Perspective

Emmanuel Reynaud*

Several international instruments affirm that every human being has the right to social security. They all were adopted between the end of World War II and the mid-1960s. The Declaration of Philadelphia, adopted in 1944 by the International Labour Conference, recognised ILO's obligation 'to further among nations of the world programmes which will achieve ... the extension of social security measures to provide a basic income to all in need of such protection and comprehensive medical care' (para. III (f)). The Universal Declaration of Human Rights, adopted in 1948, states that 'everyone, as a member of society, has the right to social security ...' (article 22) and refers explicitly to several specific rights (article 25). The International Covenant on Economic, Social and Cultural Rights, in 1966, recognises 'the right of everyone to social security, including social insurance' (article 9).

ILO's social security conventions constitute technical extensions dealing with the practical implementation of this right.[1] The most important of these conventions is the Social Security (Minimum Standards) Convention, 1952 (No. 102). It defines nine branches of social security and the corresponding contingencies covered: medical care, sickness benefit, unemployment benefit, old-age benefit, employment injury benefit, family benefit, maternity benefit, invalidity benefit and survivors' benefit. In addition, it introduces the idea of a general social security minimum level that must be achieved by all member States. To take into account the different national situations, it contains flexibility clauses in terms of the population covered as well as the scope and level of benefits provided. In other words, Convention No. 102 derives from the international instruments that affirm the right of everyone to social security, but at the same time it recognises the major practical difficulties in actually implementing this right in the various social realities that prevail worldwide.

Since World War II and the following two decades, where these important international instruments were adopted, the world has undergone profound transformations and social security systems are facing today multiple challenges. This

---

* Senior adviser on the Informal Economy, Social Protection Sector, at the International Labour Office (ILO) in Geneva.

1 For a clear review of these standards, see: Martine Humblet and Rosinda Silva, *Standards for the XXIst Century – Social Security* (ILO, 2002).

is true for the developed as well as for the developing countries. This paper begins by describing the main characteristics of the complete change of context that affects social security issues. Then, it turns to the challenges involved in adapting the existing systems providing social security. Finally, it deals with the dramatic lack of social security coverage that affects most countries in the developing world.[2]

1. A Complete Change of Context

The context in which social security issues arise today has changed dramatically since the post-war era when international instruments establishing the right to social security were adopted. This includes economic, social and political transformations as well as a doctrinal shift in mainstream economics.

1.1 Economic, Social and Political Transformations

During the past three decades, the world has undergone major economic, social and political transformations. These wide-ranging changes are multi-faceted and their combination created a totally different overall context. In industrialised countries, the wage earner model based on a male breadwinner in full-time employment has given way to a much less standard situation and, in developing countries, it has not spread to the extent that was expected; the informal economy has strongly increased in many of them. Concern over poverty and social exclusion has been significantly renewed, even in the wealthiest countries. Relations between men and women have undergone profound changes. Gender equality has become, during this period an increasingly important political objective. In addition, most industrialised countries experienced exceptionally rapid changes in family structure and marriage patterns, including rising rates of divorces, birth out of marriage and single-parent families. These trends also affect many developing countries, even if to a lesser extent.[3]

On a more global level, the period witnessed the collapse of communist regimes and the related expansion of the market economy. There has also been a re-

2 The meaning of social security is regularly questioned. There is no well-established definition. In this paper, social security is defined as the protection a society provides to individuals and households to ensure access to health care and to guarantee income security. This broad definition derives from the objectives laid down in the Declaration of Philadelphia. In addition, social security and social protection will be considered as synonyms (which is generally the common understanding, especially in Europe). To avoid the confusion between the objective (social security) and the instruments (e.g., social security institutions), it can be for example useful to speak of social protection systems that provide social security.

3 See: ILO, *World Labour Report 2000: Income Security and Social Protection in a Changing World* (ILO, 2000) at 32-34.

newed process of globalisation of the economy, which came about through the combined effect of policy decisions to reduce national barriers to international economic transactions and the impact of new technology in the sphere of information and communications.[4] It is characterised by the liberalisation of international trade, the expansion of foreign investment and the emergence of massive cross-border financial flows. It resulted in increased competition in global markets. This created new opportunities for the production of goods and services, but it also involved heavy social costs and introduced new and major instabilities. One of the most patent examples is the increase in frequency of financial crises in developing countries. The Asian financial crisis of 1997-98 showed that even countries with excellent past records of economic performance can suffer widespread social distress.[5]

Health disasters have also taken on a new dimension during the last decades with the development of the HIV/AIDS pandemic, especially dramatic in sub-Saharan Africa. Another change with a major impact in the field of social security is the ageing of the population. This is due to the combine effect of falling fertility rates and increasing life expectancy. In terms of social security provision, this represents an immediate concern in industrialised countries, but the issue will gradually spread as population is rapidly ageing in most parts of the world.[6]

By and large, the profound economic, social and political transformations experienced during the three last decades have created new forms of insecurity and uncertainties. This is leading to a growing sense of insecurity among people all around the world, including in rich countries where reference is made increasingly to 'social insecurity'.[7]

1.2 A Doctrinal Shift in Mainstream Economics

Parallel to these transformations, and strongly influencing them, there was a doctrinal shift in mainstream economics during this period. In short, there has been a movement away from Keynesianism, where economic and social objectives where seen as reinforcing each other, to a neoclassicism that privileges tight fiscal and monetary rules and open competition and where social protection expenditure tends to be seen as conflicting with economic objectives. This shift played a key role in the emergence of the current globalisation process. It also had major implications in the field of social security. In this domain, the recommendation deriving from the prevailing neoclassical theory consists in reducing taxes and social security contributions, shrinking the overall role of the state and fostering individual responsibility through the promotion of private arrangements. This thinking was

4 See: World Commission on the Social Dimension of Globalization, *A Fair Globalization: Creating opportunities for all* (ILO, 2004) at 24-49.

5 See: Eddy Lee, *The Asian Financial Crisis: The challenge for social policy* (ILO, 1998).

6 See: ILO, *World Labour Report 2000* (ILO, 2000) at 37-39.

7 See, for example, Robert Castel, *L'insécurité sociale: qu'est-ce qu'être protégé ?* (La République des Idées/Le Seuil, 2003).

influential in industrialised countries, even though the existing social protection systems demonstrated probably a stronger resilience than expected and public social expenditure did not really drop (in some countries it even continued to grow). Still, it was instrumental in determining new policy approaches, for example in the European Union, especially after the introduction of the European Monetary Union and the adoption of the Stability and Growth Pact.

In developing countries, the new neoclassical doctrine played a central role in shaping the economic, social and political development since the early 1980s. The World Bank and the IMF translated it into policy recommendations that they imposed on indebted developing countries seeking assistance to confront their debt crisis. This led to structural adjustment programmes that systematically downplayed the role of the state and had major implications for social security systems and the provision of health care, in particular in most countries governments could no longer guarantee access to free health care. The change in views with regard to the previous period and the pre-eminence of the new doctrine in development policies were so overwhelming that it was encapsulated in the idea that a new worldwide consensus was reached, the 'Washington consensus'.[8]

In the social security field, the shift in mainstream economics thinking had also a very specific and decisive influence on pension issues with the design by the World Bank of a new pension model, the three-pillar model.[9] This model became a new reference point and the World Bank has taken a leading international role in pension reforms (indeed, it has overshadowed the ILO which was the leading international agency on this subject during the previous period). Basically, this model allots a residual role to the state and a limited scope for solidarity (confined to the first pillar) and relies extensively on mandatory privately managed arrangements (second pillar), with special emphasis on individual savings accounts. This new form of social security has been implemented in several countries, especially in Latin America and Central and Eastern Europe. The World Bank made recently a critical assessment of the results achieved in Latin America and, more generally, of the assistance it has given to 68 countries in reforming their pension systems between 1984 and 2004[10]. In 2005, it also reformulated its multi-pillar model.[11] The major difference consists in the addition of a basic non-contributory component ('zero pillar') to alleviate old-age poverty.

The World Bank approach to pension systems carries a new vision of social security objectives limited to poverty reduction and consumption smoothing. This

8 For the initial definition of the term, see: John Williamson, 'What Washington Means by Policy Reform', in John Williamson (ed.) *Latin America Adjustment: How Much Has Happened?* (Institute for International Economics, 1990).

9 See: World Bank, *Averting the Old Age Crisis: Policies to Protect the Old and Promote Growth* (Oxford University Press, 1994).

10 See: Indermit S. Gill, Truman Packard and Juan Yermo, *Keeping the Promise of Social Security in Latin America* (World Bank, 2004); Independent Evaluation Group – World Bank, *Pension Reform and the Development of Pension Systems: An Evaluation of World Bank Assistance* (World Bank, 2006).

11 Robert Holzmann and Richard Hinz, *Old-Age Income Support in the 21st Century: An International Perspective on Pension Systems and Reform* (World Bank, 2005).

means that other objectives, which were previously considered essential (and which are still viewed by the ILO as being crucial), are neglected. These include protection against the uncertainties of life in a market economy, implementing principles of justice (e.g., redistribution and gender equality), strengthening social cohesion, promoting social inclusion and democracy. In addition, the influence of the World Bank and neoclassical economics thinking on social security issues led to the emergence of the financial institutions (banks, insurance companies, pension industry) as a new set of actors in the field. They represent extremely powerful and influential players and constitute a major interest group that can create a prejudicial imbalance in political decisions.

On the whole, in this totally renewed context, there are today two main types of challenges in the field of social security: to adapt the existing systems to the new risks and needs and to tackle the dramatic lack of coverage in most developing countries.

2. Adapting Existing Social Protection Systems to New Needs

In the industrialised countries, the current social protection systems were mostly set up and developed during the post-World War II period. The socio-economic circumstances today are drastically different. The economy has entered a post-industrial era, new risks and new needs have emerged and there have been serious concerns expressed with regard to the capacity of industrialised countries to maintain their comprehensive social protection systems, their 'Welfare States', in the future. Still, these have shown a strong resilience and have already undergone wide transformations since the beginning of the 1980s.[12]

2.1 New Context, New Needs and Main Transformations Under Way

The move towards a post-industrial economy has major implications for the functioning of social protection systems and social security needs. The emerging service-dominated economy creates greater inequalities and is potentially dualistic with the parallel development of high-skilled and low-end jobs. It produces substantial long-term unemployment, job insecurity, low-paid jobs, poverty and social exclusion. In addition, it leaves less scope for productivity increases, which were essential to finance social protection systems during the three post-war decades. Moreover, the process of globalisation has created greater insecurity and puts pressure on governments and companies to reduce labour costs (including social

[12] For a comprehensive overview, see: Hedva Sarfati and Giuliano Bonoli (eds.), *Labour Market and Social Protection Reforms in International Perspective: Parallel or converging tracks?* (Ashgate, 2002). For the priorities in the context of the EU, see: Gøsta Esping-Andersen (ed.), *Why We Need a New Welfare State* (Oxford University Press, 2002).

security contributions). It means increased competition, between companies (on costs) as well as between states (on taxes). The threat to transfer capital or production abroad to reduce costs is a credible and potent lever.

Relationships between men and women have undergone profound transformation during the last three decades. Gender equality is now established as an objective to achieve and changes in family structure and marriage patterns have created new forms of insecurity. This calls for adapting social protection systems that were based on assumptions about family structure and gender roles which do not reflect present reality (the male breadwinner model where the woman is a dependent undertaking unpaid caring and domestic work). In addition, social protection systems are faced with a demographic challenge related to the ageing of the population. Two major changes are affecting dramatically the financing of pension schemes: the baby-boom generation will gradually retire (starting in 2005) and life expectancy at the age of retirement will probably continue to increase steadily (about 1.5 year by decade). Population ageing has also major implications for the financing of health care and the provision of long-term care and home help services.

Moreover, social protection systems are confronted with new social aspirations. Notably, there are very strong expectations with regard to retirement, especially in Europe. This is due to the very existence and success of pension systems. Retirement is a major achievement of industrialised democracies in the twentieth century: a period of security and leisure outside of work available to many. There is also a growing importance given to individual choices and diversity.

Since the beginning of the 1980s, social protection systems have undergone wide transformations in industrialised countries to adapt to the new context. There has been a diversity of approaches, but there is still a common trend to emphasise employment promotion and to downplay the role of income maintenance, which was the key element of social protection in the previous period. This includes so-called 'active' measures (meaning for example training and life-long learning) to facilitate and encourage access to the labour market for specific groups, especially women, long-term unemployed and persons with disabilities; these measures being combined with reinforcing work incentives ('to make work pay' as it was summed up in EU policies). The extreme of this approach was implemented in English-speaking countries through what became known as workfare schemes, where working is a conditionality for receiving benefits. In other words, the right to benefits depends on the requirement to work to force benefit recipients into employment. In addition, several countries introduced minimum income schemes to reduce poverty and promote social inclusion.[13]

In brief, the current challenge for social protection systems is two-fold: providing adequate protection in a context of heightened uncertainties in the labour market and fighting against poverty and social exclusion, especially to avoid processes of entrapment in deprivation and exclusion. On the one hand, this means to reconcile mobility and protection, which has, for example, been encapsulated in the term 'flexicurity'. On the other hand, there is a pressing need to combine income

[13] See: Guy Standing (ed.), *Minimum Income Schemes in Europe* (ILO, 2003).

maintenance guarantee with inclusion policies and it should be stressed that adequate income maintenance is a precondition for any type of long-term inclusive strategy.

Moreover, social protection systems in industrialised countries are confronted with a serious pension challenge. Old age and survivors pensions represent the major public social security expenditure in almost all these countries and there is special concern with regard to their financial sustainability.

2.2 The Pension Challenge

To ensure the financial sustainability of pension systems in industrialised countries involves not only a demographic challenge (the ageing of the population), but also a labour market challenge. The prospect of population ageing should not overshadow the fact that a rising number of persons of working age are inactive. Employment is key in financing pensions. In all financing methods, pensions are paid out from the production of the working population, either through taxes and social contributions revenues or investment returns from bonds and equities. The different methods are just alternative ways for working age individuals to register a claim on future production. It is widely agreed now that both pay-as-you-go and advance-funded schemes are affected by population ageing and that there is no way out but to face an increase in the cost of supporting the retirees. The main policy challenge posed by population ageing is in fact distributional: how to allocate the rising cost of pensions within and between generations?

An overarching issue in the pension debate relates to the level of public expenditure. It is an issue of prioritisation between different policy objectives for public spending in a context of high financial constraints. There is a shared objective amongst governments in industrialised countries to limit public expenditure and this is coupled with strong pressure on labour costs (including social security contributions) by globalisation. This reduces drastically the flexibility in the pension debate to tackle the distributive challenge. To stabilise public finances, most governments are making efforts to shift pension costs off the public budget in favouring the development of supplementary private provision. But cost shifting to the private sector does not solve the distributive challenge of allocating the additional pension costs. It is the entire pension budget, public and private costs, which needs to be taken into account. Favourable tax regimes available to private schemes call for giving them explicit social goals and not have them, as is often the case, benefit the part of the working population that needs less support. Tax expenditure is an increasing means to finance pension and it should be an essential and explicit component of the pension debate. Moreover, relying on private provision can mean shifting the risk to the individual, especially in defined-contribution arrangements. The long-term implications that could arise are shown in the example of the UK, where the Independent Pensions Commission estimates that around 9.6

million people aged 35 and over in work are not currently contributing at a level required to provide adequate pensions.[14]

There is broad agreement amongst policy-makers and analysts that extending the working life by postponing retirement is a necessity in the long run. The case is made that it is a logical response to the fact that people are living longer. But in most countries it is politically extremely difficult to implement such a solution. Increasing the retirement age is probably one of the least, if not the least popular reform option. The situation is even more complex in that the issue is not only to increase the legal retirement age, but also to increase the *actual* retirement age. As of today, in many countries, a vast proportion of workers are no longer in regular employment when they get their pension paid. On the whole, there is wide consensus that solutions to the pension challenge should be sought above all through measures to increase employment rates, notably of women, older workers, youth and persons with disabilities.

In addition, the protection package provided by pension systems has to be redesigned to reflect the profound changes underway in industrialised societies. A main policy issue is to design a system which corresponds to upcoming security needs in old age. It is crucial here to adopt a dynamic perspective. Time is a key factor for pension issues. Tomorrow's retirees will have on average very different career profiles and family patterns than today's. The same generational life course logic cannot be applied to them. The pension system should reflect this change, and the protection it provides should be redefined to respond to the future security needs in old age of current young workers. This policy objective calls for a relatively long transition period for the gradual introduction of the new measures to take account of the generational differences. Moreover, a general tendency in recent pension reforms is to achieve more transparency with regard to the redistribution mechanism operated by the system. This increased transparency brings explicitly into the political arena the issues of how much redistribution, for whom and financed by whom. In that respect, two issues deserve special attention: gender equality, as women tend to be major losers in previous reforms, and the possibility of introducing an adequate minimum pension to respond to the tendency of the new service-dominated economy to produce more uncertainties and wage inequalities.

Special mention should be made to the partial privatisation of public schemes. Some countries in Central and Eastern Europe, which had achieved full pension coverage under communist regimes, adopted radical reforms in the late 1990s. These reforms meant scaling down social insurance in favour of privately managed individual savings accounts. This is especially the case of Poland and Hungary.[15] Early experience shows that this approach poses several problems and brings a new set of challenges. First, the individual savings accounts are built up

---

[14] See: Pensions Commission, *Pensions: Challenges and Choices: The First Report of the Pensions Commission* (The Stationary Office, 2004).

[15] See: Elaine Fultz (ed.), *Pension Reform in Central and Eastern Europe, Volume 1: Restructuring with Privatisation: Case Studies of Hungary and Poland* (Budapest: ILO, 2002).

by diverting a portion of existing pension contributions to the privatised tier. This creates a 'hole' in the financing of the public pension scheme, which must continue to meet the benefit obligations earned in earlier periods. The size of this hole is important, it ranges between 0.5 and 2.5 per cent of GDP per year for the next fifty years, and it raises the question of who will have to bear the burden. Second, although privatisation was promoted as a means to reduce state involvement, experience points to the need for governments to perform many new and complex tasks. Among these, a crucial one is to ensure that administrative charges are kept to a reasonable level and do not erode pension savings (the problem is particularly urgent as the charges are currently high in the countries concerned). Third, privatisation requires stable and well-developed financial markets as well as a properly regulated and supervised annuity market. Fourth, there are serious concerns related to the adequacy of future pensions, especially for women and low-income workers. Privatisation, combined with a more individualised public pension scheme, will increase the risk of poverty in old age for these two groups. This is a challenge that governments will very likely have to face in the coming years.

2.3 Reform Process and Democratic Participation

Adapting social protection systems represents major and very diverse challenges. Some measures have already been taken, but in most countries much still needs to be done. Emphasis is generally given to the technical aspects of the reforms, while the actual process of definition and implementation of the reform itself is overlooked. Yet it is a key factor, as there is no standard solution to the series of policy issues involved in pension reform as well as in other social protection areas. Each society needs to define its own way to respond to the various challenges posed by the adaptation of existing social protection systems. The quality of the reform process is crucial. This is especially true in the field of pensions.[16] Pensions play a very specific role in contemporary democracies. They are a major aspect of the security which industrialised societies provide to their citizens and they have to be guaranteed over the very long term. To avoid conflict between this long-term perspective and the relatively short-term political alternation typical of parliamentary democracies, it is essential for the sustainability of the system to arrive at a consensus among political and social forces. The involvement of employers' and workers' organisations, which embody the major economic and social interests at stake, is particularly important in the process.

By and large, in industrial democracies, social protection systems are potent instruments to make collective choices concerning the actual implementation of principles of justice and the concretisation of rights set in their constitutions. What is essential is to provide ways and means for making these collective policy choices and ensure wide democratic participation in the decision-making process. Social protection systems were developed in the last century to protect people against the harshness of market forces and they appeared to be a necessary ingre-

16 See: Emmanuel Reynaud (ed.), *Social Dialogue and Pension Reform* (ILO, 2000).

dient of a well-functioning market economy. This lesson from history should not be forgotten within industrialised countries, but it is also equally relevant for developing countries.

3. Lack of Social Security Coverage Worldwide

The key global challenge facing social security today is the fact that more than half the world's population is excluded from any type of social security protection. They are covered neither by a contribution-based social insurance scheme nor by tax-financed social benefits, while a significant additional proportion is covered for only a few contingencies. The situation varies among the different regions. In sub-Saharan Africa and South Asia, it is estimated that only 5 to 10 per cent of the active population is covered by a statutory social security scheme, most of these being old-age pension schemes, and in some cases access to health care, but coverage is tending to decrease. In Latin America coverage ranges from 10 to 80 per cent according to the country, and is mainly stagnating. In South East and East Asia, it can vary from 10 per cent to almost 100 per cent, and in many cases was until recently increasing. In most industrialised countries, coverage is close to 100 per cent, although in a number of these countries, especially those in transition, compliance rates have fallen in recent years. In general, it can be taken that only 20 per cent of the world's population has adequate social security.

3.1 A Growing Problem and a Growing Need

The problem of low coverage in the developing world is not a new one, especially in countries where large numbers of people work in subsistence agriculture. However, hopes that the developed country models might gradually spread to developing countries have been disappointed. The issue of lack of social security coverage has taken a dramatic new dimension with the growing proportion of the urban labour force working in the informal economy. In many developing countries, and particularly in Latin America and Africa, most of the jobs created during the last decade have been in the informal economy.[17] Today, informal employment comprises between one-half and three-quarters of non-agricultural employment in developing countries: 48 per cent in North Africa, 51 per cent in Latin America, 65 per cent in Asia and 72 per cent in sub-Saharan Africa (78 per cent if South Africa is excluded). If informal employment in agriculture is included in the estimates, the proportion of informal employment increases significantly: from 83 per cent to 93 per cent in India, from 55 per cent to 62 per cent in Mexico and from 23 per cent to 34 per cent in South Africa.[18] Informalisation is such a widespread phenomenon that the informal economy cannot be considered as a 'sector' as such. It

[17] See: ILO, *Decent Work and the Informal Economy* (Report VI, International Labour Conference, 90th Session, 2002).

[18] See: ILO, *Women and Men in the Informal Economy: A statistical picture* (ILO, 2002).

is to be found in all sectors. Informal employment is comprised of both self-employed in informal enterprises and wage employment in informal jobs. Moreover, informal employment is generally a larger source of employment for women than men (except in North Africa): 60 per cent or more of women workers in the developing world are in informal employment (outside of agriculture).

The paradox is that the lack of coverage is concentrated where social security protection is most needed. Here, the historical experience of industrialised countries is very relevant. The current situation in the developing world calls to mind the 'double movement' described by Karl Polanyi where, in 19th century England, the laissez-faire movement to expand the scope of the market was confronted by a protective countermovement, involving all groups in society, to resist the disembedding of the economy from social relations.[19] In that context, the establishment of social protection arrangements is seen as a protective reaction to the attempt of transforming human labour into a commodity. Today in developing countries, the traditional forms of protection provided by the extended family and the community have been eroded with the process of urbanisation and industrialisation. There is an urgent need for new forms of collective arrangements to ensure the protection of individuals who can no longer rely on traditional solidarity networks. This was well exemplified by the Asian financial crisis of 1997-98.[20] The underdevelopment of social protection systems in the three most affected countries – Indonesia, Thailand and the Republic of Korea (especially in the two former) – was a major element of the widespread social distress that hit these countries. It evidences that successful economic performance cannot by itself ensure the well-being of a society and the security of people. It calls for rethinking a model of development primarily based on economic development.

Even though the lack of social security protection is a wide-ranging phenomenon in developing countries, there are many attempts throughout the world to improve the situation and successes have been achieved in extending coverage.[21]

3.2 Experiences in Extending Social Security

A large variety of policies and institutions are available to extend social security coverage. Statutory schemes (i.e., social insurance, universal schemes and social assistance programmes) can extend existing or modified benefits to previously ex-

---

19 Karl Polanyi, *The Great Transformation: The Political and Economical Origins of Our Time* (Beacon Press, 1944).

20 See: Eddy Lee, *The Asian Financial Crisis: The challenge for social policy* (ILO, 1998).

21 The ILO publishes a working paper series on the extension of social security (ESS Papers), available on www.ilo.org/coverage4all. For general overviews, see: Emmanuel Reynaud, *The Extension of Social Security Coverage: The approach of the International Labour Office* (ESS Paper No. 3, 2002); Wouter van Ginneken, *Extending Social Security: Policies for developing countries* (ESS Paper No. 13, 2003); Clive Bailey, *Extending Social Security Coverage in Africa* (ESS Paper No. 20, 2004); K.P. Kannan, *Social Security, Poverty Reduction and Development* (ESS Paper No. 21, 2004).

cluded groups or contingencies. They may also enhance their effectiveness through improved governance and design. New schemes can be set up. Another option may be to encourage and support the development of micro-insurance and innovative decentralised social security schemes to provide social protection through communities, social partners or civil society organisations. In addition, various forms of linkages can be developed between the different schemes and other public policies, including a wide range of public-private or public-third sector partnerships.[22] Several examples can illustrate the variety of paths that can be followed.

The Republic of Korea adopted a gradual approach. It has extended health insurance coverage to the entire population in a period of 12 years.[23] It introduced the scheme to employees in large corporations in 1977 and increased progressively the coverage to other groups until 1989 where the last group, the self-employed in urban areas, joined the scheme. Tunisia also went through a process of gradual extension. It increased health and pension coverage from 60 per cent of the working population in 1989 to 84 per cent in 1999.[24] Costa Rica too is a good example of a progressive extension of health coverage through a combination of health insurance and free access to public health services.[25] Colombia illustrates a new strategy in the field of health that consists in subsidising the demand for care (health insurance arrangements) instead of primarily the supply (health services). It introduced in 1993 a mechanism which subsidises contributions for categories traditionally excluded from health insurance.[26] Brazil has reached remarkable benefit coverage among the elderly over the last decades. This is largely due to two basic pension programmes: a rural pension scheme (for persons with low or no contributory capacities in the rural economy) and social assistance pensions targeted at the indigent aged 67 or more and the disabled. Overall, it has been estimated that pension income in Brazil is lifting 14.6 million persons out of extreme poverty.[27]

In the recent years, a new type of scheme has attracted a lot of interest, especially in middle-income countries: conditional cash transfer programmes. The principle is to condition the provision of the cash benefit to behaviour, such as school attendance for children, regular visits to health centres and participation in different educational programmes. In 1997, the federal government of Mexico introduced, for example PROGESA (Programa de Educación, Salud y Alimentación) for poor rural families. The programme provided cash transfer linked to children's enrolment and regular school attendance and to clinic attendance. It

22 For a typology of the different possibilities, see: P.K. Kannan (ESS Paper No. 21) *supra* note 21 at 24-30.

23 See: Soonman Kwon, *Achieving health insurance for all: Lessons from the Republic of Korea* (ESS Paper No. 1, 2002).

24 See: Mohamed Chaabane, *Towards the universalization of social security: The experience of Tunisia* (ESS Paper No. 4, 2002).

25 See: Wouter van Ginneken (ESS Paper No. 13), *supra* note 21 at 14.

26 See: Emmanuel Reynaud (ESS Paper No. 3) , *supra* note 21 at 6.

27 See: Helmut Schwarzer and Ana Carolina Querino, *Non-contributory pensions in Brazil: The impact on poverty reduction* (ESS Paper No. 11, 2002).

also included in-kind health benefits and nutritional supplements for children up to age five, and pregnant and lactating women. It was fully implemented in early 2000 and covered then 2.6 million families, that is around 40 per cent of all rural families.[28] In 2003, the government of Brazil launched the Bolsa Familia Programme, which integrates previous cash transfer programmes into a single one. The transfers are made preferentially to women in each family and are conditioned to children's school attendance, use of health cards and other social services. The programme, which is supported by the World Bank, has grown exponentially since its launch: in January 2005, it covers about 26 million people. It is expected to cover about 44 million people by the end of 2006, at least two-thirds of whom are extremely poor.[29]

A completely different approach to the extension of coverage consists in community-based schemes, such as micro-insurance and mutual health organisations. These schemes are growing rapidly in many developing countries to respond to the priority needs of the excluded segments of the population, mainly with regard to health care, maternity protection and life insurance. The development of these schemes is especially important in Asia (India, Bangladesh and the Philippines) and in Western and Central Africa.[30] In India, for example, the Self-Employed Women's Association (SEWA), a trade union of self-employed women workers in the informal economy, set up in 1992 a social security scheme for its members. Today it comprises more than 100 000 beneficiaries and covers health care, death and property insurance. Another example is the Yeshasvini scheme which had been set up for the cooperative farmers of the state of Karnataka, also in India. It was introduced in 2003 and by 2004 it already had 2.1 million people contributing. The scheme covers surgical interventions in accredited hospitals and outpatient consultations. In Africa, the development of mutual-health organisations is a new phenomenon, but it has been rapidly growing in importance over the past few years, especially in countries such as Senegal and Mali.

These examples evidence the fact that the extension of social security is possible, even in poor countries. Still, the lack of coverage remains dramatic in the developing world. The widespread need for protection in developing countries is so important that it could lead to making a distinction between basic social security and contingent social security.[31] Basic social security would primarily take into

---

28 See: Emmanuel Skoufias, *PROGRESA and its Impacts on the Human Capital and Welfare of Households in Rural Mexico* (International Food Policy Research Institute, 2001).

29 See: Kathy Lindert, 'Brazil: Bolsa Familia Program Scaling-up Cash Transfers for the Poor' in *Principles in Action: Sourcebook on Emerging Good Practice* (Managing for Development Results, draft, 2005) at 3.3-3.13.

30 See: ILO/STEP, *India: An inventory of micro-insurance schemes* (Community-Based Schemes Working Paper No. 2, 2005); ILO/STEP, *Inventory of Micro-Insurance Schemes in the Philippines* (Community-Based Schemes Working Paper No. 1, 2005); Concertation entre les acteurs du développement des mutuelles de santé en Afrique, *Inventaire des systèmes d'assurance maladie en Afrique: synthèse des travaux de recherche dans 11 pays* (La Concertation, 2004).

31 See: K.P. Kannan (ESS Paper No. 21), *supra* note 21.

account the dimension of deficiency: the absence or inadequacy of basic capabilities to access to goods and services for a dignified life in a given society. The four realms of security that could constitute basic social security are: food security, health security, housing security and education security. Contingent social security primarily takes into account the dimension of adversity, that is contingencies and uncertainties arising out of life and work, such as ill-health, injuries and accidents, maternity, unemployment, old age, death of a breadwinner. In terms of rights, this distinction between basic and contingent social security calls for linking the right to social security to other rights, such as the right to an adequate standard of living, the right to be free from hunger, the right to physical and mental health and the right to education.

4. Towards Social Security for All

In 2001, the International Labour Conference stated that 'of highest priority are policies and initiatives which can bring social security to those who are not covered by existing schemes'.[32] Accordingly, the Conference directed the ILO to launch a major campaign in order to promote the extension of coverage of social security. In response to this request, the ILO designed a global campaign with the overall objective to develop awareness to ensure access to health care and income security to all. The Global Campaign on Social Security and Coverage for All was officially launched at the International Labour Conference in June 2003.[33] Within the framework of the Campaign, the ILO is presently active in about 40 countries. The main thrust of the activities undertaken are of three types: to promote the extension of social security through social dialogue, to promote and strengthen community-based social security organisations, and to strengthen the governance of existing schemes and the capacities of social partners to intervene. This implies to develop broad partnerships, particularly with other international organisations, donor countries and development agencies.

The international context is today especially favourable for the extension of social security. The fight against poverty has become the integrative framework for development aid, through the Millennium Development Goals (MDGs) and the Poverty Reduction Strategy Papers (PRSPs) approach supported by the World Bank and the IMF. Social security has a major role to play in that undertaking. Historical experience in industrialised countries shows that it is a powerful tool to prevent and alleviate poverty as well as an instrument for sustainable social and economic development. The needs in terms of social security are infinite and the means limited, so it is crucial for a society to define its priorities. There is no standard solution in this domain and the quality of the decision-making process is essential. The ILO is currently working on a new mechanism that will provide to

[32] ILO, *Social Security: A new consensus* (ILO, 2001) at 2, para. 5.
[33] See: www.ilo.org/coverage4all.

member countries a framework and a methodology to define and implement a national strategy for extending social security.[34]

The world has undergone tremendous changes since the right of everyone to social security has been established. The magnitude of the transformations affecting social security is immense. At its 89th session in June 2001, the International Labour Conference held a general discussion on social security to take stock of the present situation and confront the current challenges. The representatives of governments, employers' and workers' organisations reached at this occasion a new international consensus on social security.[35] The Conference adopted conclusions which re-affirm that social security is 'a basic human right' and provide a vision of social security in accordance with the needs of the time.[36] It is built on the Declaration of Philadelphia and relevant ILO social security standards viewed in the light of the decent work concept and the 2001 conclusions.

In a totally transformed world, the International Labour Conference remains faithful to the Declaration of Philadelphia. This re-affirmation of the right of everyone to basic income and access to comprehensive medical care is a call for action to pursue the actual implementation of the recognised right.

---

34 See: Alain Supiot, *Standards-Related Activities and Decent Work: Prospects in the Field of Social Security – Summary Report* (ILO, mimeo, 2005).

35 For the main elements related to this general discussion, see: ILO, *Social Security: A new consensus* (ILO, 2001), also available in French, Spanish, Portuguese and Chinese.

36 *Ibid.* at 1-6.

The Human Right to Social Security: Some Challenges

Eibe Riedel*

1. Introduction

The right to social security in article 9 of the International Covenant on Economic, Social and Cultural Rights (ICESCR) has not received the attention it deserves.[1] The Committee entrusted to oversee the Covenant has regularly asked questions on the human right to social security, but until recently, not in a systematic or fully consistent manner. This could be explained by the brevity of the article; it is the shortest in the entire Covenant,[2] and is formulated in highly abstract and vague language.[3] The Committee members consequently have not spent a great deal of time elucidating the meaning of that right, instead concentrating their efforts on other rights. Experience of 'Committee practice' has shown that the quality of questions put to States parties improves greatly, once the Committee has produced a General Comment on that particular article.[4] So far, eighteen General Comments

---

* Professor of Comparative Public Law, European and International Law and Director, Institute of Medical Law, Public Health and Bioethics, University of Mannheim, and member of UN Committee on Economic, Social and Cultural Rights.

1 United Nations General Assembly Resolution (UNGA Res.) 2200A (XXI) of 16 December 1966.

2 Art. 9 of the ICESCR states that 'the States Parties to the present Covenant recognize the right of everyone to social security, including social insurance.'

3 For an analysis of general criticisms levelled against economic, social and cultural rights, see: Eibe Riedel, 'International Law Shaping Constitutional Law. Realization of Economic, Social and Cultural Rights', in Eibe Riedel (ed.), *Constitutionalism – Old Concepts, New Worlds. German Contributions to the VIth World Congress of the International Association of Constitutional Law* (Berliner Wissenschafts-Verlag, 2005) 105-121.

4 See generally: Eibe Riedel, 'The Examination of State Reports', in Eckart Klein (ed.), *The Monitoring System of Human Rights Treaty Obligations* (Berlin Verlag Arno Spitz, 1998), 95-105; Eibe Riedel, 'Der Internationale Pakt über wirtschaftliche, soziale und kulturelle Rechte (ICESCR)', in Ulrich Becker (ed.), *Implementierung internationaler Sozialstandards und –rechte (IISR)* (in print). On General Comments, see Eibe Riedel,

have been produced in the last fifteen years, and several more are in the pipeline, for example on article 2(2) (non-discrimination), and 15(1)(a) and (b) (right to culture) to name but a few. And, of course, the quality of the State reports has also improved as a result of such General Comments. The same applies to non-governmental organisations (NGOs) at the national and international levels when drafting alternative or shadow reports.

Social security and insurance issues have, however, sometimes been raised in other General Comments, en passant, such as in General Comments on older persons, persons with disabilities, housing, food, education, health and water.[5] The biggest obstacle to a more in-depth and comprehensive analysis of article 9 has been the feeling that when one opens the lid of this article, one opens a Pandora box, or at least a singularly involved and highly technical scenario that few of the Committee members profess to be expert in. There is also the feeling that as the International Labour Organization (ILO) has been working in this field for at least half a century, it would look dilettante if the Committee started systematic work on its own. For this reason alone, the Berlin workshop that led to this book, and the increased cooperation amongst Committee members who are experts on the topic, will prove to be most useful and helpful in developing a future General Comment on the topic.

2. Social security in historical perspective

A few introductory words about the right to social security will follow, before the challenges will be discussed.[6] As is well-known, it was the industrial revolution of

'Kurzeinführung', in Deutsches Institut für Menschenrechte (ed.), *Die General Comments zu den VN-Menschenrechtsverträgen* (Nomos, 2005), 160-171.

5 Committee on Economic, Social and Cultural Rights, General Comment No. 6, The economic, social and cultural rights of older persons, (Thirteenth session, 1995), U.N. Doc. E/1996/22 at 20 (1996); General Comment No. 5, Persons with disabilities, (Eleventh session, 1994), U.N. Doc E/1995/22 at 19 (1995); General Comment No. 4, The right to adequate housing, (Sixth session, 1991), U.N. Doc. E/1992/23, annex III at 114 (1991); General Comment No. 7, Forced evictions, and the right to adequate housing, (Sixteenth session, 1997), U.N. Doc. E/1998/22, annex IV at 113 (1997); General Comment No. 12, Right to adequate food (art 11 of the Covenant) (Twentieth session, 1999), UN doc. E/C.12/1999/5 (1999); General Comment No. 13, The right to education (Twenty-first session, 1999), U.N. Doc. E/C.12/1999/10 (1999); General Comment No. 14, The right to the highest attainable standard of health (art 12 of the Covenant) (Twenty-second session, 2000), UN doc.E/C.12/2000/4 (2000); General Comment No. 15 The right to water (arts 11 & 12 of the Covenant) (Twenty-ninth session 2002), UN doc. E/C. 12/2002/11 (2003). Full text versions of all General Comments of the Committee can be accessed via www.ohchr.org/english/bodies/cescr/comments.htm.

6 See generally: Jef van Langendonck, 'The Right to Social Security and Allied Rights', in Franz Ruland, Bernd Baron von Maydell and Hans-Jürgen Papier (eds.), *Verfassung, Theorie und Praxis des Sozialstaats: Festschrift für Hans F. Zacher zum 70. Ge-*

the nineteenth century that changed agrarian societies into urban settlements, bringing in its wake a great deal of personal hardships, economic instability, as Charles Dickens in his famous novels has so brilliantly outlined. But Karl Marx and Friedrich Engels also left their imprint on the latter half of the nineteenth century, and with their social pathos criticised increasing poverty, exploitation and general economic insecurity for the marginalised and disadvantaged groups of society, singling out children working in the mines, the lack of social protection for the sick, old, disabled and orphaned.[7] The social democrats, in their turn, initiated the group rights movement to institute what we now call rights of the second generation; particularly rights in work and social security.[8]

But it was Otto von Bismarck as German Chancellor, who in 1883-84, in order to quell socialist support and to pacify public unrest, set up a system of social security, which has since been copied by many developed states. The 'Reichsversicherungsordnung', or Social Security Code, was an impressive model of legislation, that proved to be highly successful and influential long after Bismarcks's death. It outlived the 'First Reich', the Weimar Republic, Hitler's Third Reich, and the two Germanys after 1949.[9] The basic idea was simple: workers and employers would each pay contributions, in order to finance workers' compensation and sickness benefits by way of sickness insurance. Later this system was supplemented by old-age insurance, which was partly financed through taxation[10].

Other States have since developed various modalities of social security, ranging from contribution-based, employment-focused schemes, to welfare or social assistance components paid for by the state, such as the welfare state model elaborated by Aneurin Bevin in the United Kingdom, to mixed models of financing, and sectoral sub-systems. Social security benefits were generally reserved for workers and their families, and were therefore regarded as 'earned social security benefits', while other individuals or groups, not in a position to earn their living, would re-

---

burtstag (C.F. Müller Verlag, 1998), 477-488; *Bertram Schulin*, 'Techniken und Instrumente sozialer Sicherheit', in Bernd Baron von Maydell, Eva-Maria Hohnerlein (eds.), *Die Umgestaltung der Systeme sozialer Sicherheit in den Staaten Mittel- und Osteuropas* (Duncker & Humblot, 1993), 173 et seq.; Betram Schulin (ed.), *Sozialgesetzbuch*, (Beck, 33rd editon, 2006) IX-XLVIII.

7 See: Friedrich Engels, 'Die Lage der arbeitenden Klasse in England', in *Marx-Engels-Werke*, Vol. 2 (1972), 225-506.

8 See, for example, Asbjørn Eide and Allan Rosas, 'Economic, Social and Cultural Rights: A Universal Challenge', in Asbjørn Eide, Catarina Krause and Allan Rosas (eds.), *Economic, Social and Cultural Rights: A textbook* (Martinus Nijhoff Publishers, 2001), 3-7 at 4.

9 Guy Perrin, 'L'assurance socials – ses particularités – son rôle dans le passé, le présent et l'avenir', in Peter A. Köhler and Hans F. Zacher (eds.), *Beiträge zur Geschichte und aktueller Situation der Sozialversicherung* (Duncker & Humblot, 1983), 29 et seq.

10 See: Margaret S. Gordon, *Social Security Policies in Industrial Countries* (Cambridge University Press, 1988), 134 et seq.; Martin Scheinin, 'The Right to Social Security', in Asbjørn Eide, Catarina Krause and Allan Rosas, *supra* note 8, 211-221 at 211 et seq.

ceive needs-based social assistance from public funds, raised through tax revenues, and usually distributed at the local level.
The literature relating to social security offers dozens of typologies and definitions,[11] and I will therefore single out a couple of most frequently cited definitions:

Schulin[12] defines social security as an individual's possibility to lead a life in human dignity – based on a reliable living basis. Some authors regard social security as referring to protection against situations of hardship or needs, to provide protection for the foundations of life.

Others opt for a functional analysis and postulate that social security is provided in order to enable an individual or group to lead an adequate life in dignity, and elaborate concrete areas of application which includes health care. All those participating in work and employment should receive pensions at the end of their active work period, and in cases of work interruption due to disease, accidents, maternity, invalidity or unemployment such payments should be provided.[13]

Franz and Keebet von Benda-Beckmann[14] widen the definition to include all institutions which provide members of society who are not in a position to look after themselves, with food, housing, health care, education and protection by way of social assistance.[15] Referring to Article 1 of the German Social Code, social security is defined by *Bauer*[16] as an attempt to realise social justice and social protection for a life in dignity, based on equal access, free development of one's personality, free choice of workplace, and to be able to meet the challenges of life by self-reliance.[17] Still others stress the target to guarantee for each individual the so-called "existence minimum", and to reduce poverty, create more equality of treatment, guaranteeing security and allowing each individual to have his/her share in the wealth of society[18]. By using the word 'social' as a prefix to "security", the emphasis is on that task being transferred from the shoulders of individuals to the community – at large -, thus signifying 'solidarity'.

---

[11] For an overview see: Christoph Steiner, *Das Recht auf soziale Gesundheitsversorgung* (Peter Lang, 2004), at 57 et seq.

[12] See: Bertram Schulin, *supra* note 6 at IX et seq.; Bertram Schulin/Gerhard Igl, *Sozialrecht* (Werner Verlag, 2002), marginal note 9.

[13] Jef van Langendonck, *supra* note 6, at 486.

[14] Franz and Keebet von Benda-Beckmann, 'Rural Populations, Social Security and Legal Pluralism in the Central Moluccas of Eastern Indonesia', in John Dixon and Robert P. Scheurell (eds.), *Social Security Programs: A cross-cultural perspective* (Greenwood Press, 1995), 75 et seq., at 79.

[15] The inclusion of social assistance is persuasively argued for by Franz and Keebet von Benda-Beckmann, ibid.

[16] Rudolph Bauer, *Lexikon des Sozial- und Gesundheitswesens, vol. 3* (R. Oldenbourg Verlag, 1992) at 1806.

[17] Christoph Steiner, *supra* note 11, at 59.

[18] Bernd Baron von Maydell, 'Fundamental approaches and concepts of social security', in Roger Blanpain (ed.), *Law in motion – International Encyclopedia of Laws, World Law Conference* (Kluwer Law International, 1997), 1029-1058, at 1039 et seq.

Social security, in all variants mentioned, thus embraces community action in solidarity, by which living conditions will be improved, while at the same time avoiding very low standards.[19]

If one summarises the various definitional attempts, three particular linkages can be discerned: Social security definitions frequently concern access to health care (i. e. art. 12 ICESCR), to work (arts. 6-8 ICESCR) and to an adequate standard of living (art. 11 ICESCR). Social security, thus understood, means the guarantee of a conceivably constant level of standard of living above a minimum level, largely geared towards restitution of the capacity to work, by means of social insurance and social assistance. As soon as workplaces are mentioned, insurance models usually come up with the need for payment of premiums, and the capacity to pay for contributions usually is linked to employment. Where this precondition is lacking, social assistance comes to the fore, in order to prevent people from becoming destitute. Von Maydell has characterised this as an approach giving each member of society, irrespective of whether that person contributes actively or passively, a share in the general material welfare of a particular state.[20]

3. Social security in the Social Covenant

If one examines the travaux préparatoires for the ICESCR, one finds that originally the draft text said 'the States parties recognize the right of everyone to social security.' Later the Soviet Union suggested widening the text to embrace 'and to social insurance, the cost of which should be borne by the state or the employer'. Syria proposed adding to this the wording 'or both of them jointly'. Afghanistan suggested the additional rider: 'in accordance with the organization and resources of each state'. Although there was majority consensus that social security embraces social insurance, it was finally decided to explicitly add 'including social insurance' to the text. The Afghani suggestion was rejected on the ground that that point was already covered under Article 2 (1) ICESCR.

The Third Committee and the General Assembly (GA) ultimately opted for the very wide wording of article 9, without giving specific descriptions of individual elements of social security, thus highlighting the comprehensive nature of the right. The drafters clearly were of the opinion that article 9 would have to be seen in conjunction with Articles 22 and 25 of the Universal Declaration of Human Rights (UDHR),[21] and in particular ILO Convention No. 102, Social Security (Minimum Standards) Convention of 1952.[22] The ILO Convention 102[23] offers a

19 Christoph Steiner, *supra* note 11, at 59.

20 Bernd Baron von Maydell, *supra* note 18, at 1039 et seq.

21 United Nations General Assembly Res. 217 A III.

22 See: Jef van Langendonck, *supra* note 6, at 480; Martin Scheinin, *supra* note 10, at 214; Bård-Anders Andreassen, 'Article 22', in Gudmundur Alfredsson and Asbjørn Eide (eds.), *Universal Declaration of Human Rights – A common standard of achievement* (Martinus Nijhoff Publishers, 1999), 453-488, at 469 et seq.; General Assembly Offi-

full menu of social security instruments which covers most of the types of social security modalities to be found, namely nine specific branches of social security: (1) medical care; (2) sickness benefit; (3) unemployment benefit; (4) old-age benefit; (5) employment injury benefit (6) family benefit (7) maternity benefit (8) invalidity benefit, and (9) survivors' benefit.

These specific branches of social security should be seen in the context of the ILO tripartite system, and the general focus is on work-related risks and contingencies, although a number of them extend beyond that. The Article 9 of the ICESCR formulation is potentially wider. But the Committee, not having outlined independently the normative content of Article 9, has in practice raised many questions based on the definition of the right in ILO Convention 102. This is partly because the ILO regularly gives valuable information concerning particular countries' performance in those social security branches, enabling Committee members to ask more poignant questions. Moreover, in the Revised Reporting Guidelines, dating back to 1991, eight separate types of questions are listed on which States parties should report:

1. If the State party has joined ILO-Convention 102, and subsequent ones (121, 128, 130 and 168) and has submitted reports to the supervisory committees of ILO, then those findings should be included in the State party report.
2. The nine special branches of social security are listed and the State party is requested to indicate which ones they have adopted.
3. Data is requested on the comprehensiveness of coverage, both at an aggregate level and with respect to different groups within society, the nature and level of benefits, and the method of financing the schemes.
4. Additional data is requested in relation to the percentage of the Gross Domestic Product (GDP) devoted to social security at the national and/or regional level.
5. The State party should report on whether the social security schemes are supplemented by any informal (private) arrangements.
6. The issue of marginalisation of groups is addressed, and in particular, the situation of women. The Committee asks States parties to report on by policy measures or by targeted measures to improve the situation of the vulnerable and disadvantaged groups of society.
7. Legislative, judicial and administrative changes are to be reported upon.
8. The role of international assistance regarding Art. 9 is raised.

This catalogue of questions already shows that the CESCR clearly takes a very broad and comprehensive approach regarding social security under Article 9.

---

cial Records (GAOR), 11th Session, 1956/57, 3rd Committee, 727th meeting, paras. 10, 25, 33; 728th meeting, para. 6; Commission on Human Rights, UN-Doc. E/CN.4/669, at 17, paras. 117, 118.

[23] For full text versions of this and all other ILO Conventions see: www.ilo.org/ilolex/english/convdisp2.htm.

4. Social security and the Universal Declaration of Human Rights

If one also analyses articles 22 and 25 of the Universal Declaration of Human Rights (UDHR), this approach by the Committee finds support. Art. 22 UDHR states that 'everyone, as a member of society, has the right to social security', and Art. 25 UDHR supplements that umbrella provision or 'chapeau', by providing:

> 1. Everyone has the right to a standard of living adequate for the health and well-being of himself and of his family, *including* food, clothing, housing and medical care *and the necessary social services*, and the *right to security in the event of unemployment, sickness*, disability, *widowhood, old age or other lack of livelihood* in circumstances beyond his control.
> 2. *Motherhood* and *childhood* are entitled to special care and assistance. All *children*, whether born in or out of wedlock, shall enjoy the same social protection. [Emphasis added.]

These two UDHR provisions were the result of protracted negotiations. Article 22 does not contain a reference to social insurance, because it was felt that it is covered by the concept of social security as a generic term. By referring to national measures and international cooperation, article 22 foreshadowed article 2(1) of the ICESCR later on. Article 25, by contrast, reflects much of what was later to go into article 11 ICESCR, i.e., article 25 contains rights which are essential for the survival or subsistence of individuals or groups.

5. Social assistance as part of social security

One key question, which neither the wording of articles 22 and 25, nor ILO-Convention 102 made crystal-clear, is the question as to whether social assistance is covered by Article 9. The literature seems to be divided on the issue.[24] Some maintain,[25] and I subscribe to that view, that the concept of the right to social security was deliberately left open, to reflect the comprehensiveness of the provision, to include social assistance, a view since supported by the European Social Charter (Revised)[26] and the draft European Union (EU) constitutional document.[27]

---

24 Martin Scheinin, *supra* note 10, at 215 and Jennifer Tooze, *The Right to Social Security* (unpublished doctoral dissertation Nottingham, 2005) passim: against location in article 9, but coverage in "adequate standard of living" in Article 11.

25 Christoph Steiner, *supra* note 11, 97 et seq.; Eibe Riedel, 'Kapitel IV, Solidarität: Artikel 27 bis 38', in: Jürgen Meyer (ed.), *Kommentar zur Charta der Grundrechte der Europäischen Union* (Nomos, 2006) Art. 34, at 390.

26 European Social Charter (Revised), 3.5.1996, European Treaty Series (ETS) No. 163.

27 For the full text of the Draft Treaty establishing a Constitution for Europe (2003) see: europa.eu/constitution/futurum/constitution/index_en.htm.

Chapter IV of the EU Charter of Fundamental Rights (EU-Charter) clearly follows that approach in its article 34.[28] But whether or not social assistance as a taxation-based, non-contributional modality is covered by the global term social security is an open question, needing further reflection.

The Committee's practice is not conclusive. Jennifer Tooze[29] analysed five sessions of the Committee, and found that of the 27 State party reports considered during the 20th – 25th sessions, only 10 (i.e. 37 per cent) placed social assistance under article 9. Those wishing to place social assistance in the context of article 11, usually argue that by including it in article 9 social security might be watered down, since the right might be reduced to some minimal form of social assistance without the State party incurring any violation of human rights for failing to develop something more substantive with regard to social insurance. If social assistance were to be excluded from Article 9, a minimum core obligation in relation to social insurance would exist, and a more solid and unified content of the right could be articulated together with a greater focus on whether cuts and retrogression are permissible.

The counter-position stresses the disadvantages that would arise by separating social assistance from social security. For one, guarantees found in article 11 already are substantial and further categories might be unacceptable to States parties. Secondly, the distinction between social security and assistance is somewhat artificial, particularly in practice, as benefits often straddle the two categories, rendering distinctions very difficult. Thirdly, State delegations to the Committee often include governmental experts from the social ministries which engage in a dialogue with the Committee on all social security issues, including social assistance. The inter-relationship of social security and assistance might also be undermined by such an approach.

My own position is to read social assistance into the broadly defined 'social security' and thus see it safeguarded by article 9. Article 9 is doctrinally linked with article 11, but this also applies to articles 10, 12 and 6 – 8 ICESCR.

As a result of this position, realistic minimum standards of social security can be required of a State parties to the Covenant. Even though States may have a

---

[28] The Charter of Fundamental Rights of the European Union (2000/C364/01). Art. 34 states that:

1. The Union recognises and respects the entitlement to social security benefits and social services providing protection in cases such as maternity, illness, industrial accidents, dependency or old age, and in the case of loss of employment, in accordance with the procedures laid down by Community law and national laws and practices.

2. Everyone residing and moving legally within the European Union is entitled to social security benefits and social advantages in accordance with Community law and national laws and practices.

3. In order to combat social exclusion and poverty, the Union recognises and respects the right to social and housing assistance so as to ensure a decent existence for all those who lack sufficient resources, in accordance with the procedures laid down by Community law and national laws and practices.

[29] Jennifer Tooze, *supra* note 24.

wide margin of discretion in this sphere, they will nevertheless have to extend social security protection as resources permit. This follows directly from article 2(1) ICESCR which requires utilisation of available resources for the rights guaranteed in Part III of the Covenant which, in turn, includes the right to social security.

But even if one follows this line of argument, the Committee will have to look very carefully into how the mixture of social security insurance and assistance, actually operates in the country concerned, and how it affects the level of social security coverage as such.

One last argument in favour of regarding social assistance as covered by Article 9 relates to the fact that very many states since 1956 when article 9 was drafted, and ILO Convention 102 of 1952,[30] have actually decided for a mixture of social security *and* social assistance. For example, in the European regional context, this was effected by article 13 of the Revised European Social Charter, and by article 34 of the EU Charter which is now part of the Union Treaty, presently still undergoing the ratification process.[31] It is only a question of time before the European Court of Justice will pronounce on article 34 EU-Charter. It might say that that article does not represent progressive development, but is merely declaratory of existing obligations that have developed by customary law since 1976.

6. Social security benchmarking

It is for this reason that the Committee's more recent approach of asking for *indicators and benchmarks* makes sense. If States parties themselves report on the degree of contributory/ non-contributory mix in fulfilling their obligation to guarantee to every person a right to social security in the wider sense, the question of the ultimate legal validity of the definitional exercise can be by-passed. If the State party takes this approach, then the Committee can make use of such information, and base its concluding observations on information gained in this manner. The process has been described in General Comments Nos. 12 (food), 14 (health), 15 (water), 17(work), and 18 (authors' rights),[32] and although States parties are yet to react to this Committee request, it seems likely that they will comply in the foreseeable future. Without going into detail, this Indicators, Benchmarking, Scoping and Assessments procedure, the 'IBSA-process', initially involves finding suitable indicators. The ILO Conventions could be a basis from which States parties select certain benchmarks as targets to be achieved during the next reporting cycle, al-

---

30 On the *travaux préparatoires* of ILO-Convention 102 see: Angelika Nußberger, *Sozialstandards im Völkerrecht* (Duncker & Humblot, 2005), 64 et seq.; Christoph Steiner, *supra* note 11, at 57 et seq.; Danny Pieters, *Introduction into the Basic Principles of Social Security* (Klawer Law International, 1993) at 2; John Dixon, 'Social Security and the Ghosts that haunt it', in John Dixon and Robert P. Scheurell, *supra* note 14) 3-14.

31 See: Eibe Riedel, *supra* note 25, at 390 et seq.

32 Full text versions of all General Comments of the CESCR can be accessed via www.ohchr.org/english/bodies/cescr/comments.htm.

though the right to social security is broader and different in nature as Langford explores within this volume. The Committee engages in a dialogue ('scoping') with the State party on the benchmarks selected, and after 5 years, the assessment stage is to be based on those agreed benchmarks. The advantage of that procedure lies in focussing the questions that are to be addressed by the State parties, showing more clearly where human rights efforts have to be increased.

7. The universality claim of the right to social security

Perhaps the greatest challenge which the Committee will have to face is the question as to whether the human right to social security can be applied universally. Quite a number of developing countries either have no social security scheme, or provide only rudimentary, sectoral aspects of it. Instead, the private and informal sectors have to fill the gap, and often poorly. It is frequently said that the role of social security schemes in more highly developed countries is taken up by family protection in less developed countries. Children look after their parents, or groups of individuals cater for themselves. Considering the rapid urbanisation in developing countries, the decreasing role of the family unit, and, if one bears in mind that many developing countries will soon suffer from the effects of an aging population, to which Emmanuel Reynaud has referred, social security and generational compacts become more and more precarious.

8. Resource-independent obligations

Any future General Comment will undoubtedly have to give a prominent place to non-discrimination as set out in articles 2(2) and 3 of the Covenant. The position of the most vulnerable sectors of society, the marginalised and disadvantaged groups, will need special attention in relation to the right to social security. At the same time, it is precisely those provisions which mark out the minimum obligations that even very poor countries will have to meet because they impose obligations that are not wholly resource-dependent. The Committee has described this in greater detail in its General Comment No. 16 on the equal right of men and women to the enjoyment of all economic, social and cultural rights (article 3).[33]

---

[33] A full text version of this General Comment can be accessed via www.ohchr.org/english/bodies/cescr/comments.htm.

9. The level of protection and non-retrogression

In sum, the Committee should opt for a fully comprehensive approach, making sure that social security is provided universally, even though the levels of realisation may vary on account of article 2(1) ICESCR. The minimum level of protection could be covered by either non-contributory or contributory schemes, but the former will be essential for reaching for the most vulnerable members of society. In this fashion, the 'existential minimum' or 'subsistence level' protection for every individual as a member of society would serve as a safety net, while the progressive realisation promised in article 2(1) would require positive steps by State parties to fully guarantee the right to social security.

States, naturally, will find themselves in very different starting positions – which incidentally led the ILO to require adoption of merely three types from the nine offered in ILO Convention 102 to allow many States to join, although ideally all nine categories should be embraced. But only about 40 States have done so, and this may require careful analysis as to how State parties have fulfilled their obligations under article 9. Article 9 is thus all the more important for providing a legal platform for monitoring State activity with regard to social security. State parties have to show what they intend to do to ameliorate the situation during the next reporting cycle.

The Committee gives special attention to the question of non-retrogression. If retrogressive steps have to be taken, the State party will have to give good reasons why the protection standard could not be maintained. While the State enjoys a considerable margin of discretion in this respect, that discretion is not unbounded. The fundamental responsibility resting on every State party is to guarantee the minimum requirements of the right to social security for all, particularly for the most marginalised and disadvantaged groups of society, within the available resources at the disposal of the State.

As the Committee has pointed out in General Comment No. 3, lack of financial resources cannot serve as a general excuse for non-fulfilment of Covenant obligations, but requires careful consideration of the policy choices available within their budgetary constraints. Even the less developed countries will have to show that their allocation of resources respects the Covenant obligations of guaranteeing non-discrimination and securing equal treatment for men and women under the available resources.

The right to social security, including social assistance and social insurance, represents one typical human right enunciated in the Social Covenant. A future General Comment on the right to social security would undoubtedly stress these aspects, bringing them in line with the general approach that the Committee has adopted for all economic, social and cultural rights, and which most State Parties have accepted willingly, and in a spirit of cooperation. Through constructive dialogue, the Committee tries to strike a fair balance between the need to provide a social security system and to leave a reasonable margin of discretion to each State party in making policy choices in this sphere, but always bearing in mind that

State parties have Covenant obligations to progressively realise and guarantee without discrimination the right to social security for all.

The Right to Social Security and Implications for Law, Policy and Practice

Malcolm Langford*

1. Introduction: Added value?

Literature emanating from the 'social security sector' reveals an increasing tendency to deploy the right to social security not only as a rhetorical flourish, as was common with social rights before the 1990s, but as a legal entitlement grounded in international law. For example Wouter van Ginnekin of the ILO concludes:

> This situation of low coverage reflects a failure by governments by countries and the international community to meet their obligations under Article 9 of the International Covenant on Economic, Social and Cultural Rights [ICESCR] which 'recognizes the right of everyone to social security, including social insurance.'[1]

Others have gone further. At the general discussion on social security at the International Labour Conference in 2001, worker's representatives highlighted the individualised nature of the right to social security, which meant that pension systems that linked women's entitlements to discriminatory labour markets or a spouse's entitlement should be re-examined to ensure conformity with the principle of non-discrimination, inherent in the right to social security.[2] An NGO participant asserted that individual savings accounts for social security should not be used since 'the great majority of low-paid workers in precarious employment' would be excluded, a result inconsistent with the right to social security in ICESCR and ILO conventions which the speaker said should be 'universal, comprehensive and based on the principle of solidarity'.

---

* Senior Legal Officer, Centre on Housing Rights and Evictions (COHRE). He is also a Senior Researcher, at the University of Mannheim and a Research Associate at the Australian Human Rights Centre, University of NSW.

1 Wouter van Ginneken, *Extending social security coverage: Policies for Developing Countries*, (ESS-Paper No.13, 2003), at 2.

2 International Labour Office, *Social Security: A New Consensus* (International Labour Office, 2001) at 19.

But questions remain as to whether the right to social security offers more than a principled and legal justification for supporting the current, and very comprehensive, ILO framework on social security. If the right to social security has a more sophisticated content, representing what we might call a quiver of arrows, then what are the consequences for law, policy and practice?

What is immediately noticeable is that the potential content of the right, as contained in the ICESCR and the conventions on race, women and children, speaks directly to the difficult issues faced by the ILO in applying the current framework:[3] These challenges include:

- The need for protection of those persons excluded from coverage of social security systems, particularly in the informal sector and rural areas.
- The greater calls for market-based solutions and reductions of non-employee contributions. Both ideas have spurred greater marketisation of social security systems, particularly in Latin America and Eastern Europe, as well as the reduction of government and employer expenditures on social security. Proponents have argued that such policies will increase economic efficiency, spur economic growth through the release of public finances and increase incentives.
- Ensuring non-discriminatory outcomes for women, migrants and people with disabilities. The employment-based nature of the ILO framework is perhaps partly the problem, but the causes of unequal outcomes run much deeper.
- The need to address the rise of voluntarism and self-regulation in the labour and social sectors. Some authors have recently argued that this is partly attributable to the soft law 1998 ILO Declaration on Fundamental Principles and Rights at Work.[4]
- The general lack of effective national and international systems of accountability for both individual and collective violations of international social security rights.

Whether the right to social security can provide comprehensive or non-controversial answers to these issues though is another matter. Nevertheless, we can point briefly to some potential benefits of a 'right to social security approach'.

The first is the *universal nature* of the right to social security, which potentially avoids the bias towards formal employment in the ILO framework, particularly as manifested in the earlier standards. Such an approach is likely to benefit those working in the informal sector, long-term unemployed, as well as women, children, migrants and asylum seekers, persistently excluded minorities and those suf-

3 See, for example, International Labour Office, Social Security: A New Consensus, *ibid.* and Emmanuel Reynaud, *The extension of social security coverage: The approach of the International Labour Office*, (ESS-Paper No. 3, 2002).

4 See: Philip Alston and James Heenan, 'Shrinking the International Labor Code: An Unintended Consequence of the 1998 ILO Declaration on Fundamental Principles and Rights at Work', 36 (2004) *New York University Journal of International Law and Politics,* 221-264.

fering from permanent disabilities. This extension of the definition also enables NGOs and other associations working with these groups to more easily join the trade union movement - suffering a declining base in the face of globalisation and expanding services sector - in defending social security rights. Amartya Sen, while strongly endorsing this aspect of a human rights based approach to work, notes however the danger of neglecting 'the hard-earned gains of people in organized industry, through an attempt – often recommended (if only implicitly) – to level them down to the predicament of unorganized and unprotected workers'.[5]

The second benefit is the greater *ratification* of human rights instruments addressing social security in comparison to ILO Conventions. For example, as at 8 May 2006, 153 States had ratified the International Covenant on Economic, Social and Cultural Rights and 192 had ratified the Convention on the Rights of the Child, both of which provide explicit provisions on social security. At the same time, the principal ILO Convention on social security – No. 102 – has received 42 ratifications despite it being adopted in 1952. The figures for other ILO social security conventions are lower with the exception being the more specialised Workmen's Compensation (Agriculture) Convention, 1921 (No. 12) Equality of Treatment (Accident Compensation) Convention with 75 and 120 ratifications respectively. Although it must be said that many countries have followed the ILO approach even though they have not ratified the standard.

The pervasiveness of ratification of human rights treaties also means that there can be a more comprehensive response to the negative impacts of globalisation on social security: States are able, or should be compelled, to refer to their international obligations when faced with unreasonable demands for structural adjustment, cuts in social security spending etc. Furthermore, many countries have incorporated the right to social security or the above human rights treaties in their national constitutions, which means the potential for national application of the right. A greater emphasis on the content on the right would help guide court decisions and policymaking. However, while national courts and other adjudicatory and political bodies will have the opportunity to monitor the right, it is difficult to conclude that the international enforcement mechanisms for the human rights treaties can rival the ILO system, both in terms of focus upon the respective contributions and the high-level participation of employee and employer groups, which increases the likelihood of implementation.

A third benefit is the focus upon *participation* and *accountability* that are inherent in the right to social security. The practice of the Committee on Economic, Social and Cultural Rights makes clear that participation rights and the provision of remedies – both individual and collective - are a key and indispensable part of the mechanisms for the realisation of economic, social and cultural rights.[6] Indeed,

5 Amartya Sen, 'Work and Rights' 139 (2000) 2 *International Labour Review* 119-128 at 120.

6 In the case of remedies for violations, the Committee has indicated to States it will require them to justify their absence in the domestic legal system. See: Committee on Economic, Social and Cultural Rights, *General Comment 9, The domestic application of the Covenant* (Nineteenth session, 1998), U.N. Doc. E/C.12/1998/24 (1998).

the emphasis on participation and accountability goes to the heart of the human rights approach. Decision-makers must not only listen to the views of the beneficiaries of human rights, but they must account for the reasonableness of their decisions in a public and transparent manner, which can be achieved through some form of independent review. As Amartya Sen notes, 'unscrutinized feelings' and 'very rudimentary reasoning' are not the foundations for the crafting of social security policy.[7]

2. Content of the Right

It is certainly possible to tease out a detailed interpretation of the right to social security in light of the previous General Comments of the UN Committee on Economic, Social and Cultural Rights ('Committee') and the emerging human rights jurisprudence on social security from national and regional courts around the world. There is of course a genuine question as to whether such an interpretation should be the only legitimate version. Whose 'voices' does the Committee capture in its interpretive process, particularly since General Comments are developed without reference to a particular case or violation, as is normal in the common law world. In response, it can be said that the Committee has express authority from States to develop General Comments in order to give them guidance on their substantive obligations under the ICESCR[8] - the former UN Human Rights Commission also annually adopted a resolution encouraging the Committee to draft further general comments[9] - , and the Committee does draw to a certain extent on its extensive experience in monitoring the performance of States parties to the ICESCR. Another more potent critique is the length and occasionally ambitious and repetitious nature of some recent General Comments, a result of the template adopted by the Committee in the late 1990s' and the adoption of new but overlapping catego-

---

7 Amartya Sen, *supra* note 5, at 121.

8 The United Nations Economic and Social Council encouraged the Committee to 'continue using that mechanism to develop a fuller appreciation of the obligations of State Parties under the Covenant.' Economic and Social Council Resolution 1990/45, para. 10.

9 See: Question of the realization in all countries of the economic, social and cultural rights contained in the Universal Declaration of Human Rights and in the International Covenant on Economic, Social and Cultural Rights and study of special problems which the developing countries face in their efforts to achieve these human rights, Commission on Human Rights, resolution 2003/18, para. 11(a)(ii). Alston and Heenan also make a pertinent point about the value of expert development of human rights standards at the international level: 'creating 'Habermasian' dialogues that lead to 'shared convictions' and common standards is not always possible at the international level, nor perhaps even desirable if the result is an unwieldy heterogeneity or the emasculation of the content of human rights through the over-representation of non-democratic polities.' See: Philip Alston and James Heenan, *supra* note 4, at 251.

ries, particularly the extension of the idea of the minimum core obligations.[10] But even this approach can be partially defended.[11]

With this jurisprudence in mind, we might posit a number of key elements of the right that should apply to everyone. These aspects are often 'existential' in nature, representing the key concerns of individuals. A number of authors have attempted to define these key elements for the right to social security.[12] The 'claim' or 'normative' aspects of the rights are usually then covered under the 'State obligations' due to bifurcation of rights and obligations in the ICESCR. While the binary approach enables the more precise identification of State responsibility, Amartya Sen correctly points out that the sometimes over-obsessing by lawyers with such dualistic approaches can detract attention from the general force of the idea of human rights: 'The recognition of such claims as rights may not only be an ethically important statement, it can also help to focus attention on these matters, making their fulfilment that much more likely – or quicker.'[13] A marriage of the two approaches would certainly be possible by conceptualising obligations as equivalent to rights, combined with a defence for state incapacity.[14] But for present purposes the Committee's current approach will be followed.

The key element of the right would invariably include at a minimum:

1. *Adequate* benefits that ensure the rights to family protection, an adequate standard of living and right to health, as respectively contained in Articles 10, 11 and 12 of the ICESCR. A key question is the extent to which the level of benefits should be informed by the respective ILO Conventions. On one hand, the relativist approach of the ILO bodes well for the ICESCR since the minimum is often defined in relation to average wage levels in the national economy. For example, in ILO Convention 102, unemployment and sickness benefits must be 45 per cent (or 50 per cent in a later convention) of the wage of a

---

10 See: Malcolm Langford, 'Ambition that overleaps itself? A Response to Stephen Tully's 'Critique' of the General Comment on the Right to Water', 26 (2006) 3 *Netherlands Quarterly of Human Rights,* and Matthew Craven, 'Assessment of the Progress on Adjudication of Economic, Social and Cultural Rights', in John Squires, Malcolm Langford and Bret Thiele (eds.), *The Road to a Remedy: Current Issues in the Litigation of Economic, Social and Cultural Rights* (Australian Human Rights Centre, Distributed by UNSW Press, 2005), 27 – 42.

11 See: Malcolm Langford, Ambition that overleaps itself?, *ibid.*

12 See: Lucie Lamarche, 'The Right to Social Security in the International Covenant on Economic, Social and Cultural Rights', in Audrey Chapman and Sage Russell (eds.), *Core Obligations: Building a Framework for Economic, Social and Cultural Rights* (Intersentia, 2002), 87-114 and Malcolm Langford, Aoife Nolan and Bret Thiele, *Litigating Economic, Social and Cultural Rights: Legal Practitioners Dossier (Revised)* (Centre on Housing Rights and Evictions, 2006). See also discussion of the South African context by Sandra Liebenberg, 'The right to social assistance: The implications of *Grootboom* for policy reform in South Africa' 17 (2002) 2 *South African Journal on Human Rights*, 232.

13 Amartya Sen, *supra* note 5, at 124.

14 See: Malcolm Langford and Bret Thiele, 'Introduction' in Road to a Remedy, *supra* note 10.

skilled manual male employee plus any family benefits available to such workers. It is debatable though whether the percentages applied by the ILO Convention represent the 'minimum essential level' or a higher level of adequacy. Chantal Euzéby argues, for example, that flat-rate pensions in Europe should correspond to 50 to 60 per cent of the median income or poverty line. This corresponds to the ILO Recommendation 131 of 1967 which provides for 55 per cent of the reference wage and coverage of a minimum standard of living.[15] But the earlier ILO Conventions Nos. 102 and 128 respectively provide for 40 and 45 per cent. It should be noted that this incremental approach of the ILO suggests that ILO Convention 102 of 1952 is closer to the minimum than any level of adequacy necessary for a dignified life, the cornerstone of economic and social rights.

2. *Coverage* of all *risks and contingencies,* particularly those articulated in ILO Convention 102. As is well known, the ILO conventions provide benefits for nine risks: medical care, sickness benefits, unemployment benefits, old-age benefits, employment injury benefits, family benefits, maternity benefits, invalidity benefits and survivors' benefits. The Committee on Economic, Social and Cultural Rights has dealt explicitly with a number of these categories. In General Comment on people with disabilities it emphasised the importance of social security and income-maintenance schemes and noted that such schemes should 'reflect the special needs for assistance and other expenses often associated with disability' and, as far as possible, such support should also cover carers of people with disabilities.[16] In General Comment No. 6 on Older Persons, the Committee required States parties to guarantee the provision of survivors' and orphans' benefits on the death of the breadwinner who was covered by social security or receiving a pension, and noted further that Article 9 of ICESCR implicitly recognises the right to old-age benefits and that States parties should, within the limits of available resources, provide non-contributory old-age benefits and other assistance for all older persons, who are not entitled to an old-age pension or social security benefit or assistance under a contributory scheme and have no other source of income.[17] However, other risks associated with inability to realise economic, social and cultural rights must also need to be included,[18] for example risks from natural disasters and emergencies.
3. *Affordable* contributions, if a social insurance scheme is used. Contributors should be informed in advance of the extent of their liabilities. Affordability

---

15 Chantal Euzéby, 'Rethinking social security in the European Union' 57 (2004) 1 *International Social Security Review*, 85-103.

16 Committee on Economic, Social and Cultural Rights, *General Comment No. 5, Persons with disabilities*, (Eleventh session, 1994), U.N. Doc E/1995/22 at 19 (1995), para. 28.

17 Committee on Economic, Social and Cultural Rights, *General comment No. 6, The economic, social and cultural rights of older persons*, (Thirteenth session, 1995), U.N. Doc. E/1996/22 at 20 (1996).

18 See: Martin Scheinin, 'The Right to Social Security', in Asbjørn Eide, Catarina Krause, Allan Rosas (eds.) *Economic, Social and Cultural Rights* (Martinus Nijhoff Publishers, 2001) 211-221, at 215.

should be defined, as in previous jurisprudence of the Committee, with respect to an individual's or family's budget for covering economic, social and cultural rights. Bettie goes further, and argues that many define affordability in relation to the future benefits they expect to derive from the scheme and concludes, perhaps provocatively, that contribution-based schemes may be viewed as more affordable than tax-based schemes.[19]

4. *Non-discrimination* in the guaranteeing of the rights. This requires that the social security system should not only provide objectively unjustifiable differential arrangements directly or indirectly based on prohibited grounds – such as race, sex, marital status, disability, age – but that there is a positive obligation to eradicate such differences over time.

Lucie Lamarche, however, adds two more elements, which will later take us to the heart of the discussion in this paper. The first is that *all persons* are covered and while this is intrinsic in the right and all the elements expressed above, the real question is the extent to which the Government covers all persons immediately and progressively. Secondly, and more importantly, she argues that social security must be defined as a collective arrangement in accordance with the ILO definitions.[20] While this accords with sectoral understandings, the tripartite approach of the Committee to State obligations means that the right may have a wider definition, encompassing self-help forms of social protection. This will be taken up in section 3.1 below. It also potentially clashes with the Committee's previous non-committal approach to the involvement of the market although they do require the states to engage in a variety of ways with the market: see section 3.3 below. But Lamarche includes private arrangements within the ambit of collective arrangements, so long as certain minimum requirements are met, notably those articulated in ILO Convention 102.[21]

The second leg of the Committee's approach is State obligations. In addition to the duty to guarantee the right without discrimination,[22] States parties to the Covenant must take steps, including through international assistance and cooperation, to progressively achieve the realisation of the rights with the maximum available

---

19 Roger Beattie, 'Social Protection for all: But how?' 139 (2000) 2 *International Labour Review,* 129 at 137.

20 She states: '[S]ocial security, as a human right and not a commodity, relies on collective funding. This can be of different types: public, professional community, private (if risks are assessed on the basis of a determined group and benefits paid to this group) or even mixed. In all cases, it is a basic and minimal requirement of the right that it be supervised by an independent, participatory and regulated body.' Lamarche, *supra* note 12, at 103.

21 Articles 71 and 72. In particular, contributions must be affordable, the public authority must regulate the system, beneficiaries must be able to participate in the system and have the right to appeal decisions negatively affecting them. See: Lamarche, *ibid*, at 94.

22 Article 2(2) of ICESCR states: 'The States Parties to the present Covenant undertake to guarantee that the rights enunciated in the present Covenant will be exercised without discrimination of any kind as to race, colour, sex, language, religion, political or other opinion, national or social origin, property, birth or other status.'

resources.[23] This duty has been broken down below, somewhat awkwardly at times, into a set of duties. It has been done in summarised format since many of the issues will be picked up in the analysis of implications.[24]

Domestic Obligations

1. *Respect* existing arrangements for right to social security – private and public - and permit individuals to self-organise, or provide adequate alternatives as a result of any interference.
2. *Protect* from interference by private actors the existing arrangements for social security and permit individuals to self-organise, or ensure provision of adequate alternatives as a result of any interference.
3. *Fulfil* the right which means:
   a) Reviewing legislation and policy to ensure consistency with right to social security.
   b) Adopting and implementing appropriate measures, including legislation, to ensure provision of social security with effective participation of potential and current beneficiaries.
   c) Ensuring progressive realisation of the right to social security over time as resources permit.
   d) Ensuring a minimum essential level of social security immediately.
   e) Avoiding unjustifiable deliberate retrogressive measures that cannot be justified.
   f) Monitor the realisation of the right and provide remedies for violations.

With respect to the first two, and possibly three, aspects of the obligation to fulfil, the Committee would obviously be influenced by the 'menu' system for the different pillars of social security (e.g. unemployment benefits, old age benefits etc) and incremental coverage under the ILO system. But the ILO approach may represent more of a guide rather than an exclusive definition of appropriate measures, particularly in light of uneven ratification and selection by states of different risk pillars.

International obligations

The international obligations of States relate to persons outside their jurisdiction:

1. *Respect* existing the right to social security of such persons.

---

[23] Article 2(1) states: 'Each State Party to the present Covenant undertakes to take steps, individually and through international assistance and co-operation, especially economic and technical, to the maximum of its available resources, with a view to achieving progressively the full realization of the rights recognized in the present Covenant by all appropriate means, including particularly the adoption of legislative measures.'

[24] Note that I have ignored the so-called 'minimum core obligations' category since it largely repeats the immediate obligations.

2. *Protect* the right to social security of such persons from interference by private actors based in the State or international organisations of which the State is a member. For example, ensuring that policies of international financial institutions do not negatively impact on the right to social security.
3. *Fulfil* the right to social security of such person's through international aid and cooperation.

3. Potential Implications

The paper now turns to analyse the implications of the right to social security for a number of crucially important issues. These include the coverage of the excluded, the elimination of discrimination and the challenge of 'market' approaches.

3.1 Covering the Excluded

> Generally, the extension of social protection to uncovered populations raises a fundamental question: should one try to extend the existing coverage – which benefits only a minority – to all the population, or create specific mechanisms that provide a lower level of protection for the uncovered population?[25]

One of the key challenges for the achievement of the right to social security is the slow, stagnant or even declining coverage of both persons and risks in developing countries, and even some transition countries.[26] While the European experience clearly indicates that the development of fully-functioning and comprehensive systems of social insurance and assistance can take a significant period,[27] the situation in many regions is alarming: 5-10 per cent are covered in sub-Saharan Africa and South Asia (in most cases only pension schemes), 10 to 80 per cent are covered in Latin America, in South East Asia and East Asia coverage is between 10 and 100 per cent, while in European transition countries the figures are 50 to 80 per cent.[28]

The ILO has evaluated whether the current system of incrementally extending formal coverage through financially sound and well-organised schemes – as required by ILO Convention 102 and others – should be the sole method for reaching the excluded, particularly those working and living in the informal sector and rural areas. Emmanual Reynaud of the ILO concedes that in poor, as opposed to

---

25 Emmanuel Reynaud, *supra* note 3.

26 Wouter van Ginneken, *supra* note 1.

27 See: Peter Koehler, Hans Zacher in collaboration with Martin Partington, The Evolution of Social Insurance 1881-1981: Studies of Germany, France, Great Britain, Austria and Switzerland (Frances Pinter, 1982).

28 See: Emmanuel Reynaud, *supra* note 3, at 1. See also: An Maes, 'Informal economic and social security in sub-Saharan Africa' 56 (2003) 3-4 *International Social Security Review,* 39-58.

transition, countries, alternative approaches will be critical since the State's capacity is limited.[29] But the ILO emphasis is upon drawing the informal sector into the formal sector, and it perhaps has in mind the 19th Century German experience where fragmented public, private and informal arrangements gradually evolved into a system characterised by almost comprehensive coverage of all risks and persons, the collective sharing of risks and a strong role for the State.[30] Otherwise, dual systems of protection may result. Other major international actors, such as the World Bank, are however, more accepting of differentiated results and systems – particularly if the private sector has a significant role - although they also express concern at the current levels of coverage.

Before considering such alternatives, it is important to analyse the legal requirements of the right to social security. On one hand, it is clear that ICESCR calls for the progressive realisation of the right to social security and therefore the incremental expansion of a formal 'system' – the nature of such a system will be considered below – at a pace consistent with a country's capabilities. On the other hand, the Committee's jurisprudence indicates that certain measures will be needed in at least the short to medium term.

Protection of assets etc

First, the *obligation to respect* represents the more classically liberal notions of human rights since it calls for State abstention from injurious acts that may impinge upon an individual's self-organised access to social security.[31] Similarly, the obligation to protect requires measures to prevent other actors interfering with self-organised protection. Such measures ordinarily include regulation and a system of accountability, including remedies. These protections extend both to the financial resource itself as well as the systems and associations connected with its realisation.

The ILO acknowledges that there have been calls to widen the definition of social security to include the wider sense of social protection, for example protection of assets, resources and livelihoods intrinsically connected with social security. The traditional definition reads as follows:

---

29 Emmanuel Reynaud, *supra* note 3, at 3.

30 Reynaud, *ibid*, states at 4: 'The extension of social protection calls for a dynamic approach. The process involved is long, and the ultimate aim is to build a generalized national social security system in order to guarantee to all a secure income and access to health care at a level corresponding to the economic capacity and political will of the country. Moreover, it is essential from the outset to provide for linkages and bridges between the arrangements designed for uncovered categories and other social protection mechanisms.' For the German experience see: Detlev Zoellner, 'Germany', in Peter Koehler, Hans Zacher and Martin Partington, *supra* note 27, 1-92.

31 It is to be noted that the obligation to respect could also apply to retrogressive measures that reduce publicly funded or organised social security. However, this aspect of the 'respect obligation' is still unclear in the literature on economic, social and cultural rights and will be dealt with under the obligation of 'non retrogression' in section 3.3 below.

> [T]he protection which society provides for its members through a series of public measures, against the economic and social distress that otherwise would be caused by the stoppage or substantial reduction of earnings resulting from sickness, maternity, employment injury, invalidity and death; the provision of medical care; and the provision of subsidies for families with children.[32]

Of course, it can be argued that such resources would be protected under many other economic and social rights and that the right to social security should remain confined to systemic or 'public' measures. Nevertheless, assets, resources and livelihoods of the poor are commonly destroyed in forced evictions, particularly in informal settlements in rural areas and peasants and fisher-folk that live with precarious security of tenure. Likewise, it is important for semi-formal networks and associations – for example savings and insurance schemes – to be protected from malevolent State interference. This is certainly not a new phenomenon. Before Bismarck's reforms in the late 1880s, one of the only two demands the German Socialist Labour Party made with respect to social security in 1875 was 'complete self-administration for all worker relief and benevolent funds'.[33]

The argument carries strong resonance in developing countries but is not without its contradictions and there is a need to ensure that the *method* of protecting the rights does not compromise the rights of other vulnerable and marginalised groups. For example, slum-upgrading schemes are increasingly, and appropriately targeting tenants but elderly 'slum landlords', particularly women, should be taken into consideration since rental income effectively constitutes their 'pension'.[34] Similarly, in rural areas women and poorer families are often discriminated against in traditional systems. While many commentators have increasingly focused on the positive effects of traditional systems,[35] the discriminatory aspects of family and community based systems are sometimes overlooked, for example 'fewer and weaker' general resource rights for women and exclusion of women and children from inheritance laws.[36] In conjunction with the focus on micro-insurance, in which women often predominate and therefore undertake the greatest

---

32 ILO, *Introduction to Social Security*, (ILO, 1984, 3rd edition), at 2-3.

33 Quote from the Gotha Programme in Detlev Zoellner, *supra* note 30, at 12. However, it is difficult draw generalisations from the German experience. Bismarck's social security reforms can be largely understood as a way to justify restrictions on the labour movement and remove worker support for the political arms of the labour movement.

34 See: COHRE, *Listening to the Poor: Housing Rights in Nairobi, Kenya* (COHRE, 2005) at chapter 5. Available at www.cohre.org/kenya.

35 For a review see: Johannes Jutting, 'Social security systems in low-income countries: Concepts, Constraints and the need for cooperation' 53 (2000) 4 *International Social Security Review*, 3-24.

36 See: Deborah Kasente, 'Gender and social security reform in Africa' 53 (2000) 3 *International Social Security Review,* 27-41 and COHRE, *Women's Inheritance Rights in Africa* (COHRE, 2004).

risks, some authors have called for positive measures to restrain male behaviour and norms that adversely affect access to social security.[37]

Minimum essential level

The second relevant aspect of the Committee's jurisprudence is the obligation to provide the minimum essential level of each rights:

> [T]he Committee is of the view that a minimum core obligation to ensure the satisfaction of, at the very least, minimum essential levels of each of the rights is incumbent upon every State party. Thus, for example, a State party in which any significant number of individuals is deprived of essential foodstuffs, of essential primary health care, of basic shelter and housing, or of the most basic forms of education is, prima facie, failing to discharge its obligations under the Covenant.[38]

However, even these obligations are tempered by the availability of resources but the State party to ICESCR must demonstrate that there is sufficient evidence that this is indeed the case.[39]

As can be seen in the list of minimums enumerated, only 'existential' entitlements are included but it is relatively straightforward to recognise some form of minimum entitlement to basic protection against risks, particularly those which may impinge upon other economic, social and cultural rights. While the minimum under the European Social Charter has been defined as those obligations existing under the relevant ILO Conventions or, more lately, the European Code of Social

---

37 A critique on the South African Governments White Paper on Social Welfare stated: 'Compared to the relative space that is devoted to women and other special groups it is in fact rather astonishing how little is said about men as a social group.... Despite mentioning family violence against women and children, a problem that is highly prevalent in South Africa, the report does not discuss how this might be caused by specific conceptions of male behaviour. There is no thorough discussion of male negligence and neglect (refusal to pay child support for example) and the abandonment of wives and children.' See: Selma Sevenhuijsen, Vivienne Bozalek, Amanda Gouws and Marie Minaar-McDonald, 'South African social Welfare Policy: An analysis through the Ethic of Care', Paper, University of Utrecht, The Netherlands, 2003 at 16 quoted in Rune Ervik, *Global Normative Standards and National Solutions for Pension Provision: The World Bank, ILO, Norway and South Africa in Comparative Perspective,* Working Paper 8-2003, Stein Rokkan Centre for Social Studies, April 2003.

38 Committee on Economic, Social and Cultural Rights, *General Comment 3, The nature of States parties' obligations*, (Fifth session, 1990), U.N. Doc. E/1991/23, annex III at 86 (1991), para. 10.

39 The Committee states: 'By the same token, it must be noted that any assessment as to whether a State has discharged its minimum core obligation must also take account of resource constraints applying within the country concerned. Article 2 (1) obligates each State party to take the necessary steps "to the maximum of its available resources". In order for a State party to be able to attribute its failure to meet at least its minimum core obligations to a lack of available resources it must demonstrate that every effort has been made to use all resources that are at its disposition in an effort to satisfy, as a matter of priority, those minimum obligations.' General Comment No. 3, *ibid*, para. 10.

Security, it is likely that the ICESCR requires that States go beyond their incremental obligations under ILO conventions and address the excluded with some alternative measures in the short-term. The Committee frequently encourages States to consider low-cost and small-scale alternatives as a way to extending the reach of economic and social rights.[40]

But what can a State be expected to do for those who are not yet covered for all or any risks? For example, workers who have access to a pension scheme, but not unemployment, health or maternal assistance or insurance, or those in the informal sector with no coverage. The difficulty of identifying clearly a minimum was one of the key reasons the South African Constitutional Court did not endorse the concept as part of its interpretation of constitutional socio-economic rights. But in the absence of any safety net, there is a likelihood that all economic, social and cultural rights will be at risk in the event of unemployment, injury or the birth of a child. Should the Committee accept the principle of 'all for some' but not 'some for all' as a recognition of the State's limited capacities, or is there a minimum obligation to provide some form of assistance for all?

There are of course some examples in developing countries, for example the grain ration system in India[41] although the challenges of administering such a scheme are demonstrated by the recent hunger-related suicides of two women in rural areas.[42] At the same time, advocates have secured a series of Supreme Court judgments for the improved implementation of the scheme.[43] In slightly wealthier countries, for example South Africa, cash payments have been made to all older persons, which has had a significant impact on rural economies and poverty. Others advocate for the adoption of a basic income[44] in developing countries, although the administrative costs in some countries may make such a scheme unfeasible.

An alternative approach is to focus on the risks identified by the population itself. While pensions have traditionally been the first scheme developed, a number of countries have responded to the demand of workers for more immediate and culturally relevant needs, in particularly health expenses but also funeral expenses. In Namibia, a scheme for sickness, maternity and death expenses was introduced in 1995 and now covers 80 per cent of the formal sector.[45]

---

40 See, for example, Committee on Economic, Social and Cultural Rights, *General Comment 15, The right to water* (Twenty-ninth session, 2003), U.N. Doc. E/C.12/2002/11 (2003).

41 See interview with Colin Gonsalves in Malcolm Langford, *Litigating Economic, Social and Cultural Rights: Achievements, Challenges and Strategies* (COHRE, 2003), chapter 3.

42 Letter from Asian Human Rights Commission to UNICEF, dated 15 March 2005 (on file with author).

43 *People's Union for Civil Liberties v Union of India*, No. 196 of 2001, Interim Order of 2 May 2003.

44 See, for example, Rick van der Ploeg, *Pros and Cons of Basic Income*, presented at 'Basic income versus subsidized employment' of the 6th B.I.E.N. International Congress 1996, United Nations Office at Vienna, 12-14 September 1996.

45 Emmanuel Reynaud, *supra* note 3, at 5.

Secondly, what steps can be undertaken to reach the informal sector, who are unlikely to benefit from collective schemes for a significant period? One approach that has growing support – although it is certainly not new in historical terms - is micro-insurance[46] or what Jutting refers to as member-organisation-based organisations. Jutting defines such organisations as follows:

> We are thinking here of civic organisations in the form of various sorts of self-help groups organized to improve social security at the community level. Major activities could encompass the provision of health insurance, access to credit and saving, or giving people a voice to formulate their needs and interests. [47]

In the case of health micro-insurance, Reynaud argues that State should assist such schemes through design kits for schemes, control and regulatory mechanisms, decentralising public health services to enable engagement with such schemes, training and co-financing. The State should then seek to replicate the schemes nationwide. But one obstacle to well-functioning schemes is communal wide risks, which such schemes cannot cope with. For example, risks include crop failure, natural disaster or large-scale evictions or home/business demolitions, all common in developing countries. In some cases, the State is directly responsible for the destruction of the scheme: i.e., cases of forced eviction of small businesses, homes and community facilities.

But there are other voices of scepticism. Workers' Representatives at the ILO stated that 'while micro-insurance schemes might contribute to extending coverage in a limited way, they were unlikely to provide a solution for large numbers of people' and supported further research on the question to the extent that 'it showed potential for expansion and that such schemes could be integrated with national security schemes'.[48] Jutting also notes the tendency for schemes to be captured by the wealthier poor.[49]

3.2 Equal Treatment and Non-Discrimination

The equality implications of the right to social security are significant, and perhaps remain only partially explored. The 'negative' aspects of the right to non-discrimination have received much attention with respect to gender and race,[50] but the common exclusion or unequal treatment of other groups, for example migrants and asylum seekers, may raise significant issues. On the other hand, the 'positive' obligations arising from the right to social security may have important implications for women and people with disabilities since they address unequal outcomes. This is sometimes ignored in the literature. Luckhaus' analysis of the right to so-

---

46 See: Johannes Jutting, *supra* note 35 and Reynaud, *supra* note 3.

47 Johannes Jutting, *supra* note 35, at 7.

48 ILO, *supra* note 2, at 13.

49 Jutting, *supra* note 35.

50 See: Linda Luckhaus, 'Equal Treatment, social protection and income security for women' 139 (2000) 2 *International Labour Review,* 149.

cial security in the EU for example, situates the relevant international legal framework wholly within the 'negative obligations' approach of the European Court of Justice to the EU equality regulations and relegates other important and potentially further-reaching international standards to a footnote.[51]

As will be seen, it is clear from the ICESCR that the right to social security requires both abstention from discrimination as well as a duty to take positive steps. Article 2(2) states:

> The States Parties to the present Covenant undertake to guarantee that the rights enunciated in the present Covenant will be exercised without discrimination of any kind as to race, colour, sex, language, religion, political or other opinion, national or social origin, property, birth or other status.

Direct and indirect discrimination has been criticised by UN human rights treaty committees. The Human Rights Committee declared that unemployment benefit legislation that excluded married women – on the assumption that their husbands would provide for their needs – discriminated on the basis of marital status and sex.[52] In its concluding observations on Canada, the Committee on Economic, Social and Cultural Rights noted that cuts to social security most adversely affected women who constitute the majority of the poor: 'The Committee notes with grave concern that with the repeal of CAP and cuts in social assistance rates, social services and programmes have had a particularly harsh impact on women, in particular single mothers, who are the majority of the poor, the majority of adults receiving social assistance and the majority among the users of social programmes.'[53]

However, while the European Court of Justice have adopted a more formal approach to non-discrimination, allowed for 'equalising down' or 'levelling down' in its application of equality directives,[54] the UN system,[55] including the more con-

---

51 *Ibid.,* at 153.

52 '[A]lthough article 26 [right to equality and non-discrimination] requires that legislation should prohibit discrimination, it does not of itself contain any obligation with respect to the matters that may be provided for by legislation. Thus it does not, for example, require any State to enact legislation to provide for social security. However, when such legislation is adopted in the exercise of a State's sovereign power, then such legislation must comply with article 26 of the Covenant.' See the following decisions of the UN Human Rights Committee: *Zwaan-de Vries v the Netherlands*, Communication No. 182/1984, (9 April 1987) at para. 12.4.

53 Concluding observations of the Committee on Economic, Social and Cultural Rights: Canada, 10/12/98, E/C.12/1/Add.31, para. 23.

54 For example, in *Taylor v United Kingdom* Case-382/98, 16 December 1999, the European Court of Justice ruled that the lower-age threshold for a winter fuel benefit discriminated against elderly men.

55 In its General Comment No. 15 on Right to Water, the Committee on Economic, Social and Cultural Rights states: The obligation of States parties to guarantee that the right to water is enjoyed without discrimination (art. 2, para. 2), and equally between men and women (art. 3), pervades all of the Covenant obligations. The Covenant thus proscribes any discrimination on the grounds of race, colour, sex, age, language, religion, political or other opinion, national or social origin, property, birth, physical or mental disability,

servative Human Rights Committee,[56] have hued more tightly to the expansive definition of discrimination set out in the Convention on the Elimination of All Forms of Racial Discrimination, which calls for the elimination of discrimination in practice.[57] This approach has been accepted by quite a number of national courts in applying similar provisions. For example, the Canadian Supreme Court declared that 'The principle that discrimination can accrue from a failure to take positive steps to ensure that disadvantaged groups benefit equally from services offered to the general public is widely accepted in the human rights field.'[58] In the *Eldridge* case, the Committee found that the protection from discrimination entailed a positive right of the deaf to interpretive services in hospitals, despite the additional costs.[59]

Further, in its first substantive General Comment concerning a group vulnerable to discrimination, the Committee on Economic, Social and Cultural Rights has underlined the influence of the explicitly affirmative character of the Covenant:

> The obligation of States parties to the Covenant to promote progressive realization of the relevant rights to the maximum of their available resources clearly requires Governments to do much more than merely abstain from taking measures which might have a negative impact on persons with disabilities. The obligation in the case of such a vulnerable and disadvantaged group is to take positive action to reduce structural disadvantages and to give appropriate preferential treatment to people with disabilities in order to achieve the objectives of full participation and equality within society for all persons with disabilities. This almost invariably

---

health status (including HIV/AIDS), sexual orientation and civil, political, social or other status, which has the intention or effect of nullifying or impairing the equal enjoyment or exercise of the right to water. The Committee recalls paragraph 12 of General Comment No. 3 (1990), which states that even in times of severe resource constraints, the vulnerable members of society must be protected by the adoption of relatively low-cost targeted programmes. See: General Comment No. 15, *supra* note 40, para. 13.

56 The Human Rights Committee has commented: [T]he principle of equality sometimes requires States parties to take affirmative action in order to diminish or eliminate conditions which cause or help to perpetuate discrimination prohibited by the Covenant. For example, in a State where the general conditions of a certain part of the population prevent or impair their enjoyment of human rights, the State should take specific action to correct those conditions. Such action may involve granting for a time to the part of the population concerned certain preferential treatment in specific matters as compared with the rest of the population.' Human Rights Committee, *General Comment No. 18: Non-discrimination* (1989), para. 10.

57 Article 1(1) states: 'In this Convention, the term "racial discrimination" shall mean any distinction, exclusion, restriction or preference based on race, colour, descent, or national or ethnic origin which has the purpose or effect of nullifying or impairing the recognition, enjoyment or exercise, on an equal footing, of human rights and fundamental freedoms in the political, economic, social, cultural or any other field of public life.'

58 *Eldridge v British Columbia* (Attorney General) [1997] 3 S.C.R., para. 78.

59 *Ibid.*

> means that additional resources will need to be made available for this purpose and that a wide range of specially tailored measures will be required.[60]

While two of the Committee's General Comments have focused on people with disabilities and older persons, the remainder of this section will explore the position of women and migrants. Unequal outcomes for women in the field of social security are overwhelming in their number and scope. First, the rights of women to maternity protections, including maternity leave benefits for a minimum period, are protected in ILO Convention 102 and strengthened in the Maternity Protection Convention 2000 (No. 183), but ratification remains low and maternity protections are very weak in many countries. Even where some protection is provided, Arun and Arun note that women in India fear claiming their benefits since they may lose their jobs.[61] Therefore, States will not only need to ensure that a system of protection develops for maternity benefits – even it means allowing women in developing countries to claim other forms of social assistance (e.g. pensions for a short-term) – but will need to eradicate the other obstacles that women face in accessing the benefits such as actual or perceived employer discrimination.

Secondly, discrimination in the workplace is responsible for perhaps the most intractable element of discrimination in social security, the replication of unequal work outcomes in insurance-based systems, particularly where insurance benefits such as pensions and unemployment benefits are based on a percentage of previous earnings or qualifying periods and hours do not take account of women's intermittent labour market participation, often due to child rearing and domestic duties, and part-time work.[62] Since the gender wage gap is unlikely to disappear in the foreseeable future, even in developed countries,[63] and women will continue to dominate part-time work, reliance on corrections to the labour market are unlikely to solve the problem. Increased child-care is obviously one clear remedy but redressing the structural wage inequalities whereby occupations dominated by women receive lower wages is extremely difficult with the decline of centralised wage fixation and the neo-liberal emphasis on competitiveness in the setting of wages.[64] Therefore, States will need to attempt to redress some of the problems in their social security system, and this will invariably require additional resources. But there are some positive examples. For example, various European countries have taken some steps to address the problem by crediting unpaid caring work (e.g. Finland) or by omitting periods of unpaid work from calculation of benefits (e.g. Switzerland).[65] Italy on the other hand has established a new fund for 'home-

---

60 General Comment No. 5, *supra* note 16, para. 9.

61 Shoba Arun and T.G. Arun, 'Gender issues in social security policy of developing countries: Lessons from the Kerala experience' 54 (2000) 4 *International Social Security Review,* 93-110, at 98.

62 See generally: Linda Luckhaus, *supra* note 50.

63 See: Malcolm Langford, 'The Gender Wage Gap in the 1990's' (1995) 34 *Australian Economic Papers,* 62-85.

64 *Ibid.*

65 See: Linda Luckhaus, *supra* note 50, at 168-169.

makers'.[66] In Canada, the earnings and hours thresholds were abolished for unemployment benefits.[67] However, such schemes will require either State budgetary support or increased contributions from employer and employee.

In the area of survivor's pensions, the position of women is actually under significant pressure. Luckhaus notes the increasing trend to dismantle the protections granted to widow's under social insurance and occupational schemes, which linked benefits to the earnings of their deceased spouses.[68] Schemes across Europe have introduced various reforms that decrease the levels of payments of female survivors or make them subject to a means test. While financial viability of the schemes must obviously be taken into account, and perhaps result in less regressive redistribution of incomes, the system increases the income gaps between men and women, potentially contravening Article 3 of ICECR.

A fourth, and perhaps most critical issue is the over-representation of women in all the disadvantaged groups as they relate to social security, for example those relying on minimum or flat pensions, unemployment benefits, survivor's pensions, or who are working in the informal economy of developing countries.[69] Ensuring coverage for the excluded is therefore synonymous with protection of women's rights, and the discussion in the section above becomes immediately relevant. However, there are some fundamental contradictions in policy responses. Pragmatic strategies to increase the level of protection for women mean ensuring that women benefits are more closely linked to their partner's benefits, for example through the practice of pension or pension splitting. However, others decry this approach on principled grounds and argue that the right to social security should reduce dependency, not increase it.[70]

Turning to the issue of migrants and social security, perhaps one the most explosive political issues in developed countries and in even in wealthier countries in less developed regions such as South Africa and Malaysia. Despite this, exclusion of migrants from social insurance and assistance schemes has been a relatively regular topic for international and European supervisory bodies and national courts. (Note that I will concentrate migrants in general and not on specific categories such as asylum seekers. Helen Bolderson covers the social security rights of this latter group in a chapter in this volume).

What is striking is that courts and quasi-judicial bodies principally concerned with civil and political rights – and who have greater enforcement powers, have issued far-reaching decisions, particularly on rights to social assistance, which are the most controversial due to the limited nature of a migrant's contribution to taxation. This is particularly the case for the European Court of Human Rights. In *Gaygusuz v Austria*, the Court characterised social assistance benefits as *property* and therefore a protected right for residents. However, the fact that the worker from Turkey had made contributions to an unemployment benefit scheme seemed

66 *Ibid.* at 169.
67 *Ibid.* at 165.
68 *Ibid.* at 158.
69 For an overview, see: Shoba Arun and T.G. Arun, *supra* note 61.
70 See: Linda Luckhaus, *supra* note 50, at 164.

to be decisive factor in the case.[71] Similarly the ruling by the UN Human Rights Committee that Senegalese ex-soldiers who served with the French army had equal rights to the same level of pension benefits[72] is certainly 'far-reaching' as Scheinin and Krause conclude, but it is not clear whether it applies to all pensions as they suggest.[73] The case is slightly different from normal claims since the soldiers were now living in Senegal but instead claimed French pension rights on the basis of their service. Therefore, the link with *a contribution* is made, which made it easier for the Committee to find that the distinction based on nationality was not based on reasonable and objective criteria. However, a number of national courts have struck down exclusion of migrants from social assistance schemes, for example in Spain.[74] Courts in the United Kingdom have consistently battled with the executive over the denial of social security rights to asylum seekers, even elevating the exclusions to the category and 'cruel and degrading treatment'.[75]

However, economic and social rights most likely provide a higher level of protection, since those excluded can rely directly on the right as opposed to claiming the more complex and stretched application of civil and political rights. The recent *Khosa* decision in South Africa is emblematic of this. The Constitutional Court of South African read the equality and social assistance provisions together and ruled that permanent residents had the right to social security, a significant decision given the large numbers of non-nationals from Africa working in South Africa (see further discussion by Liebenberg in this book).[76] Similarly Swiss courts relied on an implied constitutional right to assistance and extended access to illegal migrants.[77]

The European Committee on Social Rights in applying the European Social Charter has consistently found national practices on exclusion of non-nationals – particularly through residency and qualifying period requirements – to violate the

---

71 See: Martin Scheinin and Catarina Krause, 'The meaning of article 1 of the First Protocol for social security rights in the light of the *Gaygusuz* judgement', in Stefaan Van den Bogaert (ed.), *Social Security, Non-discrimination and Property* (Antwerpen-Apeldoorn, 1997), 59-73 and Martin Scheinin and Catarina Krause, 'The Right not to be Discriminated Against: The Case of Social Security', in Theodore S. Orlin et al. (eds.), *The Jurisprudence of Human Rights: A Comparative Interpretive Approach* (Turku: Åbo Akademi University Institute for Human Rights, 2000), 253-286, at 265.

72 *Gueye et al v France*, Human Rights Committee, Communication No. 196/1983 (3 April 1989).

73 Martin Scheinin and Catarina Krause, *supra* note 71, at 262.

74 Decision of the Constitutional Court of Spain, Case No. 130/1995, (1995) 3 Bulletin on Constitutional Case Law 366, quoted in Nihal Jayawickrama, *The Judicial Application of Human Rights Law: National, Regional and International Jurisprudence* (Cambridge University Press, 2002).

75 *R ex parte Adam and others v Secretary of State for the Home Department* [2004] EWCA Civ. 540.

76 *Khosa v Minister of Social Development; Mahlaule v Minister of Social Development* 2004 (6) BCLR 569 (CC).

77 *V v Einwohnergemeinde X und Regierungsrat des Kantons Bern* (BGE/ATF 121 I 367, Federal Court of Switzerland, of 27 October 1995).

rights to social security and social assistance.[78] However, there are some key restrictions in the Charter. A party to the Charter is only obliged to ensure the protection of the rights in the Charter to non-nationals of other Contracting Parties who are lawful resident or working regularly in their territory, unless refugee and stateless person conventions cover them.[79] This exception in a multilateral treaty in essence attempts to reflect the reciprocal approach that many States adopt to the social security rights of non-nationals.[80] While restrictiveness is tempered by provisions urging State to apply such regulations for non-nationals in a 'spirit of liberality' and simplify visa requirements, it is clear that the rights of non-nationals from outside Western Europe are quite circumscribed. However, a recent decision by the Committee on the right to health care for illegal immigrants in France indicates that the Charter could be read more expansively.[81]

Yet, the ICESCR contains none of these limitations and there is a key question as to the extent to which States parties to the ICESCR can limit access to social security assistance and insurance schemes to non-nationals, particularly those from countries they have not signed bilateral agreements with or who are working or living illegally in the country. The Committee in its General Comment No. 14 on the Right to Health, to the consternation of some States, has found that illegal migrants are entitled to health care:

> States are under the obligation to respect the right to health by, inter alia, refraining from denying or limiting equal access for all persons, including prisoners or detainees, minorities, asylum seekers and illegal immigrants, to preventive, curative and palliative health services.[82]

Therefore, the Committee certainly appears to take a relatively principled stand on the importance of access to social and economic rights for non-nationals, but the key question may be the extent of access to benefits. Health care is often closely linked to right to life and there is a question as to whether assistance for non-nationals will or should be set at the maximal or minimal levels in accordance with the ICESCR.[83]

---

78 For a review see: Martin Scheinin and Catarina Krause, *supra* note 71, at 269-277.

79 See appendix to original and revised European Social Charters.

80 See: Simon Roberts, 'Migration and social security: Parochialism in the global village', presented at *The Year 2000 International Research Conference on Social Security*, Helsinki, 25-27 September 2000 at 8.

81 See: *FIDH v France,* Complaint No. 14, European Committee on Social Rights. For a comment on the implications of this decision, see: Malcolm Langford, 'Gathering Steam? A Review of Recent Cases from the European Committee on Social Rights', 2 (2005) 2 *Housing & ESC Rights Law Quarterly*, 4-6.

82 Committee on Economic, Social and Cultural Rights, *General Comment 14, The right to the highest attainable standard of health* (Twenty-second session, 2000), U.N. Doc. E/C.12/2000/4 (2000), para. 34.

83 See: Malcolm Langford, *supra* note 82.

3.3 Markets and Social Security

The confluence of the beliefs that market provision is more efficient, that smaller governments promote economic growth, that generous social security provisions provide perverse work incentives and that current levels of social security, particularly benefits, cannot be financed in the future have generated significant debate and substantial reforms in social security provision. These beliefs have been strengthened by attitudes in many countries which some have characterised as 'post-emotionalism' and 'downwards envy' whereby solidarity with the poorer segments of society has been replaced with more harsher Victorian notions of deserving and undeserving poor. The reduction in universal entitlements has also helped undermine middle-class, and even working class, support for social security. Two of the key issues are the privatisation of social security through increasing the role of market-based insurance and secondly the pressure to reduce benefit and financing levels.

Privatisation of social security

While the scope and definition of privatisation differs according to the context (and various models are possible), the content of the debate over the push for privatisation is relatively uniform across the relevant sectors.[84] Proponents for an increased role for the private sector point to the failings of the public sector, the inability of the public sector to provide sufficient capital and finance, and, when faced with the development and human rights discourses, argue that the private sector is more able to reach the excluded. Opponents of privatisation point to increased administrative costs of schemes, the vulnerability of beneficiaries to shocks to the economy and exchange rates and the financial disincentives for the market to reach the excluded, which are unlikely to be corrected through regulation due to weak governments, particularly in developing countries. They also claim that the various institutions who denounce the public sector failings are partly responsible for that failure, for example through structural adjustment programs and the refusal to provide public support. One critic called it a policy of 'defund and defame'. While the World Bank has recently stated in various publications that it will look at mixed approaches, its emphasis on resolving the issue at the national level means that it retains significant leverage over the debate since this is where its power is greatest *vis-a-vis* other international organisations such as the ILO, which are more supportive of collective and public-based systems. Further, supporters of social security privatisation point to the politicisation of social security funds while detractors are nervous about the social security capital being placed in the hands of managers over whom they may have little control.

---

[84] For an overview of the debate on pension reform see sources listed in: Monika Queisser, 'Pension reform and international organizations: From conflict to convergence' 53 (2000) 2 *International Social Security Review* 2, in particular debates between McGillivray and Beattie with Estelle James and Robert Holzmann.

The Committee on Economic, Social and Cultural Rights has generally refrained from declaring that private sector participation is contrary to ICESCR. From its beginning it has interpreted the Covenant to mean that States have flexibility in choosing their economic system – see particular General Comment No. 3. As former Committee member, Paul Hunt has stated:

> [I]nternational human rights law is interested in the *destination* - the full realisation of all human rights - and is less interested in the *road* by which that destination is reached.[85]

But the Committee is clear on three things. First, the involvement of the private sector must be consistent with *democratic principles*, particularly the right to participation. A constant critique of privatisation processes in social security is the lack of transparency, particularly when international financial institutions are involved. Indeed, Mueller's analysis of social security privatisation in Latin America and Eastern Europe demonstrates that higher levels of civil society and parliamentary participation ordinarily result in more modest reforms.[86] Further, many social insurance schemes were previously characterised by high levels of employee participation, something that the market model does not provide for.

The second requirement is *regulation*. In its General Comment on the Right to Water, the Committee has been clear that the private sector must be independently monitored and penalties are to be imposed for non-compliance. During their process of periodically reviewing the performance of countries, they have often been critical of governmental failure to properly regulate private actors operating in the area of social and economic rights.[87] At the national level, some Courts have been

---

85 Paul Hunt, *The international human rights treaty obligations of State parties in the context of service provision*, Submission to UN Committee on the Rights of the Child, Day of Discussion on The Private Sector as Service Provider and Its Role in Implementing Child Rights, Office of the High Commissioner for Human Rights, Palais Wilson, Geneva, 20 September 2002 at 2. Available at www.crin.org/docs/resources/treaties/ crc.31/Paul_Hunt-Legal-Obligations.pdf.

86 See: Katharina Müller, *Privatising Old-Age Security: Latin America and Eastern Europe Compared* (Edward Elgar, 2003).

87 In the case of social security, the Committee pertinently stated in its concluding observations on Chile: 'The Committee is deeply concerned that the private pension system, based on individual contributions, does not guarantee adequate social security for a large segment of the population who do not work in the formal economy or are unable to contribute sufficiently to the system, such as the large group of seasonal and temporary workers. The Committee notes that women are particularly affected in this regard: "housewives" and about 40 per cent of working women do not contribute to the social security scheme and are consequently not entitled to old age benefits. Moreover, the Committee is concerned at the fact that working women are left with a much lower average pensions than men as their retirement age is five year earlier than that of men. The Committee recommends that the State party take effective measures to ensure that all workers are entitled to adequate social security benefits, including special measures to assist those groups who are currently not able to pay into the private social security system, paying special attention to the disadvantaged position of women and the large number of temporary and seasonal workers and workers in the informal economy.' See:

willing to apply the right to social security to this issue: A Latvian law that established an ineffective mechanism for ensuring that employers paid their contributions was struck down by the Constitutional Court of Latvia for its failure to ensure the right to social security of the relevant employees.[88] Many commentators in social security have noted the very poor enforcement mechanisms for regulating social security, particularly in developing countries. This is particularly the case where a defined contributions scheme is used and private social security managers build up large capital assets. The incentives for corruption are no less than in the public sector.

The third stipulation is that the government must ensure that private actors, at the end of the day, take the *necessary steps* to assist in the realisation of the right to social security or accept the responsibility itself to correct market failures. The debate over whether private managers are better or worse at improving access to social security is heated. But three observations can be made. First, the use of defined contribution, and not defined benefit, schemes is almost problematic by definition. While the multi-pillar approach of the World Bank provides for a first tier basic pension, a defined contributions scheme for the second tier potentially undermines the obligation of progressive realisation. First, it is likely to increase unequal outcomes since it will mean greater links between labour markets and social security payments. While many countries have contribution-based insurance schemes, a long-term effort has been made to ensure greater equity. But perhaps more striking is the reliance on pre-funding and no defined benefits, which leaves savings or insurance contributions more vulnerable to inflation and the prospect that benefits will not be paid or will be lower. Of course the obverse is true and benefits may be higher if real interest rates and wages are high but it is difficult to conclude that the system provides *security*. While a pre-funded defined contributions scheme is not automatically inconsistent with the right to social security, it raises significant issues that will need to be dealt with in the design and implementation of the scheme, for example as was done in Sweden. The second major issue is whether private managers will engage in cherry-picking and creaming by excluding poorer workers – where administrative costs may be comparatively too high – or avoiding minimum benefits mandated for such schemes.

Benefits: Reductions and restrictions

Many social security reforms as McGillivray points out in his paper, seek to reduce benefit levels and introduce greater restrictions on eligibility. Since social security is often a major budget item, the pressure to institute retrogressive reforms is significant. While retrogression is not prohibited under the Covenant, it is

Conclusions and recommendations of the Committee on Economic, Social and Cultural Rights, Chile, U.N. Doc. E/C.12/1/Add.105 (2004), paras. 20 and 43 respectively.

88 See: Case No. 2000-08-0109, Constitutional Court of Latvia, 2001. The right to social security and the International Covenant on Economic, Social and Cultural Rights are respectively enshrined and incorporated in the constitution.

deemed immediately suspicious since it contradicts the duty of progressive achievement. The Committee has therefore stated:

> [A]ny deliberately retrogressive measures in that regard would require the most careful consideration and would need to be fully justified by reference to the totality of the rights provided for in the Covenant and in the context of the full use of the maximum available resources.[89]

Further, Article 4 of the Covenant states that 'the State may subject such rights only to such limitations as are determined by law only in so far as this may be compatible with the nature of these rights and solely for the purpose of promoting the general welfare in a democratic society.' The European Committee on Social Rights has captured this necessity for objective and rational review of retrogressive measures as follows: 'It recalls that this provision of the Charter leaves the Contracting Party concerned a certain latitude in the choice of occupations to be classed as dangerous or unhealthy. This choice is however still subject to review by the Committee.[90] In the periodic review of one country, the Committee actually sanctioned the reduction of social security benefits after reviewing the justifications.

The importance of providing such a review is undeniable. Amartya Sen has stated that 'The need for trade-offs is often exaggerated and is typically based on very rudimentary reasoning. Further, even when trade-offs have to be faced, they can be more reasonably – and more justly – addressed by taking an inclusive approach, which balances competing concerns, than by simply giving full priority to just one group over another.'[91] But what form should the review take? A number of principles of non-retrogression can be advanced, in circumstances where the reforms are carried out in a democratic society and in promotion of the general welfare:

1. Alternatives to the problem at hand should be comprehensively examined, including budgetary reviews to determine whether the objectives can be reached without affecting the right to social security.
2. There should be genuine participation of affected groups in examining proposed measures and alternatives that threaten their existing human right to social security protections.
3. The burdens, where necessary, should be shared as far as possible in order not to exacerbate poverty.
4. The reform should not be directly or indirectly discriminatory.
5. The reform must as far as possible avoid beneficiaries losing the achievement of the right to an adequate standard of living, particularly if the reduction is to be sustained.

---

[89] General Comment No. 3, *supra* note 38, para. 9.

[90] *STTK ry and Tehy ry v Finland*, Complaint No. 10, para. 20.

[91] Sen, *supra* note 5, at 120-121.

6. The reform must not further deprive an individual of access to the minimum essential level of housing, health care, education etc unless all maximum available resources have been used, including domestic and international.
7. Review procedures should be instituted at the national levels, for example Senate review Committees in Finland.

4. Conclusion

In a field congested by standards and existing actors, it appears at first glance that the right to social security may simply provide a supporting and affirming role. However, the above analysis indicates that the right to social security may have a much more substantial role to play since it not only greatly extends the reach of the international legal framework and mandates a system of accountability, but may require new approaches in the field of social security.

Social Security Reforms and the Right to Social Security

Latin America and Eastern Europe Compared

Katharina Müller*

1. Introduction

During the 1990s, many Latin American countries introduced compulsory pre-funded social security schemes, run by private pension funds that either compete with, substitute or complement the pre-reform public pay-as-you-go (PAYG) schemes. A similar wave of 'structural' or 'systemic' pension reforms has occurred in the transition countries of Central-Eastern Europe (CEE). These reforms imply a substantial rewrite of the underlying social contract, which does not usually occur in the case of changes to entitlement conditions, commonly referred to as 'parametric' reform.

This paper comes in five parts. After this introduction, two sections give an overview on the pre-reform legacies, the regional background and the systemic pension reforms in both Latin America and Eastern Europe. Thereafter, a critical evaluation of pension privatisation in both regions is ventured and followed by a discussion on the right to social security in the context of pension privatisation.

2. Regional Background: Old-age Security in Latin America

The origins of Bismarckian-style pension schemes in Latin America can be traced back to the first decades of the 20th century. Mesa-Lago[1] distinguishes between the 'pioneer countries', an 'intermediate group' and the 'latecomer countries'. The pioneers – Brazil, Uruguay, Argentina, Cuba, Chile – set up the first pension schemes in the 1920s and 1930s. Mexico, Costa Rica, Ecuador, Panama, Colombia, Peru – the intermediate group – introduced their first pension programmes in

---

* Economist, German Development Institute (DIE), Bonn, Germany.

1 Carmelo Mesa-Lago, *Social Security and Prospects for Equity in Latin America* (World Bank, Discussion Paper No. 140, 1991), XI.

the 1940s, while the latecomers – Nicaragua, Bolivia, Venezuela, Guatemala, El Salvador, Honduras, the Dominican Republic – did so between the 1950s and 1970s.[2]

The expansion of coverage was based on populist-corporatist state action and the influence of pressure groups, reflecting the extreme stratification of Latin American society.[3] Benefits were first accessible to powerful constituencies (the military, public servants, unionised private sector workers), whereas weaker groups – agricultural workers, domestic servants, informal sector workers – were covered only much later, if at all.

The favourable age structure of the insured population and the progressive integration of new contributors into the pension schemes ensured that the schemes were financially sound during the first decades. Yet, in a context of mounting inflation, the existing scaled premium systems turned into de facto PAYG schemes. Reserves, invested largely in public bonds, rendered negative real rates of return and decapitalised rapidly. Pension programmes in the pioneer countries matured, reaching the limits of coverage expansion. In the wake of the 1980s' debt crisis, economic stabilisation and structural adjustment programmes only contributed to a further decline of available resources, just when the need for compensatory state measures had become most pressing.[4]

Apart from their financial problems, pension programmes in Latin America suffered from a number of other shortcomings. A weak contribution-benefit link coincided with generous entitlement conditions and replacement rates. Consequently, contribution rates and state subsidies were high, while evasion and underreporting of income increased. Furthermore, the existing old-age security systems were fragmented, consisting of multiple funds with different legislation and management, benefits and contribution rates. This situation generated high costs, as well as problems of equity. Moreover, an ever-growing part of the labour force lacked formal employment and, thus, coverage.

Chile was the first country to privatise its pension system. In 1981, in the context of an anti-statist ideology and the extraordinary powers of the Pinochet regime, the existing public PAYG system was replaced by a compulsory prefunded scheme run by private pension fund administrators. The significance of the Chilean reform was not the development of a substantially new concept for old-age security, but the putting of existing neoliberal reform proposals into practice, thereby establishing a precedent.[5]

---

[2] Carmelo Mesa-Lago and Fabio Bertranou, *Manual de Economía de la Seguridad Social* (CLAEH, 1998).

[3] Carmelo Mesa-Lago, *Social Security in Latin America: Pressure Groups, Stratification, and Inequality* (University of Pittsburgh Press, 1978).

[4] Carmelo Mesa-Lago, 'Die Reform der Renten in Lateinamerika und die Position der internationalen Organisationen' 11 (1997) *Zeitschrift für ausländisches und internationales Arbeits- und Sozialrecht* 3.

[5] Monika Queisser, *Vom Umlage- zum Kapitaldeckungsverfahren: Die chilenische Rentenreform als Modell für Entwicklungsländer?* (Weltforum, 1993); *Silvia Borzutzky, Vital Connections: Politics, Social Security, and Inequality in Chile* (University of Notre Dame Press, 2002).

Table 1: A comparison of Latin American pension privatisations[6]

	Chile	*Peru*	*Argentina*	*Colombia*	*Uruguay*
Type of public mandatory tier	Phased out	Traditional PAYG; alternative to private tier	Traditional PAYG; private tier complementary	Traditional PAYG; alternative to private tier	Traditional PAYG; private tier complementary
Mandatory membership in private pre-funded tier[7]	New entrants to labour market; others may opt to switch from public tier	Membership in either the private or the public tier is mandatory for all	All workers may redirect their contribution to the private tier	Membership in either the private or the public tier is mandatory for all	Mandatory for earners > US$800; optional for smaller earners and those aged 40+ to redirect part of their contribution to private tier
Contribution to prefunded tier (net of administrative costs)	Individual rate: 10%	Individual rate: 8%	Individual rate: 4.48%[8]	Individual rate: 10.5% (split between employees and employers)	Individual rate: 12.14%
Reform type	Substitutive	Parallel	Mixed	Parallel	Mixed
Starting date	1981	1993	1994	1994	1996

	Bolivia	*Mexico*	*El Salvador*	*Costa Rica*
Type of public mandatory tier	Closed down	Closed down	Phased out	Traditional PAYG; private tier complementary
Mandatory membership in private pre-funded tier[7]	Mandatory for all workers	Mandatory for all workers	Mandatory for new entrants to labour market and insured up to age 35, optional for those aged 36–50 (women) / 36–55 (men)	Mandatory for all workers
Contribution to prefunded tier (net of administrative costs)	Individual rate: 10%	7.09% (split between employees, employers and state)	10.01% (split between employees and employers)	4.06 % (split between employees and employers)
Reform type	Substitutive	Substitutive	Substitutive	Mixed
Starting date	1997	1997	1998	2001

6 Source: Based on Katharina Müller, *Privatising Old-Age Security: Latin America and Eastern Europe Compared* (Edward Elgar Publishing, 2003).

7 Although the prefunded tier is dominated by private pension administrators, some countries also admit publicly run pension funds.

8 Withholdings were substantially reduced in the aftermath of the 2001 economic crisis.

While it seemed a bold, but isolated experiment of an autocratic regime at first, reference to the Chilean pension reform became 'politically palatable'[9] in the early 1990s, when a democratic government took over from the Pinochet regime. The Chilean reform soon evolved as a paradigm for Latin America and beyond, yet without being replicated identically. Currently, more than half of all Latin American countries have legislated and/or implemented variations of the so-called 'Chilean model', most of them under democratic regimes (Mesa-Lago 2004).[10]

Table 2: Latin America: some relevant pension indicators[11]

	System dependency rate[12]	Old-age dependency rate[13]	Pensioners (as % of population)	Coverage rate[14]	Replacement rate[15]	Pension spending (in % of GDP)
Argentina	64.0	27.0	13.8	53.0	46.7	4.1
Bolivia	40.0	16.2	2.0	11.7	45.3	2.5
Brazil	60.0	14.1	10.0	36.0	30.3	4.9
Chile	24.3	17.5	10.4	70.0	67.5	5.9
Colombia	11.0	16.1	1.5	33.0	63.6	1.1
Costa Rica	14.0	14.5	2.5	47.0	47.2	3.8
Ecuador	18.0	13.9	1.7	26.0	24.5	1.2
El Salvador	8.6	14.3	0.9	26.2	67.9	1.3
Guatemala	15.0	12.5	1.4	28.9	14.3	0.7
Honduras	4.0	12.0	0.4	24.0	n.a.	0.6
Mexico	12.5	12.9	1.6	30.0	66.9	0.4
Nicaragua	21.0	11.2	1.0	13.6	29.4	4.3
Panama	n.a.	14.6	3.4	50.0	50.3	4.3
Paraguay	12.5	12.0	1.5	31.0	n.a.	n.a.
Peru	31.0	14.3	2.3	20.0	22.3	1.2
Uruguay	70.0	34.5	25.8	82.0	65.0	8.7
Venezuela	5.0	13.0	0.7	23.6	n.a.	0.5

The substitutive model, which replaces the public pension scheme entirely with mandatory pension funds, is most frequent among Latin America's structural pension reforms (see Table 1). It was chosen in Chile (1981), Bolivia (1997), El Sal-

[9] Carmelo Mesa-Lago, 'Social Welfare Reform in the Context of Economic-Political Liberalization: Latin American Cases' 25 (1997) *World Development* 498.

[10] Carmelo Mesa-Lago, 'La reforma de pensiones en América Latina. Modelos y características, mitos y desempeños, y lecciones' in Katja Hujo, Carmelo Mesa-Lago and Manfred Nitsch (eds), *¿Públicos o privados? Los sistemas de pensiones en América Latina después de dos décadas de reformas* (Nueva Sociedad, 2004).

[11] Data are mostly for the mid-1990s. Source: Katharina Müller (*supra* note 8).

[12] Pensioners as a percentage of contributors.

[13] 60+ years old as a percentage of 20-59 years old.

[14] Contributors as percentage of labour force.

[15] Average pension as percentage of average wage.

vador (1997) and Mexico (1997), while Nicaragua and the Dominican Republic have legislated similar reforms. Peru (1993) and Colombia (1994) are the only two countries that adopted the parallel model, under which the public and private pension schemes compete for contributors. The mixed model, that adds a mandatory prefunded tier to a downsized public pension scheme, was implemented in Argentina (1994), Uruguay (1996) and Costa Rica (2001).

While the pension reforms adopted are rather similar, all implying the introduction of a mandatory prefunded tier, the reform context is not. An intra-regional comparison of relevant pension indicators highlights substantial disparities (see Table 2). In all Latin American countries but Uruguay, Argentina, Brazil and Bolivia there are more than three contributors per pensioner, while the ratio is above 10:1 in Honduras, Venezuela and El Salvador. Moreover, most Latin American countries still have young populations, with seven or eight persons in active age for every person aged 60 or above. Only Uruguay and Argentina exhibit European levels of demographic ageing, with an active/passive ratio of around 3:1. Thus, population ageing is clearly not the main issue in Latin America.

Instead, Table 2 shows that the real challenge facing Latin American pension schemes is coverage. In all countries but Uruguay, Chile, Argentina and Panama, less than half of the labour force contribute to the pension scheme. As little as one-fifth of the economically active population contributes in Bolivia, Nicaragua and Peru. On the other hand, in most countries less than 3 per cent of the total population receive a retirement benefit, reflecting both low coverage and the relatively recent introduction of a mandatory pension insurance. Exceptions are Brazil, Chile, Argentina and – most notably – Uruguay, where more than a quarter of the population were drawing a pension in the mid-1990s. Compared with the OECD average of 10.5 per cent of GDP,[16] public pension expenditure is low in Latin America, exceeding 5 per cent of GDP only in Uruguay and Chile, while falling below 1 per cent in some Central American countries. Thus, a heterogeneous panorama emerges. While the Southern Cone countries and Brazil face pension-related challenges that may be considered as roughly comparable to the European ones, all other Latin American countries have young populations, favourable system dependency ratios and a small number of pensioners.

3. Regional Background: Old-Age Security in the Transition Countries

Bismarckian-style pension insurance was established at the end of the 19th century in Central Europe. These early schemes were fragmented and did not protect the rural population. During the socialist era, pension provision in Eastern Europe and the Soviet Union followed similar lines. Pension schemes were unified and integrated into the state budget. Individual contributions were mostly abolished,

16 Colin Gillion, John Turner, Clive Bailey and Denis Latulippe (eds.), *Social Security Pensions: Development and Reform* (ILO, 2000).

rendering employers' contributions the only source of financing. A major achievement was the gradual expansion of coverage, rendering it virtually universal by the 1960s or 1970s.

Table 3: Post-socialist countries: some relevant pension indicators[17]

	System dependency rate[18]	*Old-age dependency rate*[19]	*Pensioners (in % of population)*	*Coverage rate*[20]	*Replacement rate*[21]	*Pension spending (in % of GDP)*
Albania	95.3	18.5	14.8	32.0	34.7	5.1
Armenia	38.0	21.7	16.2	66.6	24.0	3.1
Azerbaijan	66.0	18.5	16.4	52.0	29.0	2.5
Belarus	47.0	33.3	23.5	97.0	44.1	7.7
Bulgaria	81.0	38.5	27.5	64.0	30.0	7.3
Croatia	61.7	37.6	19.0	66.0	46.1	11.6
Czech Rep.	53.0	31.3	24.2	85.0	41.5	9.8
Estonia	60.0	33.3	25.0	76.0	31.6	7.0
Georgia	66.0	31.3	21.1	41.7	36.0	2.7
Hungary	78.1	35.7	27.5	77.0	39.1	9.7
Kazakhstan	66.0	18.9	16.0	51.0	31.0	5.0
Kyrgyzstan	64.0	18.9	11.7	44.0	45.0	6.4
Latvia	65.9	34.5	25.0	60.5	62.8	10.2
Lithuania	69.2	32.3	22.5	74.3	30.8	7.3
Macedonia	50.0	22.7	12.4	49.0	63.5	8.7
Moldova	n.a.	25.6	17.4	34.5	31.6	7.5
Poland	53.7	29.4	18.2	68.0	63.5	14.4
Romania	58.3	32.3	15.1	55.0	23.9	5.1
Russia	n.a.	30.3	25.1	n.a.	38.0	5.7
Slovakia	57.0	27.8	22.0	73.0	41.0	9.1
Slovenia	58.9	31.3	22.2	86.0	68.7	13.6
Tajikistan	n.a.	n.a.	n.a.	n.a.	27.0	3.0
Turkmenistan	n.a.	n.a.	n.a.	n.a.	26.0	2.3
Ukraine	78.0	34.5	27.1	69.8	32.0	8.6
Uzbekistan	n.a.	14.9	11.4	n.a.	42.0	5.3

17 Data are mostly for the mid-1990s. Source: Katharina Müller (*supra* note 8).
18 Pensioners as a percentage of contributors.
19 60+ years old as a percentage of 20-59 years old.
20 Contributors as percentage of labour force.
21 Average pension as percentage of average wage.

Table 4: A comparison of post-socialist pension privatisations[22]

	Kazakhstan	*Hungary*	*Poland*	*Latvia*	*Bulgaria*
Type of public mandatory tier	Closed down	Traditional PAYG; private tier complementary	NDC scheme; private tier complementary	NDC scheme; private tier complementary	PAYG scheme/ pension points; private tier complementary
Mandatory membership in private prefunded tier	Mandatory for all workers	Mandatory for new entrants to labour market; optional for others to redirect part of their contribution to private tier	Mandatory for those below age 30; optional for those aged 30–49 to redirect part of their contribution to private tier	Mandatory for those below age 30; optional for those aged 30–49 to redirect part of their contribution to private tier	Mandatory for those below age 42 to redirect part of their contribution to private tier
Contribution rates to prefunded tier	Individual rate: 10%	Individual rate: 6%	Individual rate: 9%	Individual rate to be gradually increased to 10%	Contribution rate to be gradually increased to 5% and to be paid 50:50 by employees and employers
Reform type	Substitutive	Mixed	Mixed	Mixed	Mixed
Starting date	1998	1998	1999	2001	2002

	Croatia	*Estonia*	*Lithuania*	*Slovakia*
Type of public mandatory tier	PAYG scheme/ pension points; private tier complementary	Traditional PAYG; private tier complementary	Traditional PAYG; private tier complementary	PAYG scheme/ pension points; private tier complementary
Mandatory membership in private prefunded tier	Mandatory for those below age 40; optional for those aged 40–49 to redirect part of their contribution to private tier	Mandatory for those below age 18; optional for others to redirect part of their contribution to private tier	All workers may redirect their contribution to the private tier	Mandatory for new entrants to labour market; optional for others to redirect part of their contribution to private tier
Contribution rates to prefunded tier	Individual rate: 2.5%; employer's rate: 2.5%	Individual rate: 2%; employer's rate: 4%	Individual rate: 5%	Individual rate: 9%
Reform type	Mixed	Mixed	Mixed	Mixed
Starting date	2002	2002	2004/05	2005

[22] Note: Although the prefunded tier is dominated by private pension administrators, some countries also admit publicly run pension funds. Source: Based on Katharina Müller (*supra* note 8 above) modified.

Overall, the existing contribution-benefit link was weak. Pensions depended on years of service rather than on contributions made on behalf of the individual. Although there was little benefit differentiation, branch privileges (a lower retirement age and higher pensions) were granted to occupations of strategic importance, marking an important departure from universalism. The insufficient adjustment of current pensions to price–wage dynamics implied that newly granted pensions were considerably higher than average retirement benefits, giving rise to problems of inter-cohort fairness and benefit adequacy.[23]

Economic transformation, which largely commenced in 1989, affected the existing PAYG systems in several ways. At the onset of reforms, price liberalisation and the curtailment of subsidies on basic goods and services implied a shift from indirect to direct transfers, requiring rising expenditure for old-age security. Subsequently, the restructuring of state-owned enterprises had an effect on both the revenue and expenditure side of public pension schemes. When state-owned enterprises were privatised, downsized or closed down, part of the workforce retired early or took out disability pensions. Designed to disguise the employment effects of adjustment, this policy implied that the pension system was used as a substitute for welfare and unemployment benefits. The increasing number of pensioners and falling number of contributors destabilised public pension finances.

By the mid-1990s, system dependency ratios had deteriorated dramatically. In all countries but Armenia, Belarus and Macedonia, there were less than two contributors per pensioner (see Table 3). In Albania, Bulgaria, Hungary and Ukraine system dependency rates had even risen to 95, 81 and 78 per cent, respectively. The declining revenue base and the erosion of social security also showed up in a dramatic drop in coverage ratios. Before 1989, with full employment and high economic activity rates of women, coverage bordered 100 per cent of the labour force. By the mid-1990s, it had plunged to 32 and 34.5 per cent in Albania and Moldova. In Georgia, the Kyrgyz Republic and Macedonia coverage rates were 42, 44 and 49 per cent, respectively. If these trends are not reversed, over half of those currently in active age may not be entitled to a retirement benefit in the future.

In the post-socialist countries, life expectancy at birth (68.4 years) has now fallen below the Latin American average (69.3 years), while the differences are even larger at retirement age. Nevertheless, due to lower fertility rates, population ageing hit the region more severely than Latin America.[24] Central Asia, the Caucasus and Albania have young populations, but demographic dependency rates in other post-socialist countries are close to EU levels. Table 3 indicates that there are about three persons aged 20 to 59 for everyone aged 60 and above. The ratio of pensioners to the total population is much higher than in Latin America, reflecting demography but also the historically high coverage levels in the socialist world. While there were 11 pensioners per 100 Uzbeks, the ratio was almost three

---

23 Ulrike Götting, *Transformation der Wohlfahrtsstaaten in Mittel- und Osteuropa. Eine Zwischenbilanz* (Leske+Budrich, 1998).

24 Katharina Müller, 'Altern in der Dritten Welt', in Joachim Betz and Stefan Brüne (eds.), *Jahrbuch Dritte Welt 2001* (C.H. Beck, 2000).

times as high in Bulgaria, a country severely affected by the outmigration of the young.

Whereas public pension spending was on the rise in the region, only Poland and Slovenia surpassed the EU15 average, with pension expenditure amounting to 14.4 and 13.6 per cent of GDP.[25] The lowest levels can be observed in Turkmenistan, Azerbaijan, Georgia, Tajikistan and Armenia, where replacement rates are minute. With the exception of Slovenia, Poland, Macedonia and Latvia, the entire region suffers from low benefit levels. Notably in the Former Soviet Union, old-age benefits have fallen below subsistence.[26]

The old-age security systems inherited from the socialist past were undoubtedly in dire need of reform. The need for parametric changes to the existing retirement schemes was relatively undisputed among social security experts and proposals included the separation of pension schemes from other social insurance plans and from the state budget, the introduction of an employees' contribution, the raising of the retirement age, the abolition of branch privileges, the restriction of early retirement, the tightening of eligibility for invalidity pensions and the introduction of indexation rules to provide protection against inflation.

Several post-socialist countries opted for another potentially costly move by linking benefits more closely to lifetime earnings to improve contribution incentives, e.g. by introducing German-style pension points or notional defined contribution (NDC) plans. The point system used in Germany implies a close contribution-benefit link. One earnings point is acquired for each calendar year in which individual earnings are equal to the national average. Benefit calculation is essentially based on the sum of all earnings points, thus reflecting the entire labour biography. NDC schemes are also based on the entire contributions record of the insured, while integrating the logic of a prefunded tier into the public one. All contributions paid to the public scheme are recorded on individual accounts, yet capital accumulation is only virtual. Individual benefit levels essentially depend on the sum of individual contributions, while also reflecting the remaining life expectancy at retirement and the chosen retirement age.[27]

It should be noted that substantial resistance to parametric reforms, which were blocked by constitutional courts in more than one case, often induced policymakers to compromise on the speed and scope of the required reform steps. In comparison, the first move towards a different public–private mix was much less controversial: most Central European countries, Russia, Moldova and the Baltics introduced supplementary private prefunded schemes on a voluntary basis. Yet, the amount of voluntary funds collected fell short of expectations, largely reflecting income constraints.

---

25 Katharina Müller, 'Pension Reform Paths in Central-Eastern Europe and the Former Soviet Union' 36 (2002) *Social Policy and Administration* 2.

26 Jeanine Braithwaite, Christiaan Grootaert and Branko Milanovic, *Poverty and Social Assistance in Transition Countries* (St. Martin's Press, 2000).

27 Robert Holzmann and Edward Palmer (eds.), *Pension reform: Issues and Prospects for Non-Financial Defined Contribution (NDC) Schemes* (World Bank, 2006).

In the context of a generalised retreat of the state, a number of transition countries opted for a more radical approach, thereby stirring substantial controversy. Over the past few years, pension privatisation has been gaining considerable momentum in the post-socialist region. Kazakhstan is the only case of a substitutive reform, explicitly modelled on the Chilean precedent. A mixed approach was chosen by eight other transition countries, among them six new EU member states. Hungary, Poland, Latvia, Bulgaria, Croatia and Estonia implemented partial pension privatisation between 1998 and 2002, Lithuania and Slovakia followed in 2004/2005. Macedonia, Russia and Ukraine have recently legislated similar reforms.

The transition countries exhibit far more diversity in terms of first-tier design than the Latin American cases, where pension points and NDC schemes are virtually absent. Nevertheless, the strong inspiration from the subcontinent in terms of pension privatisation is obvious. In most transition countries, reform patterns share one common feature: a deliberate move from the universalist-redistributive heritage to strongly differentiated, earnings-related benefits, with an emphasis on contributory financing.

4. Social Security in Latin America and Eastern Europe: A Comparative Perspective

The advocates of pension privatisation claimed that such a move helps to reduce public pension expenditure.[28] They recommended pension privatisation in order to resolve financial difficulties in the PAYG schemes. Yet, while the diversion of mandatory contributions to the prefunded tier led to considerably reduced revenues, under almost all reforms acquired pension rights were recognised to some extent and needed to be paid for. In Chile, the annual fiscal cost resulting from pension privatisation is estimated at 3 to 6 per cent of GDP over several decades. The second-generation reformers have tried to lower the substantial fiscal burden by adjusting reform design and restricting the recognition of acquired pension rights, but transition costs remain high. In a context of low coverage, the impact of structural reform tends to be regressive.[29]

Capital market development has been another important motive for pension privatisation. The Chilean case seemed to indicate that a prefunded scheme could generate important financial resources.[30] However, these resources can be channelled to private investment only if transition costs are not covered by issuing new

---

[28] World Bank, *Averting the Old Age Crisis. Policies to Protect the Old and Promote Growth* (Oxford University Press, 1994).

[29] Katharina Müller, 'Die Privatisierung der bolivianischen Alterssicherung – eine Zwischenbilanz', in Rafael Sevilla and Ariel Benavides (eds.), *Bolivien – das verkannte Land?* (Horlemann, 2001).

[30] Robert Holzmann, *Pension Reform, Financial Market Development and Economic Growth: Preliminary evidence from Chile* (IMF Working Paper No. WP/96/94, 1996).

public debt.[31] Yet, this has been a common practice in the countries that privatised pensions, and investment in other sectors was crowded out. The private pension funds' portfolio is dominated by public instruments, reaching over 70 per cent in Mexico, El Salvador, Hungary, Kazakhstan, Bolivia and Costa Rica.[32] In some countries, there is a legal obligation to invest a large part of the funds in public instruments, while in others this reflects a scarcity of alternative instruments with a suitable risk-return profile.

Another assumption holds that in private prefunded schemes, competition between fund administrators reduces administrative costs and guarantees high rates of return. However, concentration in this new financial industry is high, amounting to an oligopoly in many countries. Bolivia is an extreme case with only two pension funds, as the number of affiliates is small and earning levels are low – a situation also faced by other Latin American and East European countries. It seems, therefore, that pension privatisation can only lead to a competitive industry when market size is above a minimum threshold.

On the other hand, the experiences in other Latin American countries indicate that competition amongst a larger number of pension funds translates into high commissions, reflecting the costs created by numerous sales agents, substantial marketing expenses and frequent fund-switching. In Latin America, affiliates are also charged a premium for private invalidity and survivors' insurance, which is no longer covered by the public scheme. The sum of these charges substantially reduces the share of contributions effectively credited to individual accounts. Converting an account into a lifetime annuity generates additional costs. Although the new industry exhibits high real rates of return, their calculation is only net of inflation, not of total costs. When internal rates of return were calculated in Peru and Poland, however, they turned out to be negative.[33]

The advocates of pension privatisation also expected the close contribution-benefit link inherent in prefunded schemes to translate into strong incentives for contribution compliance. Yet, in most Latin American countries less than half of all affiliates to private pension funds contribute regularly, suggesting that compliance is not only a function of incentives. Income levels are especially low in the informal and rural sector, with consumption patterns biased towards the short run. This indicates that pension privatisation cannot solve the most important problems facing the old pension schemes – coverage. In comparison, the post-socialist countries used to enjoy almost complete coverage, which is rapidly becoming a thing of the past.

---

31 András Uthoff, *La reforma del sistema de pensiones en Chile: desafíos pendientes* (CEPAL Serie Financiamiento del Desarrollo No. 112, 2001).

32 Katharina Müller, 'Las reformas de pensiones en América Latina y Europa Oriental: contexto, conceptos, experiencias prácticas y enseñanzas' in Klaus Bodemer (ed.), *Políticas públicas, inclusión social y ciudadanía* (Nueva Sociedad, 2003).

33 World Bank, *Report and recommendation of the President of the IBRD to the Executive Directors on a proposed Loan in an amount of US$300 million to the Republic of Peru for a second Financial Sector Adjustment Loan* (Washington DC, mimeo, 1999), UNFE, *Informacja o stopie zwrotu* (Superintendency for Pension Funds, 2001).

Finally, it should be borne in mind that pension privatisation does not only require private sector capacity. The Latin American and East European cases show that government capacity is at least as relevant. 'Classical' state functions in mandatory private schemes include the design and implementation of the new pension scheme, the regulation and supervision of the prefunded tier, the financing of the fiscal costs of the transition, and the provision of an implicit 'pension guarantee of last resort'.[34] Additional functions allocated to the state in some countries include a clearinghouse approach, the state as sponsor of pension funds, and the provision of disability and survivors' pensions. In this context, it is worth mentioning that several countries that have privatised pensions exhibit alarming levels of state capture and corruption, that are seriously threatening state capacity.[35] As noted by Barr,[36] 'if government is ineffective, any pension scheme will be at risk' – whether private or public. This has only been highlighted by the recent Argentinean experience.[37]

5. The Right to Social Security in the Context of Pension Privatisation

Undoubtedly, the number of Latin American and East European countries that have introduced far-reaching systemic and parametric reforms is significant, particularly when compared with the difficulties that Western countries have faced in attempting to implement more modest pension reform. But how has the right to social security fared in the context of pension privatisation?

Firstly, due to the move towards private prefunded schemes, replacing public PAYG schemes fully or partially in both regions, retirement benefits are no longer a right derived from a certain benefit formula (defined benefit approach) but essentially turn into a result of labour and capital market performance (defined contribution approach). This shift implies an increase in insecurity over future benefit levels, as well as higher risk, to be shouldered by the individual, making it doubtful to what extent he or she will be able to enjoy the right to social security at retirement age.[38]

---

34 Katharina Müller, 'Public-Private Interaction in Structural Pension Reform' in OECD (ed.), *Regulating Private Pension Schemes: Trends and Challenges* (OECD Private Pensions Series N° 4, 2002).

35 Joel S. Hellman, Geraint Jones and Daniel Kaufmann, *'Seize the State, Seize the Day': State Capture, Corruption, and Influence in Transition'* (World Bank Policy Research Working Paper No. 2444, 2000).

36 Nicholas Barr, *Reforming Pensions: Myths, Truths, and Policy Choices* (IMF Working Paper WP/007139, 2000) at 23.

37 Katja Hujo, *Soziale Sicherung im Kontext von Stabilisierung und Strukturanpassung: Die Reform der Rentenversicherung in Argentinien* (Peter Lang Verlag, 2004).

38 Roger Beattie and Warren McGillivray, 'A Risky Strategy: Reflections on the World Bank Report "Averting the Old Age Crisis"', 48 (1995) *International Social Security Review* 3–4.

Secondly, the move towards pension privatisation has often entailed a cutback of acquired rights to social security. Second-generation reformers in particular have tried to lower the concomitant fiscal burden by restricting the recognition of acquired pension rights. This has often been done by downsizing benefits and tightening eligibility in the old system before making the transition[39], or by recognising only part of accrued entitlements in the shift to the new prefunded scheme.[40] This cutback of social security rights, while not unknown in PAYG schemes, was thus used as a systematic strategy to increase the fiscal viability of the move to prefunding, entailing welfare losses to retirees and older workers.[41]

Finally and most importantly, however, it should be noted that in contributory pension schemes, the right to social security enjoyed at old age is determined by past coverage and contributions made. It has been shown above that the main shortcoming facing Latin American pension schemes is coverage, and that differences in level and scope of old-age protection are also widening within and among transition countries, where the current elderly generation will be the last to enjoy virtually universal pension coverage. In spite of this obvious challenge, the overall direction social security reform has taken in both regions was geared towards a strengthening of the contribution-benefit link. Coverage could not be improved by replacing public contributory schemes with private ones. In order to solve this pressing challenge, pension reformers in both regions will need to look for new answers.

Some of these may be found beyond the contributory approaches that have long marked old-age security in both regions. Several Latin American countries, such as Argentina, Bolivia, Brazil, Chile, Costa Rica and Uruguay, have reacted to the coverage gap by setting up non-contributory pension programmes in order to reduce and/or prevent old-age poverty, most of which means-tested.[42] Only in Bolivia is the benefit paid to everyone above age 65.[43] A closer look at existing retirement schemes in the post-socialist world also reveals the existence of non-contributory benefits for the elderly in most transition countries. These targeted benefits – variably known as social pension, national pension, or old-age allow-

39 Estelle James, 'The Political Economy of Social Security Reform: A Cross-Country Review' 69 (1998) *Annals of Public and Cooperative Economics* 4.

40 Katharina Müller (*supra* note 8).

41 David Lindeman, Michal Rutkowski and Oleksiy Sluchynskyy, *The Evolution of Pension Systems in Eastern Europe and Central Asia: Opportunities, Constraints, Dilemmas and Emerging Practices* (World Bank, 2000).
See, for example, Robert Palacios, Michal Rutkowski and Xiaoqing Yu, *Pension Reforms in Transition Economies* (mimeo., 1999) at 31, who argue that 'the government will *have to* renege on some pay-as-you-go commitments' in the context of pension privatisation (emphasis added).

42 Fabio M. Bertranou, Carmen Solorio and Wouter van Ginneken (eds.), Pensiones no contributivas y asistenciales: Argentina, Brasil, Chile, Costa Rica y Uruguay (OIT, 2002).

43 Katharina Müller, *Non-contributory pensions in Latin America: The case of Bolivia's BONOSOL* (Paper prepared for the XXV International Congress of the Latin American Studies Association, 7-9 October 2004, Las Vegas).

ance – are tax-financed, and eligibility generally presupposes a means and/or inactivity test. However, benefits are often so low that their poverty-reduction function is severely hampered.[44]

Recent years have witnessed a heightened international interest in non-contributory benefits.[45] The role of such benefits, which are still rather marginalised on the pension reform agenda in both regions, will need to increase if old-age poverty is to be avoided and the right to social security is to be extended to all elderly citizens of Latin America and Eastern Europe.

44 Katharina Müller, 'Post-socialist pension reform: contributory and non-contributory approaches' 5 (2005) *Journal of Public Finance and Management* 2.

45 See, for example, IDPM and HAI, *Non-contributory pensions and poverty prevention: a comparative study of Brazil and South Africa* (IDPM & HAI, 2003), HAI, *Age and security. How social pensions can deliver effective aid to poor older people and their families* (HelpAge International, 2004), Indermit S. Gill, Truman Packard and Juan Yermo: *Keeping the Promise of Old Age Income Security in Latin America* (Stanford University Press & World Bank, 2004), Robert Holzmann, *Pension Reform, Financial Market Development and Economic Growth: Preliminary evidence from Chile* (IMF Working Paper No. WP/96/94, 1996), and Roddy McKinnon and Roger Charlton (eds.), 'Special Issue on Ageing' 5 (2005) *Journal of Public Finance and Management* 2.

The Judicial Enforcement of Social Security Rights in South Africa

Enhancing Accountability for the Basic Needs of the Poor

Sandra Liebenberg*

1. Introduction

The 1996 South African Constitution[1] includes a range of justiciable socio-economic rights in its Bill of Rights,[2] including the right of 'everyone' to have access to social security.[3] In addition, the Bill of Rights includes a substantive equality clause,[4] as well as a right to just administrative action.[5]

This paper examines the nature and extent of the judicial protection of social security rights in South Africa. It explores three major avenues through which the courts can protect social security rights: social security as a socio-economic right, the intersection between equality rights and social security rights, and the protection of social security through administrative justice rights. The paper focuses particularly on the social assistance system because of its significant impact on poverty alleviation in the South African context. The paper aims to demonstrate that the courts are providing an important accountability mechanism in relation to social security reform and implementation in South Africa.

2. The historical and social context of social security in South Africa

Due to its colonial and apartheid history, the social security system in South Africa was characterised by pervasive racial discrimination. As the Constitutional

---

* HF Oppenheimer Chair in Human Rights Law, Stellenbosch University, South Africa. I would like to express my appreciation to my research assistants, Mary-Elizabeth Monyakame and Barbara Loots, for valuable research assistance on this paper.

1 Act 108 of 1996 (hereafter 'the Constitution').

2 Chapter 2.

3 Section 27(1)(c) read with (2).

4 Section 9.

5 Section 33.

Court observed in *Mashavha v President of the RSA and Others*[6] (hereafter 'Mashavha'):

> Our history is well-known. It is one of colonialisation, apartheid, economic exploitation, migrant labour, oppression and balkanisation. Gross inequalities were deliberately and legally imposed as far as race and also geographical areas are concerned. Not only were there richer and poorer provinces, but there were 'homelands', which by no stretch of the imagination could be seen to have been treated on the same footing as 'white' South Africa, as far as resources are concerned. These inequalities also applied to social assistance – an area of governmental responsibility very closely related to human dignity.[7]

The new democratic government thus inherited a social security system that was fragmented, inequitable and administratively inefficient. In addition, the apartheid social security system was premised on high levels of coverage by social insurance schemes in formal employment, with social assistance forming a residual 'safety net' function for targeted categories of vulnerable groups living in poverty, primarily, persons with disabilities, children and the aged.

Today, poverty and inequality are among the most serious challenges facing South Africa. It has been estimated that 18 million people in South Africa, representing 45 per cent of the population, live below the poverty line using an absolute measure of poverty, pegged at an income per adult of R353 per month.[8] Unemployment remains a major challenge with the official rate being 30 per cent.[9] Related phenomena of the 'working poor', peripheral forms of employment and a substantial informal sector characterised by low wages, minimal benefits, and no security.[10]

---

6 *Mashava v President of the RSA and Others* 2004 (12) BCLR 1243 (CC).

7 *Ibid.*, para. 51 (per Van Der Westhuizen J). See also: Haroon Bhorat, 'The South African Social Safety Net: Past, Present and Future' 4 (1995) 12 *Development Southern Africa* 595.

8 United Nations Development Programme (UNDP) (principal author: Vivienne Taylor) *South Africa: Transformation for Human Development* (UNDP, 2000) 55. According to another study, although South Africa is an upper-middle-income country in *per capita* terms, most households experience either outright poverty or vulnerability to poverty: Julian May (ed.) *Poverty and Inequality in South Africa* (University of Natal, 1998) 1.

9 The expanded definition of unemployment, which includes discouraged work-seekers, is 41.8%. See: Morné Oosthuizen and Haroon Bhorat, *The Post-Apartheid South African Labour Market*, (Strategies and Analysis for Growth and Access (SAGA) Working Paper, 2004) 3.

10 This covers a range of economic and legal relationships, including casual, seasonal, home-based, sub-contract work, and employment in the informal sector. See: Jan Theron and Shane Godfrey *Protecting workers on the periphery,* (Development and Labour Monographs, Institute of Development and Labour Law, University of Cape Town, 2000).

The HIV/AIDS epidemic is having a major impact on human survival and development in South Africa.[11] The poverty implications of the epidemic include increased health-costs, a fall in productivity due to the demands on household members of caring for ill members, the illness and death of breadwinners, and an increase in the number of AIDS orphans. The impact of the epidemic creates a number of new challenges for the social security system. This includes the payment of social grants to child-headed households,[12] the impact of the epidemic on grants such as the disability grant and care dependency grant, and the impact of declining life expectancy on poverty and the social grants system.[13]

3. Overview of the social security system and proposals for its reform

The current social security system is broadly comprised of an extensive social assistance programme and a number of social insurance programmes. Social assistance takes the form of social grants, which are paid in terms of the Social Assistance Act 59 of 1992. This Act has recently been replaced by the Social Assistance 13 of 2004.[14] The four main social grants are the grant for the aged,[15] the grant for the disabled,[16] the foster child grant,[17] and the child support grant.[18] Together these grants reach approximately 9 million poor people in our society.[19]

---

11 Statistics South Africa, *Mortality and causes of death in South Africa, 1997 – 2003: Findings from death notification* (Statistics South Africa, 2005), Statistical release PO309.3 [available on-line at: http://www.statssa.gov.za/publications/].

12 Beth Goldblatt & Sandra Liebenberg 'Giving money to children: The state's constitutional obligations to provide child support grants to child headed households' 1 (2004) 20 *South African Journal of Human Rights* 151. See also: Jeremy Seekings 'The broader importance of welfare reform in South Africa' 2 (2002) 28 *Social Dynamics* at 26 – 27.

13 See the discussion by Seekings, *ibid.*

14 The preamble of this Act refers explicitly to the constitutionally entrenched right of everyone to have access to social security.

15 The grant for the aged is payable to women at age 60 years, and men at aged 65 years. although this differentiation is currently the subject of an equality rights challenge. It is based on a sliding scale means test, and the maximum amount payable per month is R820 for the 2006/2007 fiscal year.

16 This grant is payable to a person, 18 years or older, who is unfit to provide for his or her maintenance because of physical or mental disability. The grant covers permanent or temporary disability, which must be confirmed by a medical officer. The grant is subject to a sliding-scale means test, and the maximum payable is R820 per month.

17 The foster care grant is paid to the foster parents of children under the age of 18 years old. In order to qualify for the grant, the income of the children should not be more than twice the annual amount of a foster care grant. The level of the grant is set at R590 per month.

18 The child support grant (CSG) of R180 per month per child is payable to the primary care giver of children under the age of 14 years. The income of the primary care giver is

The other main pillar of South Africa's social security system is social insurance schemes. These consist mainly of the Compensation for Occupational Injuries and Diseases Act (COIDA) Act No. 130 of 1993, the Occupational Diseases in Mines and Works Act 78 of 1993 (ODMWA), the Unemployment Insurance Act 63 of 2001, and a number of private workplace pension funds.[20] The Unemployment Insurance Act is a contributory scheme that provides for unemployment, illness, maternity and dependant's benefits. In 2003, coverage under the Act was extended to previously excluded categories of employees such as domestic workers and seasonal workers. However, the definition of 'employee' under the Act excludes other categories of vulnerable workers such as persons defined as independent contractors who may in fact be in an employment-type relationship[21] and casual workers 'employed for less than 24 hours a month with a particular employer.'[22] The coverage of these schemes is limited to those who are in formal employment. Given South Africa's high rate of structural unemployment, the unemployment insurance system is unable to serve as a primary mechanism of poverty alleviation. [23]

In the above context, the government's social assistance programme is a vital mechanism of poverty alleviation.[24] It is also one of the largest redistributive programmes of the government.[25] However, even this scheme has large gaps in cov-

means-tested according to a two-tier means test which sets a higher limit for primary care-givers and their children living in rural areas or in informal dwellings. On the application of the means test, see: Debbie Budlender, Solange Rosa & Katharine Hall *At all costs? Applying the means test for the child support grant* (Cape Town: Children's Institute & Centre for Actuarial Research, UCT, 2005).

19 The child support grant has the largest number of beneficiaries with over 5 million recipients.

20 For an overview, see: Anthony Asher & Marius Paul Olivier 'Retirement and Old Age' in Marius Paul Olivier, N. Smit and N.R. Kalula (eds.) *Social Security: A Legal Analysis* (Lexis Nexis, Butterworths, 2003), Chapter 8, 231 – 299.

21 See the definition of 'employee' in section 1 of the Unemployment Insurance Act, 2001.

22 Section 3 of the Unemployment Insurance Act.

23 There are also a number of other direct and indirect measures of social security such as road accident insurance, the provision of free basic services, various nutritional programmes, and subsidised health care, housing and education for the poor. Government is also currently investigating the establishment of a social health insurance scheme to provide government-mandated health insurance cover.

24 According to a recent study commissioned by the Department of Social Development, the current social security system with September 2000 levels of take-up effectively reduces the rand destitution gap by 45%. Destitution is defined as the bottom 20% of the expenditure distribution, and the resulting destitution poverty line is R180 per person per month. See: Economic Policy Research Institute, Summary Report, *The Social and Economic Impact of South Africa's Social Security System*, (Department of Social Development, 30 September 2004) at 8.

25 Social security programmes now account for 14% of consolidated non-interest expenditure, up from 9.5 % five years ago: Minister of Finance, Trevor Manuel, *Budget Speech* 2005 [available on-line at http://www.treasury.gov.za/].

erage and does not adequately provide for the needs of the poor.[26] The two main groups who currently have no access to social assistance in South Africa are poor children of 14 years and over and unemployed adults. Households without members who qualify for the child support grant, the grant for the aged or a disability grant, are left with no or minimal access to social assistance.[27]

Because poverty is gendered, the large gaps in social security coverage affect women disproportionately.[28] This is exacerbated by the lack of provisioning for the unpaid caring work performed primarily by women and the lack of adequate child care.[29] In addition, the administration of specific social security programmes such as the extension of unemployment insurance to domestic workers and the child support grant have profound gender implications. Women are the major beneficiaries of these programmes.[30] The way that these programmes are administered and the public discourses around them can serve to perpetuate negative gender stereotypes and stigmatisation.[31] On the other hand, the existence of these programmes also has a positive impact on gender equality by promoting women's economic independence and welfare.

In 2000, government appointed a Committee of Inquiry into a Comprehensive Social Security System (hereafter 'the Committee of Inquiry'). This Committee had a wide-ranging brief to review the entire social security system in South Africa, and to make recommendations for the reform of the system. The primary recommendation of the Committee to close the social protection gap and reduce poverty was the phased introduction of a universal Basic Income Grant (BIG).[32]

---

26 *Ibid.*, at 59.

27 The only exception may be the possibility of applying and receiving for a limited period of 3 months, the Social Relief of Distress Grant (SROD) which the Social Assistance Act makes provision for (section 13). There are, however, serious problems in the implementation of this grant so that as present it does not serve as effective poverty alleviation measure. See, for example, the settlement agreement made an order of court in *Kutumela v Member of the Executive Committee for Social Services, Culture, Art and Sport in the North West Province* Case No. 671/2003, 23 October 2003 (B).

28 See: Beth Goldblatt 'Gender and social assistance in the first decade of democracy – a case study of South Africa's child support grant' 2 (2005) 32 *Politikon*.

29 For a comprehensive discussion of the issue of child care in South Africa, see: Beth Goldblatt 'Citizenship and the right to child care' in Amanda Gouws (ed.) *(Un)thinking Citizenship: Feminist Debates in Contemporary South Africa* (Ashgate, 2005) 117-136.

30 Although it should be noted that entitlement to the child support grant is defined in gender neutral terms as the 'primary care giver' of young children.

31 For a discussion of the administrative barriers in accessing the child support grant as well as perceptions regarding teenagers becoming pregnant in order to gain access to the grant and women abusing the grant, see: Beth Goldblatt & Sandra Liebenberg, *supra* note 12; Beth Goldblatt 'Teen pregnancy and abuse of the child support grant: Addressing the myths and stereotypes' (2003) *Agenda* 71.

32 Report of the Committee of Inquiry into a Comprehensive System of Social Security for South Africa, *Transforming the Present – Protecting the Future* (Cape Town, March 2002), Ch. 5. Financing options for the comprehensive social protection package are discussed in Ch. 14. The Committee noted that part of the costs of the BIG would be covered by a progressive tax 'claw-back' from better-off beneficiaries (see at 134).

According to research and analysis conducted by the Committee, the BIG has the potential, 'more than any other possible social protection intervention, to reduce poverty and promote human development and sustainable livelihoods.'[33] This proposal is supported by the trade union movement and a range of other civil society organisations. However, it has not been accepted by the government, which has focused rather on strategies to reduce unemployment such as an expanded public works programme.

The new democratic government has removed all vestiges of state racial discrimination in the social security system, and is taking a range of significant measures to extend access to social security, basic services, productive assets and employment by the poor. However, as the Committee of Inquiry observed in its report:

> ...a key underlying principle of the old system remains in place, i.e. the assumption that those in the labour force can support themselves through work, and that unemployment is a temporary condition. In reality those who cannot find work (and who do not, or no longer, qualify for UIF payments) fall through a vast hole in the social safety net.[34]

Against this backdrop, I turn to consider the nature and extent of the State's constitutional obligations in relation to social security rights.

4. Social security as a constitutionally protected socio-economic right

4.1 Introducing social security as a constitutional right

The right to social security is entrenched as one of the socio-economic rights provisions contained in sections 26 and 27 of the Constitution. Section 26(1) entrenches the right of everyone 'to have access to adequate housing', and section 27(1) the right of everyone 'to have access to (a) health care services, including reproductive health care; (b) sufficient food and water; and (c) social security, including, if they are unable to support themselves and their dependants, appropriate social assistance.' These first sections of sections 26 and 27 respectively are qualified by a second subsection, which reads:

> The state must take reasonable legislative and other measures, within its available resources, to achieve the progressive realisation of each of these rights.

33 *Ibid.*, at 62.
34 *Ibid.*, at 15.

In addition to these provisions, the Constitution also entrenches a set of 'basic' rights consisting of children's socio-economic rights,[35] the right of everyone to basic education, including adult basic education,[36] and the socio-economic rights of detained persons, including sentenced prisoners.[37] The Bill of Rights also provides for the protection of labour rights (section 23), environmental rights (section 24), land rights (section 25(5) – (9), language and cultural rights (sections 30 and 31).

All these rights are enforceable by the Courts, and the Courts have a wide discretion to grant 'just and equitable' remedies.[38] The Constitution places an overarching obligation on the state to 'respect, protect, promote and fulfil the rights in the Bill of Rights'.[39] This establishes that all the rights in the Bill of Rights impose a combination of negative and positive duties on the state.[40]

Of particular importance to the practical justiciability of socio-economic rights, is the generous provisions on legal standing ('*locus standi*') enshrined in the Bill of Rights. Section 38 confers standing on a broad category of persons who may approach a court for appropriate relief, alleging that a right in the Bill of Rights has been infringed or threatened. This includes anyone acting on behalf of person who cannot act in their own name,[41] class actions,[42] actions in the public interest,[43] and associations acting in the interest of their members.[44] The leading case in South Africa on class actions in the context of socio-economic rights claims is *Permanent Secretary, Department Welfare, E Cape Provincial Government and Another v Ngxuza and Others* ('*Ngxuza*').[45] This case concerned an application for the reinstatement of the disability grant of tens of thousands of social grant recipients that had been unlawfully terminated by the Eastern Cape provincial govern-

---

35 Section 28(1)(c) gives every child the right to 'basic nutrition, shelter, basic health care services and social services'. A child is defined in section 28(3) as a person under the age of 18 years.

36 Section 29(1)(a).

37 Section 35(2)(e) confers the right 'to conditions of detention that are consistent with human dignity, including at least exercise and the provision, at state expense, of adequate accommodation, nutrition, reading material and medical treatment.'

38 Under section 172 of the Constitution, a Court must declare invalid law or conduct that is inconsistent with the Constitution to the extent of its inconsistency, and may make 'any order that is just and equitable.'

39 Section 7(2).

40 As Justice Kriegler of the Constitutional Court observed: 'We do not operate under a Constitution in which the avowed purpose of the drafters was to place limits on governmental control. Our constitution aims at establishing freedom and equality in a grossly disparate society.' *Du Plessis v De Klerk* 1996 (5) BCLR 658 (CC) at para. 147.

41 Section 38(b).

42 Section 38(c).

43 Section 38(d). The most famous case in this regard is *Minister of Health and Others v Treatment Action Campaign & Others* 2002 (1) BCLR 1033 (CC) ('*TAC*') where a non-governmental organisation successfully challenged the government's programme on the prevention of mother-to-child transmission of HIV.

44 Section 38(e).

45 *Permanent Secretary, Department Welfare, E Cape Provincial Government and Another v Ngxuza and Others* 2001 (10) BCLR 1039 (SCA).

ment. The Court held that the case was 'pattern-made' for class proceedings taking into account the circumstances of the large, disparate group of claimants, scattered throughout remote rural areas and 'lacking in protective and assertive armour.' The Court held that it is the needs of persons in this position that 'must animate our understanding of the Constitution's provisions.'[46]

In its jurisprudence, the Court has highlighted the close links between social security and the foundational constitutional values of human dignity, equality and freedom.[47]

The Constitutional Court has yet to engage substantively with the scope and content of the right to social security and assistance entrenched in section 27(1)(c).[48] However, it has developed a substantial body of jurisprudence on the obligations imposed by the socio-economic rights provisions in the Constitution. The relevance of this jurisprudence to the right to social security will be considered below.

4.2 State obligations: The duty to desist from preventing or impairing access

In the first place, the Constitutional Court has affirmed that sections 26(1) and 27(1) impose a negative duty on the state to 'desist from preventing or impairing' access to the relevant rights.[49] In its recent decision of *Jaftha v Schoeman and Others; Van Rooyen v Stoltz and Others* ('*Jaftha*'),[50] the Court illustrated the high degree of protection it would afford people against negative violations of their socio-economic rights. *Jaftha* concerned the constitutionality of provisions of the Magistrates' Court Act which permitted the sale in execution of people's homes in order to satisfy (sometimes trifling) debts. The Court accepted the appellants' arguments that legislative measures that permit a person to be deprived of existing access to housing constitute a negative violation of the right of access to housing. This negative violation is not subject to the qualifications of 'reasonable measures', 'progressive realisation', and the availability of resources in section 26(2). Instead any justification offered by the State for the violation falls to be determined in terms of the general limitations clause (section 36).[51]

---

46 *Ibid.*, paras. 11-12.

47 Section 1(a) of the Constitution. Thus in the case of *Mashavha v President of the RSA & Others* 2004 (12) BCLR 1243 (CC), the Court referred to social assistance as 'an area of governmental responsibility very closely related to human dignity.' (para. 51).

48 For a discussion of this issue, see: Sandra Liebenberg 'The Right to Social Assistance: The Implications of *Grootboom* for Policy Reform in South Africa.' 2 (2001) 17 *South African Journal of Human Rights* 232 at 239 – 241.

49 *Government of the Republic of South Africa v Grootboom* 2000 (11) BCLR 1169 (CC), at para. 34; TAC, *supra* note 43, para. 46.

50 *Jaftha v Schoeman and Others; Van Rooyen v Stoltz and Others* 2005 (1) BCLR 78 (CC).

51 *Ibid.*, paras. 31 – 34.

In the context of social security rights, government measures that deprive people of existing access to social security rights would constitute a negative violation of section 27. The burden would shift to the State to justify this deprivation in terms of the stringent requirements of the general limitations clause.[52] It is still an open question whether such 'negative' violations include a reduction in social security benefits as opposed to a total deprivation of access to any social security benefits.

4.3 State obligations: The duty to extend access to those excluded

4.3.1 The model of reasonableness review

In three landmark cases, *Soobramoney v Minister of Health, KwaZulu-Natal* ('*Soobramoney*'),[53] *Government of the Republic of South Africa v Grootboom* ('*Grootboom*'),[54] and *Minister of Health & others v Treatment Action Campaign & others* ('*TAC*')[55] the Court laid down the foundations of its jurisprudence on the review of the positive duties imposed by sections 26 and 27.
The Court rejected the notion that these provisions impose a direct, unqualified obligation on the state to provide social goods and services to people on demand. It did so in the context of arguments raised by the *amici curiae* ('friend of the court') interventions in the *Grootboom* and *TAC* cases. The *amici* sought to persuade the Court to adopt the notion of minimum core obligations as developed by the United Nations Committee on Economic, Social and Cultural Rights.[56] The

52 In terms of section 36, limitations may only be imposed in terms of 'law of general application'. Furthermore it must meet the proportionality requirements inherent in the factors which must be taken into account in determining whether a limitation is 'reasonable and justifiable in an open and democratic society based on human dignity, equality and freedom.' (see section 36(a) – (e)).

53 *Soobramoney v Minister of Health, KwaZulu-Natal* 1997 (12) BCLR 1696 (CC).

54 *Grootboom, supra* note 49.

55 *TAC, supra* note 43.

56 In its General Comment No. 3, the Committee stated that it 'is of the view that a minimum core obligation to ensure the satisfaction of at the very least, minimum essential levels of each of the rights is incumbent upon every State party. Thus, for example, a State party in which any significant number of individuals is deprived of essential foodstuffs, of essential primary health care, of basic shelter and housing, or of the most basic forms of education is, *prima facie*, failing to discharge its obligations under the Covenant… In order for a State party to be able to attribute its failure to meet at least its minimum core obligations to a lack of available resources it must demonstrate that every effort has been made to use all resources at its disposition in an effort to satisfy, as a matter of priority, those minimum obligations.' CESCR, *General Comment No. 3, The nature of States' parties obligations (article 2(1) of the Covenant)* (Fifth session, 1990), UN doc. E/1991/23, annex III at 86 (1991) para. 10. For an application of this concept in the context of the specific rights protected in the Covenant, see: CESCR, *General Comment No. 12, Right to adequate food (article 11 of the Covenant)* (Twentieth session, 1999), UN doc. E/C.12/1999/5 (1999), para. 17; CESCR, *General Comment No. 14, The right to the highest attainable standard of health (art 12 of the Cove-*

Court rejected an interpretation of socio-economic rights that would 'give rise to a self-standing and independent positive right enforceable irrespective of the considerations mentioned in section 27(2).'[57] The latter it will be recalled refers to the qualifications relating to reasonable measures, progressive realisation and the availability of resources. The Court voiced a number of concerns regarding the concept of minimum core obligations. These included practical issues concerning the definition of the rights in the context of varying social needs,[58] the impossibility (according to the Court) of giving everyone access even to a 'core' service immediately,[59] and its incompatibility with the institutional competencies and role of the courts.[60] The Court, however, did indicate that evidence in a particular case may show that there is a minimum core of a particular service that should be taken into account in determining whether the measures adopted by the State are reasonable.[61]

The Court proceeded to develop a model of 'reasonableness review' for adjudicating positive claims to the provision of social services and resources. In reviewing the positive duties imposed by the socio-economic rights provisions on the State, the central question that the Court asks is whether the means chosen are reasonably capable of facilitating the realisation of the socio-economic rights in question.[62] In the words of the Court:

> A Court considering reasonableness will not enquire whether other more desirable or favourable measures could have been adopted, or whether public money could have been better spent. The question would be whether the measures that have been adopted are reasonable. It is necessary to recognise that a wide range of possible measures could be adopted by the State to meet its obligations. Many of these would meet the requirement of reasonableness. Once it is shown that the measures do so, this requirement is met.[63]

The assessment of the reasonableness of government's programmes takes into account the social, economic and historical context, and the capacity of institutions responsible for implementing the programme.[64] Secondly, the internal limitations

---

nant) (Twenty-second session, 2000), UN doc.E/C.12/2000/4 (2000), paras. 43, 47; CESCR, *General Comment No. 15 The right to water (arts 11 & 12 of the Covenant)* (Twenty-ninth session 2002), UN doc. E/C. 12/2002/11 (2003), paras. 37 – 38.

57 *TAC, supra* note 43, para. 39.

58 *Grootboom, supra* note 49, paras. 32 and 33.

59 *TAC, supra* note 43, para. 35.

60 Thus the Court observed that 'courts are not institutionally equipped to make the wide-ranging factual and political enquiries necessary for determining what the minimum core standards' should be. (*Ibid.* para. 37). It went on to say: 'Courts are ill-suited to adjudicate upon issues where court order could have multiple social and economic consequences for the community. The Constitution contemplates rather a restrained and focused role for the courts....' (at para. 38).

61 *Grootboom, supra* note 49, para. 33; *TAC, supra* note 43, para. 34.

62 See: *Grootboom, ibid.*, para. 41.

63 *Ibid.*

64 *Soobramoney, supra* note 53, para. 16; Grootboom, *ibid.*, para. 43.

of section 26(2) require that the rights may be progressively realised,[65] and that the availability of resources is 'an important factor in determining what is reasonable.'[66] Thus the Court has held that the obligation to take the requisite measures 'does not require the State to do more than its resources permit.'[67] The availability of resources governs 'both the content of the obligation in relation to the rate at which it is achieved as well as the reasonableness of the measures employed to achieve the result.'[68]

The standard of scrutiny employed by the Court is more substantive than simply enquiring whether the policy was rationally conceived and applied in good faith. Thus, in the *Grootboom* and the *TAC* cases the Court set the following standards for a reasonable government programme to realise socio-economic rights:

- The programme must be comprehensive, coherent, coordinated;[69]
- Appropriate financial and human resources must be made available for the programme.[70]
- It must be balanced and flexible and make appropriate prevention for short, medium and long-term needs;[71]
- It must be reasonably conceived and implemented;[72] and
- It must be transparent, and its contents must be made known effectively to the public.[73]

The element of the reasonableness test that is of critical significance to the granting of short-term relief is the requirement that a reasonable government programmes must cater for those in urgent need:

> To be reasonable, measures cannot leave out of account, the degree and extent of the denial of the right they endeavour to realise. Those whose needs are most urgent and whose ability to enjoy all rights is therefore most in peril, must not be ignored by the measures aimed at achieving realisation of the right. … Furthermore, the Constitution requires that everyone be treated with care and concern. If the measures, though statistically successful, fail to respond to the needs of those most desperate, they may not pass the test.[74]

65 See the discussion of 'progressive realisation' below.
66 Grootboom, *supra* note 49, para. 46.
67 *Ibid.*
68 *Ibid.*
69 *Ibid.*, paras. 39 and 40.
70 *Ibid.*, para. 39.
71 *Ibid.*, para. 43.
72 *Ibid.*, paras. 40 – 43.
73 *TAC*, *supra* note 43, para. 123.
74 *Grootboom*, *supra* note 49, para. 44.

This requirement of the reasonableness test is justified particularly in terms of the value of human dignity.[75]

4.3.2 Progressive realisation and retrogressive measures

The Court interpreted 'progressive realisation' in sections 26(2) and 27(2) to place an obligation on the State to progressively facilitate access to the various socio-economic rights:

> It means that accessibility should be progressively facilitated: legal, administrative, operational and financial hurdles should be examined and, where possible, lowered over time. Housing [etc.] must be made more accessible not only to a larger number of people but to a wider range of people as time progresses.[76]

Of particular significance is the Court's endorsement of the views of the UN Committee on Economic, Social and Cultural Rights on retrogressive measures.[77] The Committee has held that such measures 'would require the most careful consideration and would need to be fully justified by reference to the totality of the rights provided for in the Covenant and in the context of the full use of the maximum available resources.'[78] This paves the way for challenges to measures that reduce either the level of benefits under existing schemes or the categories of eligible beneficiaries. The key consideration in this context is likely to be the adequacy of any alternative systems of social support which the government may put in place in the context of the scaling down of a particular social security programme.

4.3.3 Interpreting the unqualified children's socio-economic rights

In *Grootboom* and *TAC*, the Court also had to deal with the argument that the rights of children to shelter and basic health care services respectively had been breached. It will be recalled that the 'basic' socio-economic rights of children entrenched in section 28(1)(c) of the Constitution are not qualified as are the socio-economic rights in sections 26 and 27.[79] The question that arises is whether these provisions impose direct obligations on the State to provide a basic level of socio-economic rights to children. In *Grootboom*, the Court held that the 'carefully con-

---

75 Thus in *Grootboom (ibid.)* the Court held: 'It is fundamental to an evaluation of the reasonableness of State action that account be taken of the inherent dignity of human beings. … In short, I emphasise that human beings are required to be treated as human beings.' (at para. 83). See: S. Liebenberg 'The value of human dignity in interpreting socio-economic rights' 1 (2005) 21 *South African Journal of Human Rights* 1.

76 *Grootboom, supra* note 49, para. 45.

77 *Ibid.*

78 General Comment No. 3, 1990, *supra* note 56, para. 9.

79 Thus section 28(1)(c) reads: 'Every child has the right -….(b) to family care or parental care, or to appropriate alternative care when removed from the family environment; (c) to basic nutrition, shelter, basic health care services and social services; ….'

structed constitutional scheme for the progressive realisation of socio-economic rights would make little sense if it could be trumped in every case by the rights of children to get shelter from the State on demand.'[80] It held that section 28(1)(b) and (c) must be read together. While the former provision defines those responsible for giving care, the latter 'lists various aspects of the care entitlement.'[81] It concluded that the primary duty to fulfil a child's socio-economic rights rests on that child's parents or family.[82]

Concerns were voiced over the implications of this reasoning for children who live with parents or other care-givers who are too poor to provide them with the basic necessities of life.[83] In *TAC*, the Court clarified that the State's duty to provide children's socio-economic rights were not only triggered when children were physically separated from their families. Thus children are entitled to the protection contemplated by section 28 'when the implementation of the right to parental or family care is lacking.'[84] Here the Court was dealing with children born to mothers who were too poor to afford private medical and who were, as a result, dependent on State health care facilities.[85] However, the Court did not conclude that children therefore enjoyed an unqualified, direct claim to the provision of health care services. Instead the Court relied on the denial of the right of children to basic health care services to support its finding that government's rigid policy on Nevirapine[86] was unreasonable because the policy excluded and harmed a particularly vulnerable group. Thus it appears that the Court is more comfortable applying a model of reasonableness review to the positive obligations imposed by the socio-economic rights provisions in the Constitution.

However, jurisprudence on children's direct entitlement to socio-economic provisioning may still develop, particularly in contexts where children lack family care.[87] A critical area where the State's obligations to provide social grants and services to children remains to be tested is in relation to child-headed households created predominantly by the HIV/AIDS epidemic ravaging South Africa.[88]

80 *Grootboom, supra* note 49, para. 71

81 *Ibid.*, para. 76.

82 *Ibid.*, para. 77.

83 See, for example: Julia Sloth-Nielsen 'The child's right to social services, the right to social security, and primary prevention of child abuse: Some conclusions in the aftermath of *Grootboom*' 2 (2001) 17 *South African Journal of Human Rights*, 210.

84 *TAC, supra* note 43, para. 79.

85 *Ibid.*

86 Nevirapine is an antiretroviral drug with proven efficacy in reducing mother-to-child transmission of HIV. Government had resisted rolling out the drug for this purpose throughout the public health sector, restricting its provision to two test sites in each province.

87 See, for example, *Centre for Child Law & Ano v Minister of Home Affairs and Others* 2005 (6) SA 50. The case concerned the rights, including the socio-economic rights of unaccompanied foreign children in South Africa.

88 Beth Goldblatt & Sandra Liebenberg, *supra* note 12; Sandra Liebenberg 'Taking stock: The jurisprudence on children's socio-economic rights and its implications for government policy' 5 (2004) *ESR Review* 2.

4.3.4 Application of reasonableness review to the social security system

It is still unclear to what extent the right to social security in section 27 can be used to argue for more far-reaching reforms of the social security system, for example, the expansion of the child support grant to 18 years or even the introduction of a basic income grant.

One of the major critiques of the Court's model of reasonableness review for the positive duties imposed by socio-economic rights is its failure to engage sufficient with the substantive scope and content of the various socio-economic rights.[89] The Court's main inquiry is centered upon whether a government programme meets the various criteria for reasonableness as set out above.

The features of a reasonable government programme (outlined above) could be applied to the social security system to argue that government policy and programmes must progressively achieve a social security system that is comprehensive and cater for all major groups in society. However, the nature of reasonableness review and the latitude afforded the State of 'progressive realisation' and 'within available resources' makes it unlikely that the Court will order social security reforms with far-reaching resource implications.[90] This is particularly the case where the Court fears that the resource implications of its decisions may impact on the enjoyment of other rights.[91] However, it may be possible to require from government at least a plan of action or strategy for the progressive realisation of socio-economic rights.

The aspect of the reasonableness test that offers the most scope for obtaining tangible results through litigation is the requirement that a reasonable government programme must provide short-term relief for those in desperate need or living in intolerable conditions.[92] However, it is unclear how this group will be defined in the context of widespread structural poverty. It also remains to be tested to what extent individuals can obtain direct remedies through socio-economic rights litigation.[93]

---

89 David Bilchitz 'Towards a Reasonable Approach to the Minimum Core: Laying the Foundations for Future Socio-Economic Rights Jurisprudence' 1 (2003) 19 *South African Journal of Human Rights* at 5-11; Marius Pieterse 'Coming to terms with the judicial enforcement of socio-economic rights' 3 (2004) 20 *South African Journal of Human Rights* 383 at 406-407.

90 See the discussion of the *Khosa* case below.

91 See: *Soobramoney*, *supra* note 53, para. 28.

92 Thus, for example, it may be used to argue for an expansion of the currently very limited Social Relief of Distress Grant (SROD). See: *supra* note 27.

93 The Court's jurisprudence suggests that the Court is not favourably disposed to granting direct benefits to individuals, but prefers to focus on the reasonableness of government's programmes: *Grootboom*, *supra* note 49, paras. 68, 95; *TAC*, *supra* note 43, paras. 35, 39, 125. For a discussion of this issue, see: Sandra Liebenberg 'South Africa's Evolving Jurisprudence on Socio-Economic Rights: An Effective Tool in Challenging Poverty' (2002) 6 *Law, Democracy & Development* 159.

5. The intersection between equality rights and social security rights

The two cases concerning social security programmes that the Constitutional Court has decided both entailed an overlap between equality rights and social security rights.

In *Mashavha*'s case, the Constitutional Court declared the assignment of the administration of the Social Assistance Act 59 of 1992 to the provinces by Proclamation R7 to be unconstitutional in that it fell within the ambit of section 126(3) of the Interim Constitution. This provision excludes matters requiring uniform national norms and standards for their effective performance and minimum standards across the nation from assignment to provincial level. The Court held that the delivery of social assistance grants was such a matter. In doing so, it emphasised the importance of the right and value of equality in the delivery of social assistance rights:

> The history of our country and the need for equality cannot be ignored in the interpretation and application of section 126(3). Equality is not only recognised as a fundamental right in both the interim and 1996 Constitutions, but is also a foundational value. To pay, for example, higher old age pensions in Johannesburg in Gauteng than in Bochum in Limpopo, or lower child benefits in Butterworth than in Cape Town, would offend the dignity of people, create different classes of citizenship and divide South Africa into favoured and disfavoured areas.[94]

The decision of the Constitutional Court in *Khosa v Minister of Social Development; Mahlaule v Minister of Social Development* ('*Khosa*')[95] illustrates how equality rights and socio-economic rights can mutually reinforce each other to support a finding that a government programme unreasonably excludes a particular group.[96] The effect of such a finding is that the programme must be expanded to include the excluded group. Thus the Court held that that the provisions of the Social Assistance Act 59 of 1992 breached both section 9 (right to equality) and section 27(1)(c) (right of access to social assistance) by excluding destitute permanent residents from eligibility for social grants. The Court granted a remedy reading permanent residents into the eligibility requirements of the statute.[97]

The State had argued that the extension of social grants to permanent residents would impose 'an impermissibly high financial burden on the state.'[98] In review-

---

94 *Mashavha, supra* note 6, para. 51. The State intends establishing a Social Security Agency in terms of the Social Security Agency Act 9 of 2004 with primary responsibility for the administration of social assistance in terms of the Social Assistance Act. At the time of writing the Act had not yet brought the Act into force. See: *Ex Parte: Minister of Social Development and* Others 2006 (5) BCLR 604 (CC).

95 *Khosa v Minister of Social Development; Mahlaule v Minister of Social Development* 2004 (6) BCLR 569 (CC).

96 *Ibid.* See particularly the discussion at paras. 79 – 85.

97 *Ibid.*, paras 86 – 98.

98 *Ibid.*, para. 60.

ing the reasonableness of citizenship as a criterion of exclusion from social grants in terms of section 27(2), the Court was confronted with a lack of evidence as to 'the numbers of persons who hold permanent resident status, or who would qualify for social assistance if the citizenship barrier were to be removed.'[99] However, based on certain assumptions, the Court was able to conclude that the cost of including permanent residents in the system would be only a small proportion of the total cost of social grants.[100] Thus the State was unable to produce convincing evidence to support its argument that the costs of extending social grants to permanent residents would impose an excessively high financial burden on it.

Examining the claim through the lens of equality rights, the Court considered whether the exclusion of permanent residents from social grants amounted to 'unfair discrimination' in terms of section 9 (3) of the equality clause.[101] The Court noted that the applicants are part of a vulnerable group, and that the 'intentional, statutorily sanctioned unequal treatment of part of the South African community' has 'a strong stigmatising effect.'[102] Like citizens, permanent residents contribute to the welfare system through the payment of taxes. Consequently 'the lack of congruence between benefits and burdens created by a law that denies benefits to permanent residents almost inevitably creates the impression that permanent residents are in some way inferior to citizens and less worthy of social assistance.'[103] Analysing the impact of the exclusion, the Court held that it not only places an undue burden on the families, friends or communities of the permanent residents, but 'is likely to have a serious impact on the dignity of the permanent residents concerned who are cast in the role of supplicants.'[104] The Court concluded that the exclusion was unfair in that destitute permanent residents are 'relegated to the margins of society and are deprived of what may be essential to enable them to enjoy other rights vested in them under the Constitution.'[105] Thus the impact of the exclusion from social assistance on the life and dignity of permanent residents

---

[99] *Ibid.*, para. 61.

[100] Approximately one fifth of the projected expenditure on social grants for permanent residents is in respect of child grants. The unconstitutionality of the citizenship requirement in respect of the child support grant was already conceded by the State. The remainder 'reflects an increase of less than 2% on the present cost of social grants (currently R26.2 billion) even on the higher estimate.' *Ibid.*, para. 62.

[101] Section 9 of the equality clause prohibits direct or indirect unfair discrimination on a range of listed grounds (including race, sex, gender, sexual orientation, age, disability etc.). These do not represent a closed list. Other unlisted grounds (e.g. citizenship, HIV-status etc.) may be recognised as an analogous ground of differentiation if they have an adverse effect on the dignity of the individual, or some other comparable effect: *Harksen v Lane NO and Others* 1997 (11) BCLR 1489 (CC), para. 46. See, for example, *Hoffmann v South African Airways* 2000 (11) BCLR 1211 (CC) (HIV-positive status recognized as analogous ground of discrimination). Section 9(2) also provides expressly that restitutionary measures (affirmative action) may be taken '[t]o promote the achievement of equality.'

[102] *Khosa*, *supra* note 95, para. 74.

[103] *Ibid.*

[104] *Ibid.*, para. 76.

[105] *Ibid.*, para. 77.

outweighed the financial and immigration considerations on which the State relied.[106]

It is to be noted that the Court's finding was limited to permanent residents as a category of non-citizens. It expressly stated that: 'It may be reasonable to exclude from the legislative scheme workers who are citizens of other countries, visitors and illegal residents, who have only a tenuous link with this country.'[107]

Many aspects of the Court's reasoning on the impact of the exclusion of groups from social assistance is applicable also to the large proportion of the population living in poverty and excluded from current social assistance measures (e.g. children over 14 years, and unemployed adults below pensionable age). However, as noted above, the Court assesses reasonableness in terms of the available resources of the State. If the resource allocation implications of an expansion of the social security system are judged to be too extensive or have far-reaching ramifications for other State priorities, it is unlikely that the challenge will succeed. However, the Court can require the State to put in place a national strategy and plan of action to close the gap in social security provisioning. Such a plan should be devised through a participatory and transparent process and should include indicators by which progress can be measured. In addition, Courts can also intervene when the needs of vulnerable and disadvantaged groups are not given due priority in social security programmes.[108] A joint reading of social security and equality rights also has significant potential to assist in challenging gender and other inequalities in the social security system.

6. Administrative justice and constitutional remedies as vehicles for protecting social security rights

The vast majority of cases concerning social security have been decided in terms of the right to administrative justice. It is thus an important vehicle for protecting social security rights.

Section 33 of the Constitution enshrines the right to just administrative action.[109] This right gives everyone the right to administrative action 'that is lawful, reasonable and procedurally fair,'[110] as well as the right to be given 'written reasons' where one's rights have been 'adversely affected by administrative action.'[111] Furthermore, the provision imposes a duty on the State to enact national

---

106 *Ibid.*, para. 82.

107 *Ibid.*, para. 59.

108 The UN Committee on Economic, Social and Cultural Rights views such national strategising and planning as part of the core obligations of State Parties to the International Covenant on Economic, Social and Cultural Rights. See, for example, General Comment No. 14, *supra* note 56, para. 43 (f).

109 The common law of South Africa has also developed a substantial body of principles on just administrative action.

110 Section 33 (1).

111 Section 33 (2).

legislation to give effect to these rights.[112] In compliance with this duty the Promotion of Administrative Justice Act 3 of 2000 ('PAJA') has been enacted. This Act provides the framework for judicial review of administrative action, including, for example, the administration of social grants under the Social Assistance Act.[113] It gives substance to the constitutional right to just administrative action.

There have been a plethora of cases concerning unjust administration of social grants. Particularly in the Eastern Cape Province, there has been a persistent, systemic problem in the administration of social grants.[114] This led Froneman J to make the following observation in the case of *Kate v MEC, Dept of Welfare, Eastern Cape* ('*Kate*'):

> The failure in proper administration has led to the situation where the courts have become the primary mechanisms for ensuring accountability in the public administration of social grants.[115]

There have been a number of judgments, particularly in the High Courts, affirming the right of litigants to relief in cases concerning the cancellation of social security grants without notice, reasons or a hearing,[116] the failure to take decisions timeously in applications for social grants,[117] and the failure to pay back-pay and interest where applications were approved after long delays.[118] In all these cases, the litigants have obtained successful judgments based either on the constitutional right to just administrative action or, in terms of PAJA since its enactment.

However, these positive judgments have been overshadowed by a trend of the provincial department of Social Development to fail to give effect to the judg-

---

[112] Section 33 (3).

[113] See: Nick De Villiers 'Social Grants and the Promotion of Administrative Justice Act' (2002) 18 *South African Journal of Human Rights* 320; Clive Plasket 'Administrative Justice and Social Assistance' (2003) 120 *South African Law Journal* 494.

[114] However, as the recent KwaZulu-Natal case of *Machi & Others v MEC for Province of KwaZulu-Natal Responsible for Social Welfare and Population Development* Case No. 4392/04 (unreported judgment of 8 March 2005) (D&CLD) attests, the problems in social security administration are not restricted to the Eastern Cape Province.

[115] *Kate v MEC, Dept of Welfare, Eastern Cape* [2005] 1 All SA 745 (SE) at para. 5.

[116] A mass cancellation of social grants took place as a result of a re-registration drive aimed at eliminating fraud in the administration of social grants, but was effected in complete disregard of the basic principles of administrative justice. See, for example, *Ngxuza, supra* note 45; *Bushula & Others v Permanent Secretary, Department of Welfare, Eastern Cape Provincial Government* 2000 (7) BCLR 728 (E).

[117] See, for example, *Vumazonke v MEC for Social Development, Eastern Cape, and Three Similar Cases* 2005 (6) SA 229 ('*Vumazonke*'), para. 9. The High Court held in this case that the delay by the provincial department of social development in taking a decision on applicants' application for social grants was unreasonable in terms of section 6(2)(g) read with section 6(3)(a) of PAJA. In the previous cases of *Mahambehlala v MEC for Welfare, Eastern Cape and another* 2002 (1) SA 342 (SE), and *Mbanga v MEC for Welfare, Eastern Cape and another* 2002 (1) SA 359 (SE), the High Court held that any delay beyond three months in taking a decision on an application for a welfare grant is unreasonable in the absence of special circumstances.

[118] See: *Mahambehlala & Mbanga, ibid.*

ments, particularly to pay judgment debts sounding in money. The courts have adopted various strategies in response, including holding that the responsible Members of the Executive Committees (MEC's) of departments and other public functionaries could be declared in contempt of court where judgment debts sounding in money against the State were not paid.[119] This approach has been adopted as the State Liability Act (20 of 1957) precludes execution against the property of a provincial government, thus closing off this avenue of obtaining satisfaction of the judgment debt. However, the Supreme Court of Appeal judgment in *Jayiya* has held that a money judgment cannot be enforced against the State by contempt proceedings.[120] This effectively leaves social grant recipients without an effective remedy to vindicate their constitutional and statutory rights. In the subsequent High Court decision of *Kate v MEC for the Department of Welfare, Eastern Cape*, Froneman J observed:

> It is one thing to realise the possibility *as a matter of fact* that the government might refuse to comply with court orders. It is something completely different to hold *as a matter of law* that courts are powerless to devise ways to ensure compliance with court orders in a constitutional state such as ours... For the courts to do the latter would be to aid and abet unconstitutional government, the very antithesis of the court's duty in terms of the Constitution.[121]

Froneman J construed the *Jayiya* decision narrowly, holding that all that was bindingly decided was that in that case the wrong orders were sought against the wrong respondents, and that state functionaries cannot be found guilty of the *crime* of contempt of court for non-compliance with a money judgment.[122] The courts could still make a declaratory order that a State functionary is in contempt of a court order. They could also call upon State functionaries to explain why they had not complied with court orders and require them to explain how they intend complying with those orders. The common law rule of civil contempt could be developed in this manner without attaching criminal sanctions.[123] It also held that statements of the Supreme Court of Appeal in *Jayiya* calling into question whether backpay and interest could be claimed as constitutional damages in cases where there were unreasonable delays in approving and paying social grants, were *obiter dictum* (not binding in subsequent cases).

In the subsequent *Vumazonke* judgment,[124] the High Court (SE) reviewed the cases dealing with the systemic failures in the administration of social grants in the Eastern Cape Province. It observed that the courts were operating at the

---

119 *Mjeni v Minister of Health and Welfare, Eastern Cape* 2004 (4) SA 446 (Tk); *East London Transitional Local Council v MEC for Health, Eastern Cape, and Others* [2000] 4 All SA 443 (Ck).

120 *Jayiya v MEC for Welfare, Eastern Cape* 2004 (2) SA 611 (SCA).

121 *Kate (SECLD), supra* note 115, para 25.

122 *Ibid.*, para. 23.

123 *Ibid.*, para. 21.

124 *Vumazonke, supra* note 117.

'boundaries of the judicial function – [to] the limits of the institutional competence of the courts to engineer administrative efficiency.'[125]

In a renewed effort to redress some of the dysfunctional operation of the Department, the judge directed that the judgment be served on the chairperson of the Human Rights Commission 'so that he can consider whether to institute an investigation into the conduct of the respondent's department with a view to proposing concrete steps to ensure that it begins to comply with its constitutional and legal obligations and ceases to infringe constitutional rights on the present grant scale.'[126] In addition, it was ordered that the judgment be served on chairperson of the Public Service Commission so that he too could consider instituting an investigation into the respondent's department.[127] In the words of Plasket J:

> …the time for talk and no action has long passed. Something drastic and concrete must be done to remedy a serious and systemic infringement of the Constitution and the law – and the principles of good administration – by the respondent's department.[128]

On appeal in the Kate decision, the Supreme Court of Appeal confirmed that constitutional damages could be awarded in cases where the Department of Welfare was responsible for an unreasonable delay in the processing of an application for a social assistance grant.[129] The damages were calculated on the basis of an amount equivalent to the interest that is recognised in law to be payable when money is unlawfully withheld.[130] The Court also confirmed that a public official who is ordered by a court to do or to refrain from doing a particular act and fails to do so is liable to be committed for contempt.[131] Finally, the Bisho High Court has handed

---

125 *Ibid.*, paras 9 – 10.

126 *Ibid.*, para. 18. The SA Human Rights Commission is one of the 'State Institutions Supporting Constitutional Democracy' established in Chapter 9 of the Constitution. The powers and functions of the Human Rights Commission are set out in section 184 of the Constitution complemented by The Human Rights Commission Act 54 of 1994. These include the power to conduct investigations on human rights issues (section 9), to make recommendations and report thereon to the Present and Parliament (section 15). In addition, the Commission has the constitutional function to request relevant organs of State to provide it 'with information on the measures that they have taken towards the realisation of the rights in the Bill of Rights concerning housing, health care, food, water, social security, education and the environment.' (section 184(3)). The latest report of the Human Rights Commission on the right to social security pursuant to the exercise of this constitutional duty can be accessed on-line at http://www.sahrc.org.za/5th_esr_socialsecurity.pdf.

127 The Public Service Commission is established in terms of section 196, and its powers and functions are regulated by the Constitution and the Public Service Commission Act 46 of 1997.

128 *Vumazonke*, *supra* note 117, para. 22.

129 *The MEC for The Department of Welfare v Kate* Case No: 580/04, 30 March 2006 (SCA) [judgment unreported at the date of writing]. In this case the delay in processing and approving the Respondent's disability grant was thirty seven months (para 10).

130 *Ibid.*, para. 33.

131 *Ibid.*, para. 30.

down a recent judgment in which it made a supervisory order against the provincial government enabling the court to oversee the payment of judgment debts granted against the province in social grant applications.[132]

7. Conclusion

This paper has sought to illustrate both the potential and limits of the courts' role in advancing and protecting social security rights in South Africa.

The entrenchment of a justiciable constitutional right of access to social security has greatly enlarged the scope of the Court's ability to protect people's interests in social security. This is illustrated, for example, by the Court's recognition of the negative duty to refrain from depriving people of access to socio-economic rights, and its endorsement of the views of the UN Committee on Economic, Social and Cultural Rights regarding heightened scrutiny for retrogressive measures. There is also untapped potential in the reasonableness test developed by the Constitutional Court for the review of the positive duties imposed by socio-economic rights. Significant in this context is the requirement that a reasonable government programme must make provision for those in desperate need, and progressively expand access to social rights.

However, the assessment of reasonableness will also take into account the State's resource and capacity constraints. In this sphere, courts generally give the State a fairly large margin of appreciation given the limitations of their own institutional role and competencies. Thus in the *TAC* case the Constitutional Court held that although determinations of reasonableness 'may in fact have budgetary implications, [they] are not in themselves directed at rearranging budgets. In this way the judicial, legislative and executive functions achieve appropriate constitutional balance.'[133]

This naturally limits the potential of litigation alone to achieve far-reaching transformation of the social security system. However, as the *Grootboom*, *TAC* and *Khosa* decisions illustrate, the Court has been willing and capable of reviewing budget allocation decisions. In these cases it held that government's unwillingness to expand access to housing, health care and social grants to vulnerable groups was unreasonable. The courts will generally be more favorably disposed to interfering in the State's resource allocation priorities in cases where disadvantaged groups are deprived of access to essential social resources and services. This enables an incremental strategy to improve access to social security. This strategy has the potential to have a transformative impact over time.

This paper has also illustrated how the right to social security in conjunction with the right to equality can be invoked to require the social grants system to require uniform national norms and standards for the delivery of social grants

---

132 *Magidimisi N.O. v The Premier of the Eastern Cape and Others* Case No. 2180/04 (Bisho High Court) [judgment unreported at the date of writing].

133 *TAC, supra* note 43, para. 38.

(*Mashavha*) and the inclusion of the previously excluded group of permanent residents (*Khosa & Mahlauli*). The right to just administrative action and the willingness of the courts to develop innovative remedies is playing a critical role in attempting to protect social grant recipients in certain provinces against inefficient administration. In particular, the Eastern Cape welfare cases have illustrated how the courts have struggled creatively to assist welfare beneficiaries in a context of pervasive, systemic administrative problems.

The gender dimensions of the South African social security system remains a major issue for further research and policy development, and is also a challenge for the courts in developing a gender-sensitive jurisprudence.

It is also significant that the right to social security entrenched in the SA Constitution and in various regional and international human rights treaties is being invoked by civil society organisations in policy and political advocacy in relation to the transformation of the social security system.[134] Encouragingly, it has also featured in policy and legislative processes relating to the social security system, including the Welfare White Paper, the Report of the Committee of Inquiry into a Comprehensive Social Security System, the South African Law Reform Commission's deliberations on revised child care legislation,[135] and the amended Social Assistance Act.[136]

Perhaps the most significant contribution of entrenching access to social security as a constitutional right in South Africa is to enhance State accountability for the survival and development of the poor. Social security can no longer be characterised as charity or public largesse, but an expression of post-apartheid South Africa's commitment to the value of human dignity. As Justice Mokgoro observed in *Khosa*:

> The right of access to social security, including social assistance for those unable to support themselves and their dependants is entrenched because as a society we value human beings and want to ensure that people are afforded their basic needs. A society must seek to ensure that the basic necessities of life are accessible to all if it is to be a society in which human dignity, freedom and equality are foundational.[137]

---

[134] The rights discourse is used by a wide range of organisations campaigning in the sphere of social security, e.g. the Basic Income Grant Coalition, the Black Sash and the Alliance for Children's Entitlement to Social Security Rights (ACESS).

[135] South African Law Reform Commission Discussion Paper 103, Project 110, Review of the Child Care Act. (on-line at: http://www.doj.gov.za/salrc/dpapers/dp103_prj110/dp103_prj110_cover_2002.pdf).

[136] See, for example, the preamble of the Social Assistance Act 13 of 2004.

[137] *Khosa*, *supra* note 95, para. 52.

Social Security – International Standards and the Right to Social Security

Ursula Kulke and Germán López Morales*

Standards are the history of the ILO. As the international institution, which has produced the largest number of binding and non-binding instruments in the field of human rights, standards remain at the very centre of the ILO's mandate and its day-to-day work.[1]

Juan Somavia, Director General, ILO

1. ILO Standard-setting in the Field of Social Security

The overall objective of the ILO is to enhance social justice worldwide through 'decent work for all'. One of the ILO's principal means of action to achieve this is through the setting of applicable international labour standards. The reason for creating worldwide standards is the recognition by the international community that social justice has to be dealt with collectively, and not only as it concerns relations between individual states. The standards take the form of either Conventions or Recommendations and cover all areas that concern the objectives of the ILO. Conventions are designed with a view to being ratified, when an ILO Member state ratifies a Convention, the state becomes subject to legally binding international obligations, while Recommendations are not open for ratification, but they specify general or technical guidelines and often supplement corresponding Conventions. Standards therefore serve as globally-backed guidelines for national social policies and, when ratified, they also prevent countries from going backwards, or losing what has already been achieved.

In accordance with the mandate outlined in its 1919 Constitution, the ILO has continued to attach considerable importance to social security issues. In fact, the

* Germán López Morales, Co-ordinator, Social Security Team, International Labour Standards Department, ILO; Ursula Kulke, Co-ordinator for Standards and Legislation, Social Security Department, ILO. The opinions expressed in this paper are those of the authors and do not necessarily reflect the views of the ILO.

1 Preface to *Les normes internationales du travail: un patrimoine pour l'avenir - Mélanges en l'honneur de Nicolas Valticos* (International Labour Office, 2004), ix-xii.

Preamble to the ILO Constitution states that the organisation's mandate is to improve conditions of labour, *inter alia*, the 'prevention of unemployment, ... the protection of the worker against sickness, disease, and injury arising out of his employment, ... provision of old age and injury'. The mandate, reaffirmed in 1944 by the Declaration of Philadelphia[2] and incorporated into the ILO Constitution, recognises the 'solemn obligation of the International Labour Organisation' to further encourage among the nations of the world programmes that will achieve, *inter alia*, 'the extension of social security measures to provide a basic income to all in need of such protection and comprehensive medical care', as well as 'provision for child welfare and maternity protection'.

Since the establishment of the ILO, the International Labour Conference has adopted 31 Conventions and 23 Recommendations on social security. The first international labour convention on social security (maternity protection)[3] was adopted at the first session of the International Labour Conference in 1919, and the most recent convention on social security was adopted in 2000,[4] which revised earlier standards on maternity protection.

In 2002, the ILO Governing Body confirmed eight[5] out of these 31 Conventions as up-to-date social security conventions.

2. The Social Security (Minimum Standards), Convention, 1952 (No. 102)

Of the eight up-to-date social security conventions, the flagship treaty is Convention No. 102. It is the only agreement which sets minimum standards for the nine branches of social security, namely: medical care, sickness benefit, unemployment benefit, old-age benefit, employment injury benefit, family benefit, maternity benefit, invalidity benefit and survivors' benefit. Contrary to the first generation of ILO social security standards that were inspired by the concept of social insurance, Convention No. 102 is based on the broader conception of social security that officially emerged in 1944. The other up-to-date Conventions, either set higher standards for the different branches of social security or concern the social security rights of migrant workers.

---

2 The International Labour Organisation adopted at Philadelphia on 10 May 1944 the Declaration concerning the aims and purposes of international labour.

3 Maternity Protection Convention, 1919 (No. 3).

4 Maternity Protection Convention, 2000 (No. 183).

5 Up-to-date Social Security Conventions are: Social Security (Minimum Standards) Convention, 1952 (No. 102); Equality of Treatment (Social Security), Convention, 1962 (No. 118); Employment Injury Benefits Convention, 1964 (No. 121); Social Invalidity, Old-Age and Survivor's Benefits, Convention, 1967 (No. 128); Medical Care and Sickness Benefits Convention, 1952 (No. 130); Maintenance of Social Security Rights Convention, 1982 (No. 157); Employment Promotion and Protection against Unemployment Convention, 1988 (No. 168); Maternity Protection Convention, 2000 (No. 183).

Convention No. 102 is modelled on two Recommendations – Income Security Recommendation (No. 67) and Medical Care Recommendation (No. 69) – which, when adopted in 1944, were considered as innovative for their coherent and codified form as well as for their comprehensive coverage in respect of persons and contingencies.

According to a 1949 ILO survey[6] carried out before the adoption of Convention No. 102, 'The Recommendations from the Philadelphia Declaration were based not so much on actual experience but on the plans and Bills which various Governments were elaborating towards the end of hostilities; they constituted essentially a forecast of the tendencies that social security policy would follow in the post-war period.' This survey shows a new conception which is transforming the pre-war systems of social insurance. There is movement everywhere towards including additional classes of the population, covering a wider range of contingencies, providing benefits more nearly adequate to needs and removing anomalies among them, loosening the ties between benefit right and contribution payment, and in general unifying the finance and administrations of branches hitherto separate. The transformation of social insurance is accompanied by the absorption or co-ordination of social assistance, and there begins to emerge a new organisation for social security, which we can describe only as a public service for the citizenry at large. This new organisation now concerns society as a whole, though it is primarily directed to the welfare of the workers and their families. It tends therefore to become part of national government, and social security policy for raising the standard of welfare and, in particular, for promoting the vitality of the population.

Convention No. 102 is designed on the basis that there is no right model for social security; it initially grows and then evolves over time. Each country has the discretion to determine how best to ensure income security, thereby reflecting in its choices social and cultural values, history, institutions and levels of economic development. The Convention therefore does not prescribe specific obligations for ratifying States, but rather fixes a set of minimum objectives based on commonly agreed principles, which constitute a socially acceptable minimum for all member countries.

Minimum objectives are set as regards the percentage of the population protected in case of the occurrence of one of the contingencies, the conditions for and period of entitlement to prescribed benefits, the level and the duration of benefits, and the regular adjustment of pensions.

As for the principles anchored in Convention No. 102, they are mainly comprised of:

- the guarantee of defined benefits;
- the participation of employers and workers in the administration of the schemes;
- the general responsibility of the state for the due provision of the benefits and the proper administration of the institutions;

6 International Labour Office, 'Post-war trends in Social Security' 6 (1949) 59 *International Labour Review,* 668 and 669.

- the collective financing of the benefits by way of insurance contributions or taxation.

3. Universality vs. flexibility

In its standard setting activities, the ILO has always tried to keep a balance between two main elements – universality and flexibility. International labour standards are intended to be universal in nature, i.e., applicable to and capable of attainment by countries with very different social structures and at all stages of industrial development. To accomplish this objective, standards should be flexible instead of rigid, but must at the same time set meaningful targets for social development. As argued by Valticos,[7] 'the flexibility of standards is [indeed] the price of their universality. If standards have to be universal, and therefore applicable to States whose level of development and legal approaches differ considerably from one another, the only realistic approach is to develop standards with sufficient flexibility so that they can be adapted to the most diverse of countries'.

Convention No. 102 constitutes one of the best examples resulting from the International Labour Conference as a response to the need for balance and flexibility. As mentioned earlier, this Convention embodies the idea of a general level of social security, which must gradually be achieved everywhere, in view of the fact that the system can be adapted to prevailing socio-economic conditions for any country, irrespective of its level of development. By allowing States to accept obligations under at least three of the nine branches of social security covered by the Convention, and by allowing them to cover only a proportion of the population, the International Labour Conference wanted to make it possible to attain gradually the objective of universal coverage in harmony with the level of development. 'In these various ways the Convention is aimed at laying down at one and the same time, certain minimum standards to be observed and a plan for more comprehensive protection to be realised. It thus supplies a yardstick for measuring the extent to which existing systems reach or exceed the prescribed level.'[8] Rather than being seen as a weakness, the range of options and flexibility clauses offered by the Convention for its gradual application is an effective tool for the achievement of universal coverage.

---

7 Nicolas Valticos, 'Conventions de l'Organisation internationale du Travail à la croisée des anniversaires', 1 (1996) 100 *Revue générale de droit international public* 36.

8 International Labour Office, 'Minimum standards on social security: Conclusions regarding Reports Received under Articles 19 and 22 of the Constitution of the International Labour Organisation concerning the Social Security (Minimum Standards) Convention 1952, (No. 102)' Report III (Part IV) (1961), *Report of the Committee of Experts on the application of conventions and recommendations (Articles 19, 22 and 35 of the Constitution)* (ILO, International Labour Conference, 45th session) at 159, para. 3.

Convention No. 102 does not prescribe how to reach these objectives but leaves a certain flexibility to Member states. In this respect, the objectives can be achieved through:

- universal schemes (public service);
- social insurance schemes with earnings-related or flat-rate components, or both,
- social assistance schemes.

4. Relevance of Convention No. 102

The relevance of Convention No. 102 was also reconfirmed at the General Discussion on Social Security, which took place during the ILO 2001 International Labour Conference. The world community represented by governments, and employers' and workers' organisations, of ILO member states, decided that 'ILO activities should be anchored (...) in relevant ILO social security standards'[9]. It was further decided that the social security principles encompassed in Convention No. 102 should serve as a basis for the adoption of national strategies for working towards social security for all.

5. Impact of Social Security Standards

The history of ILO social security standards is intrinsically linked with worldwide developments in the field of social security. In this respect, it may be emphasised that, as these instruments were designed to provide a framework of standards reflecting common aims and principles on which any social security system must be based, their adoption went hand-in-hand with the establishment of social security systems in many countries and had an important impact at the regional level, particularly in Europe and Latin America.

According to the ILO 1949 survey,[10] the ILO Income Security Recommendation, 1944 (No. 67), 'has inclined the course of post-war income security legislation towards its main objectives. It is echoed in general terms, in the Universal Declaration of Human Rights, adopted by the General Assembly of the United Nations in December 1948, where it is provided, in Article 25, that *Everyone has the right to ... security in the event of unemployment, sickness, disability, widowhood, old age or other lack of livelihood in circumstances beyond his control...*'.

Indeed, ILO social security standards have had influence at the international, regional and national level. In this respect, in 2003 on the occasion of the 50th anniversary of the adoption of Convention No. 102, the Committee of Experts noted

---

9 International Labour Office, *Resolution and conclusions concerning social security* (International Labour Conference, 89th Session, ILO, 2001), at 4, para. 17.

10 *Ibid.*

that this Convention has had 'substantial influence on the development of social security in the various regions of the world, and that, therefore, it was deemed to embody an internationally accepted definition of the very principle of social security.

- The Committee further noted that in 2003, 40 countries ratified Convention No. 102[11] and have therefore incorporated its provisions into their internal legal systems and, in many cases, their national practice.
- Social security schemes exist in nearly all industrialised countries covering the nine branches to which Convention No. 102 applies.
- Many developing countries, inspired by Convention No. 102, have embarked upon the road to social security, even though nearly all their systems are more modest in scope and, in general, do not yet encompass unemployment or family benefits.
- Most of the social security schemes in Latin America, which have their origins in the era of social insurance, were greatly influenced by international labour standards and, in particular, by Convention No. 102.
- Convention No. 102 served as a model for the adoption of the European Code of Social Security, adopted under the aegis of the Council of Europe, which relied for its formulation on the participation of the International Labour Office.
- The European Social Charter provides that the contracting parties undertake to maintain a level of protection at least equal to that required by the ratification of Convention No. 102.[12]

Convention No. 102 is still of utmost relevance for ILO Member states, as is demonstrated by a number of recent new ratifications.[13] When conventions are ratified, states are bound by the legal obligations laid down in the respective instruments. Any reform or development of a social security system carried out by a ratifying State has to comply with the provisions set forth by the Convention. Thus, a country legally bound to Convention No. 102 may not slip below the minimum standards required by the Convention.

Although Convention No. 102 is primarily directed towards states,[14] who by virtue of their ratification undertake to enact and maintain appropriate social security legislation in line with the Convention, some of its provisions may, in certain countries, be applied directly by national courts if they are considered by those courts as sufficiently precise to be 'self-executing'. Most remarkable in this con-

---

[11] 42 ratifications in 2006.

[12] International Labour Office *Report of the Committee of Experts on the Application of Conventions and Recommendations* (Report III (IA), ILO, 2003, International Labour Conference, 91st Session) at 20, para. 53.

[13] Bosnia Herzegovina, 1993; Croatia, 1991; Cyprus, 1991; Czech Republic, 1993; The Former Yugoslav Republic of Macedonia, 1991; Poland, 2003; Portugal, 1994; Serbia and Montenegro, 2000; Slovakia, 1993; Slovenia, 1993.

[14] International labour standards, in general, do not grant rights to individuals, as standards are usually not directly applicable.

text are two rulings of the Swiss Federal Insurance Court of 1993[15] and 1994,[16] in both of which it was ruled that Article 69 lit. 'e' and 'f' of Convention No. 102 may even prevail over any provision of the national legislation that is contrary to them.

Even if provisions of Convention No. 102 are not always accepted as being self-executing, court rulings often refer to them in order to strengthen a decision based on national legislation.[17]

It should also be pointed out that the impact of Convention No. 102 should not only be measured in terms of the number of ratifications. Technical cooperation, which the ILO provides worldwide, is based on the principles laid down in ILO international labour standards. In the field of social security, ILO technical assistance is always based on relevant social security conventions such as Convention No. 102. The legislation and the national practice of a number of countries not having ratified this Convention are based on the principles laid down by this instrument.

6. Application of the Instruments in Practice

The Committee of Experts on the Application of Conventions and Recommendations (CEACR), which formulates comments on national legislation and practice, monitors the application by ratifying states of up-to-date conventions in the field of social security. Many of these comments consist of requests for additional information or clarifications from states on 'minor' points of divergence of national legislation and practice with the ratified Convention No. 102. Other comments by the Committee of Experts relate to more general periodic difficulties of application by ratifying States. A general overview of CEACR's comments in the field of social security identifies three main sets of problems which the CEACR regularly encounters in its assessment: the provision of full statistical information, the problem of the adjustment of long-term benefits, and difficulties in the application of Conventions arising out of the reforms of social security undertaken in the last two decades.

In assessing the difficulties related to the application and prospects of ratification of Conventions Nos. 102 and 128, the CEACR indicated that,

> Some governments state in general terms that there are difficulties involved in the ratification or application of Conventions Nos. 102 and 128. Many other govern-

---

15 II Assurance-invalidité (No.) 25. Arrêt du 25 août 1993 in Arrêts du Tribunal Fédéral Suisse (y compris les arrêts du Tribunal Fédéral des Assurances) rendus in 1993. Recueil Officiel, 119e volume, V^{e} partie : Droit des assurances sociales.

16 U 193 Arrèt du TFA du 21 février 1994 en la cause C.M., at 152 et seq. (RKUV/RAMA/RAMI 3/1994).

17 See: Decision of the Federal Tribunal (Social Affairs) (BSG), 4.10.1994, AZ:JK/AR 1/9, regarding the compatibility of Article 116 AFG with Article 69 (i) of ILO Social Security (Minimum Standards) Convention, 1952 (No. 102).

> ments report economic, financial or administrative difficulties. The economic crisis and inflation, as well as the country's level of development and the lack of human resources were also mentioned as factors impeding the application of the Conventions. Some governments also referred to the difficulty of collecting the statistical information required by the instruments.[18]

The assessment made by ILO supervisory bodies, together with the technical co-operation provided by the ILO, helps governments to identify priorities in the light of their economic capacity and to find ways to provide increasingly efficient social protection and, therefore, to better apply the international social security conventions.

7. International and Regional Instruments Containing the Right to Social Security

From the perspective of international law, the recognition of the right to social security has been developed through universally negotiated and accepted instruments that describe social security as a fundamental societal right to which every human being is entitled.

- Article 22 of the Universal Declaration of Human Rights;[19]
- Article 9 of the International Covenant on Economic Social and Cultural Rights;[20]

It may be pointed out that the latter instrument was designed with the contribution of countries that emerged from the process of decolonisation; the rights enshrined in it have never been questioned.

The recognition of the fundamental character of social security also appeared at the regional level:

---

[18] International Labour Office, *Social Security Protection in Old-Age: General Survey of the Committee of Experts on the Application of Conventions and Recommendations* (International Labour Conference, 76th Session, ILO, 1989) Chapter VII, at 113, para. 234.

[19] Article 22 states that 'Everyone, as a member of society, has the right to social security and is entitled to realization, through national effort and international co-operation and in accordance with the organization and resources of each State, of the economic, social and cultural rights indispensable for his dignity and the free development of his personality.' Universal Declaration of Human Rights adopted and proclaimed by General Assembly resolution 217 A (III) of 10 December 1948, United Nations, New York and Geneva, 1994.

[20] Article 9, states that 'The States Parties to the present Covenant recognise the right of everyone to social security, including social insurance.' International Covenant on Economic, Social and Cultural Rights, adopted by General Assembly resolution 2 200 A (XXI) of 16 December 1966, United Nations, New York and Geneva, 1994.

- The European Social Charter;[21]
- The Treaty of Amsterdam;[22]
- Regional instruments developed in Africa[23] and Latin America.[24]

From a national perspective, it should be noted that the right to social security has been enshrined as a constitutional right in several countries, such as Brazil and Germany.

These universal, regional and national perspectives are a reflection of what has been developed and promoted within the ILO itself. The ILO Constitution, the Declaration of Philadelphia, and more recently the Resolution and Conclusions Concerning Social Security, adopted by the ILC in 2001, confirmed the attachment of ILO Member states to social security as a fundamental basic human right and their commitment to 'the extension of social security measures to provide a basic income to all in need of such protection and comprehensive medical care".[25]

In this respect, any social policy has to bear in mind the need for income security protection. Any ILO Member should from the fact of its ILO membership put in place decent social protection for its people. In addition, these arguments should also guide the provision of technical assistance by the ILO to its constituents.

---

21 Article 12 states that, 'With a view to ensuring the effective exercise of the right to social security, the Contracting Parties undertake, (inter alia): to establish or maintain a system of social security; to maintain the social security system at a satisfactory level at least equal to that required for ratification of International Labour Convention No. 102 Concerning Minimum Standards of Social Security; to endeavour to raise progressively the system of social security to a higher level.'

22 According with the Preamble to the Treaty, the European Union confirms its 'attachment to fundamental social rights' Articles 136, 137, para. 1 (c), Treaty Establishing the European Union (Consolidated text), Official Journal of the European Communities, C325, 24 December 2002.

23 According with Article 16 of the African Charter on Human and People's Rights: '1. Every individual shall have the right to enjoy the best attainable state of physical and mental health. 2. States Parties to the present Charter shall take the necessary measures to protect the health of their people and to ensure that they receive medical attention when they are sick.' Adopted by the eighteenth Assembly of Heads of State and Government, June 1981 - Nairobi, Kenya.

24 According to Article 9, '1. Everyone shall have the right to social security protecting him from the consequences of old age and of disability which prevents him, physically or mentally, from securing the means for a dignified and decent existence. In the event of the death of a beneficiary, social security benefits shall be applied to his dependents. 2. In the case of persons who are employed, the right to social security shall cover at least medical care and an allowance or retirement benefit in the case of work accidents or occupational disease and, in the case of women, paid maternity leave before and after childbirth.' Additional Protocol to the American Convention on Human Rights in the area of Economic, Social and Cultural Rights, 'Protocol of San Salvador'; Done at San Salvador, 17 November 1988, OAS Treaty Series 69.

25 International Labour Office, *supra* note 10, at 1, para. 1.

8. Obligations Stemming from ILO and from Other International and Regional Instruments

It is therefore relevant to examine the level of protection legally required from ILO Member states, since it is not specified in the instruments mentioned above.[26] Formulated in ILO language, the question to be asked is: 'What is the basic minimum that needs to be ensured to comply with the decent work agenda?'

Recourse to international legal instruments may prove useful in the determination of criteria, which could measure the extent of the obligations stemming from these instruments and, therefore, the level of protection that a state should have to provide either immediately or progressively.

In fact, the rights granting social protection can be divided in two main categories, according to the nature of the legal obligation they generate, i.e. an obligation of result (*obligation de résultat*) or an obligation of behaviour (*obligation de comportement*).

As has been explained earlier, there is, for the ILO, a basic minimum protection that a state has to provide immediately to its people in order to fulfil international requirements. This is an obligation of result. This minimum social floor should not be negotiable and should cover the basic needs in social protection. It should also not be questioned from an economic perspective. The implementation of this basic social floor should not be postponed, but should be done immediately by all states, irrespective of their economic or social development.

With regard to these rights, one might ask how this basic social floor could be identified? According to the ILO 1949 survey, it became apparent that the range of contingencies covered in countries which have introduced social security were quite limited, e.g. Turkey started cautiously with employment injury and maternity benefits only, while Guatemala and India combined both of these benefits with a sickness benefit.[27]

In determining the basic social floor today, account should be taken of changing patterns in the world of work where increased unemployment and other forms of labour insecurity are a factor. In this regard, it is important to take advantage of the enormous knowledge of the ILO gained through the provision of technical assistance to Member states. This brought the ILO close to state practice and thus enabled it to identify those priorities that states are willing to address immediately and which could therefore constitute a core minimum protection. The ILO's practical experience shows that, nowadays, the access to universal basic health care and benefits due to employment injury are the social security priorities for countries. In addition, it is understood that universal basic pensions in case of inability to work due to invalidity or advanced age, or the death of the breadwinner, should be addressed immediately.

---

[26] The exception to this is represented by the European Social Charter whose Article 12, paragraph 2, provides that the Contracting Parties undertake: 'to maintain the social security system at a satisfactory level at least equal to that required for ratification of ILO Convention No. 102 concerning Minimum Standards of Social Security'.

[27] *Ibid.*

The second group of rights, linked to an obligation of behaviour, comprise important economic and social rights that, being internationally accepted, can be progressively attained according to the level of development of the Member state. So, having implemented the minimum social protection described before, states would have an obligation of behaviour to implement other rights, in the sense that they would need to show that measures have been taken towards extending the core minimum and providing more and better social protection.

To determine the progressive social protection measures required from a given state, the ILO should first look at overall state practices, which could reveal useful measures adopted for the extension of social protection that could be replicated. Second, it is important for the ILO to identify best practices from its Member states, enabling it to help Governments to set expenditure priorities in order to improve their level of social protection. Third, linked to the other two, there is a need for the ILO to develop an international social policy to assist Member states to identify and implement the minimum floor and to help them to prioritise the establishment of higher levels of protection. This international social policy, aimed at guiding ILO constituents, should be based on ILO standards and on the values and principles, which they reflect. Hereby, Recommendations Nos. 67 and 69 could serve as tools for the formulation of a policy for the establishment of a core minimum, which could help States in moving towards higher level of protection as required under Convention No. 102.

9. Conclusions

Convention No. 102, together with Recommendations Nos. 67[28] and 69, embody the idea of the gradual application of provisions for the achievement of their aims: full coverage, regarding persons (those protected) either through protection by social security or by being gainfully occupied, and regarding the material objectives (coverage of the different contingencies).

As mentioned above, there is a need for a basic minimum protection that a state has to provide immediately to its people in order to fulfil international requirements. This is an obligation of result. This minimum social floor should not be negotiable and it should cover the basic needs in social protection. Also, it cannot be questioned from an economic perspective. The implementation of this basic social floor should not be postponed; it should be implemented immediately by all states irrespective of their economic or social development.

When observing recent economic trends, it becomes evident that periods of growth and stability are the exception. Before the World War II, social insurance

[28] The survey 'Post-war trends in Social Security' (*supra* note 6) points out that: 'Reduced to its simplest expression, this Recommendation urges that the sphere of protection of income security systems should be progressively enlarged in order to assure, to every worker and his dependants, at least the means of subsistence in every common contingency which occasions the involuntary loss of the worker's earnings or their insufficiency to meet the family's necessities.'

systems developed gradually and only limited categories of workers were covered by social security. At the time, to be old or disabled meant to be poor.

In the aftermath of World War II, the world community recognised the need for comprehensive social security coverage for everybody and against all risks. In the light of these developments, European countries developed universal pension and comprehensive social security schemes based on principles of solidarity and redistribution, with the state having overall responsibility. At the time, most European countries went through economic difficulties; countries like Germany or the United Kingdom needed to invest in rebuilding and reconstruction. Social protection, however, was regarded as one of the priorities and therefore, comprehensive social protection schemes developed hand-in-hand with the economy. From these examples, the conclusion may be drawn that, even in difficult economic periods, countries can afford social security, and that it should not be seen as an impediment to growth. Therefore, social security should be considered as a question of priorities, choices and political will, rather than that of economic affordability.

Evaluating the ILO's Approach to Standard-Setting and Monitoring in the Field of Social Security

Angelika Nußberger*

1. Standard-Setting

1.1 General characteristics of the standard-setting approach of the ILO

Standard setting within the ILO has a very long-standing tradition. The first conventions entered into force in 1921.[1] While the majority of the early conventions were dedicated to problems of labour law, there were quite a few conventions tackling social protection issues. The most prominent among them is Convention No. 19 concerning equality of treatment for national and foreign workers as regards workmen's compensation for accidents. The convention has been ratified by 120 countries so far. It is true, though, that such a success story is singular for a convention in the field of social protection.[2]

Social protection can be regarded as a field for experimentation in standard-setting and during almost one century different approaches were tried out. In the first part of my paper I will give an overview of the different eras of social protection standards, describe the specific characteristics and discuss the pros and cons of the various approaches. The second part will be dedicated to the main charac-

---

* Professor of Law, University of Cologne, and member of the ILO Committee of Experts.

1 On 13 June 1921 five conventions entered into force: Convention No. 1 (Convention Limiting the Hours of Work in Industrial Undertaking to Eight in the Day and Forty-eight in the Week), Convention No. 3 (Convention concerning the Employment of Women before and after Childbirth), Convention No. 4 (Convention concerning Employment of Women during Night), Convention No. 5 (Convention Fixing the Minimum Age for Admission of Children to Industrial Employment), Convention No. 6 (Convention concerning the Night Work of Young Persons Employed in Industry).

2 Convention No. 19 concerns a question of the coordination, not of the harmonisation of social security law. Therefore it will not be dealt with in more detail in this article.

teristics of the detailed supervision procedure of the ILO. In the conclusion, the dilemma of drafting social protection standards applicable in different societies in the developed and developing countries will be addressed.

1.1.1 The social insurance approach prior to World War II

The standard-setting activity of the ILO in the field of social security can be subdivided in four periods: the social insurance period before World War II, the idealistic period during the war, the social security period in the 1950s, and the new approach in the era of globalisation.

The period between the wars was fruitful in the development of social protection systems on the national level.[3] The already existing insurance models were widened, new risks such as unemployment were included and the groups of persons covered by the protection systems were enlarged. Although the insurance model prevailed, it was not alone.[4] In the Nordic countries not only the workers, but all the inhabitants were protected.[5]

On the international level common standards were deemed necessary, not because social security was considered as a basic human right, but primarily because of the fear by States of unfair competition in the form of social dumping.[6] According to the ILO philosophy, peace could only be preserved if all the States accepted common standards in labour and social protection law and avoided distortions in the worldwide economic equilibrium.[7] The starting-point for all the reflections at that time was not the individual, but the collective of the workers. Still, it has to be seen that this approach was revolutionary at a time when the concept of sovereignty was understood as incompatible with any sort of international standards applicable in the relationship between a State and its citizens.[8]

Therefore, as a rule, the early ILO conventions in the field of social protection do not grant rights to individuals, but are addressed to the States and give clear prescriptions to them as to how the specific protection systems have to be organised in order for the systems to be as effective as possible. This effectiveness is

---

3 See: Jens Alber, *Vom Armenhaus zum Wohlfahrtsstaat. Analysen zur Entwicklung der Sozialversicherung in Westeuropa* (Campus, 1987).

4 See the different reports in: Peter A. Köhler and Hans F. Zacher (eds.), *Ein Jahrhundert Sozialversicherung in der Bundesrepublik Deutschland, Frankreich, Großbritannien, Österreich und der Schweiz* (Duncker & Humblot, 1981).

5 See, for example, the introduction of the pension for older people in Denmark and Norway in 1890; in Great Britain the tax-based 'Old Age Pensions Act' was passed in 1908.

6 See: Ernest Mahaim, 'The Historical and Social Importance of International Labor Legislation', in James T. Shotwell (ed.), *The Origins of the International Labor Organization* (Columbia University Press, 1934), 3-19 at 3 et seq.

7 See: the preamble of the Constitution of the ILO.

8 Note that international law was defined as '…the minimal law necessary to enable state-societies to act as closed systems internally and to act as territory-owners in relation to each other' (Philipp Allott, *Eunomia. New Order for a New World* (Oxford University Press, 1990) at 324).

evaluated in the perspective of the workers as a group. Thus in Convention No. 2 concerning unemployment, a system of free public employment agencies under the control of a central authority as well as a system of insurance had to be established. This State-oriented approach in the first decade of the ILO is not without any exception though. Convention No. 3 concerning the Employment of Women before and after Childbirth does not follow this scheme, but combines a prohibition on working in the six weeks following the confinement with a number of rights.[9]

The very early ILO conventions like the convention on unemployment, the convention on maternity protection and the convention on workmen's compensation (agriculture) usually do no contain technical details as to the construction of the protection systems, but are based on the idea that the social insurance model is the most effective means of protection.[10] General notions[11] are used to circumscribe the duties of the contracting parties. The conventions leave it to the national authorities to choose between different options or to determine the details of the rules to be applied. Despite the openness of the general approach, procedural rules are fixed demanding the involvement of workers' and employers' representatives in the decision-making processes.[12]

The most fruitful period for the elaboration of international conventions on social protection was during the early 1930s. Within a short period of time, conventions were elaborated on sickness insurance,[13] old age insurance,[14] invalidity insurance,[15] widows' and orphans' insurance,[16] workmen's compensation for occupa-

---

9 See, for example, Art. 3 (b) of Convention No. 3: 'a woman … shall have the right to leave her work'.

10 See: G. Tamburi, *L'organisation internationale du travail et l'évolution des assurances sociales dans le monde* (Bureau International du Travail, 1981); Guy Perrin, 'Reflections on fifty years of social security' 3 (1969) 99 *International Labour Review* 249-293.

11 See: Art. 3 (c) Convention No. 3 of the ILO: 'A woman … shall … be paid benefits *sufficient* for the full and healthy maintenance of herself and her child, provided either out of public funds or by means of a system of insurance, the exact amount of which shall be determined by the competent authority in each country …' (Emphasis added).

12 See, for example, Art. 2 I of Convention No. 2: 'Committees, which shall include representatives of employers and of workers, shall be appointed to advise on matters concerning the carrying on of these agencies.'

13 Convention No. 24 concerning Sickness Insurance for Workers in Industry and Commerce and Domestic Servants (1927), Convention No. 25 concerning Sickness Insurance for Agricultural Workers (1927).

14 Convention No. 35 concerning Compulsory Old-Age Insurance for Persons Employed in Industrial or Commercial Undertaking, in the Liberal Professions and for Outworkers and Domestic Servants (1933), Convention concerning Compulsory Old-Age Insurance for Persons Employed in Agricultural Undertakings (1933).

15 Convention No. 37 concerning Compulsory Invalidity Insurance for Persons Employed in Industrial or Commercial Undertaking, in the Liberal Professions and for Outworkers and Domestic Servants (1933), Convention concerning Compulsory Invalidity Insurance for Persons Employed in Agricultural Undertakings (1933).

tional diseases[17] and on benefits or allowances to the involuntarily unemployed.[18] Thus, in the inter-war period, the legislation of the ILO already covered the risks regarded as the most frequent causes for the loss of means of survival.

These conventions aim at selected risks and selected groups of insured persons. The material and personal scope of application is clearly defined according to a general perception of who might become needy. Thus for example the members of the employers' family or workers whose remuneration exceeds a prescribed amount can be excluded. But not all those who are in the danger of falling into poverty are expected to be covered by the insurance system. The system only covered 'ordinary wage earners'. Atypical cases are left out.[19] The conventions either aim at those employed in industrial or commercial undertakings or those employed in agriculture.

The preponderance of the regulations is dedicated to the benefits, although their actual amount is not predetermined. There are some regulations to the administration of the systems as well, whereas the problem of financing is left out.

From the very beginning, the normative approach of the ILO contains two dimensions: binding conventions and non-binding recommendations. Most of the conventions are accompanied by recommendations that contain additional details on the subject regulated by the convention, but are not legally binding.

The advantage of this system of international protection is that clear legal obligations form a sound basis for legal control. The idea of building up insurance systems for the workers is transported from the national to the international level. The common features of the dominant type of national systems are then filtered out and made compulsory for all States.

Still, this approach cannot be called successful. The systems are a mirror of the development of social protection systems in Western Europe at a given point in time. They lack flexibility and cannot be adapted to changing societal demands. The low numbers of ratifications – in most cases not more than 5 per cent of the member countries – are to be interpreted as a sign of a lack of acceptance.

Contrary to national legal systems, the revision of standards does not automatically mean that the earlier standards lose their legal force. Therefore the early conventions are still in force today, but they are no longer recommended for ratification; they are 'shelved'. Some countries have denounced them, but some are still bound by them. Thus, the control bodies have to check the compatibility of the na-

---

16 Convention No. 39 concerning Compulsory Widows' and Orphans' Insurance for Persons Employed in Industrial or Commercial Undertakings, in the Liberal Professions, and for Outworkers and Domestic Servants (1933).

17 Convention No. 42 concerning Workmen's Compensation for Occupational Diseases (Revised 1934).

18 Convention No. 44 Ensuring Benefit or Allowances to the Involuntarily Unemployed (1934).

19 See: Art. 2 (a) of Convention No. 24: 'It shall, nevertheless, be open to any Member to make such exceptions in its national laws or regulations as it deems necessary in respect of temporary employment which lasts for less than a period to be determined by national laws or regulations, casual employment not for the purpose of the employer's trade or business, occasional employment and subsidiary employment.'

tional legislation with these standards, although they are considered to be out-dated, which again shows the clumsiness of the system.

1.1.2 The idealistic approach during the war

The existence of social protection systems is not an aim in itself. It is not decisive in which way a person is insured, but it is crucial that the protection system helps to overcome material difficulties caused by the realisation of a certain foreseeable risk. Thus in the years that shortly preceded the Second World War, and during the war itself, the technical aspects, the measures of protection, were regarded as secondary. What was seen as important was the stabilising effect on society and the smoothing out of social gaps. It was not the problems of international competition but the 'dictates of humanity' and the 'principles of social justice' that were considered as the major motivation for the elaboration of international standards.[20]

Inspired by a new concept of individual, not collective social security,[21] two innovative recommendations were worked out in 1944.[22] They clearly show the way to a human rights based approach to social security. Under the new Director General of the ILO, Winant, social security was defined as 'the security that society furnishes through appropriate organisation against certain risks to which its members are exposed'.[23] It was stressed that security is a state of mind as well as an objective fact. An important pillar of this new understanding was the famous Beveridge report on social insurance that conveyed the idea of income security for all.[24]

The Recommendation Concerning Income Security and the Medical Care Recommendation can be considered the most advanced social security standards ever written. They embrace all the necessary elements of a sound and balanced concept of social protection, and are drafted in a very concise manner. Although these recommendations are more than half a century old and were written during the war, they are not out-dated and can still be referred to as basic documents for social security. The basic risks are enumerated and defined in an abstract manner that gives room for further developments in society. In contrast to later standards it is not the male-breadwinner-model that is underlying these recommendations; there are no discriminatory elements. The personal scope is not limited to dependent workers, but includes self-employed people as well, wherever that is possible without an exaggerated large administrative burden. The amount of benefits is not entirely left to the discretion of the national States but defined in a forward-looking way. It should be 'up to a level as is practical without impairing the will to resume work where resumption is a possibility and without levying charges on the productive

---

20 See the Santiago Resolution (published as a part of the Inter-American Social Insurance Code): ILO, *The International Labour Code* (ILO, 1952) 664 at 666.

21 Guy Perrin, *supra* note 10.

22 Recommendation Concerning Income Security, Medical Care Recommendation.

23 ILO, *Approaches to social security: An international survey. Studies and Reports, Series M (Social insurance) No. 18* (ILO, 1942) at 80.

24 Sir William Beveridge, *Social insurance and allied services. Presented to Parliament by Command of His Majesty November 1942* (H. M. Stationary Off., 1969).

groups so heavy that output and employment are checked'. This wisdom should be observed nowadays as well.

In contrast to the pre-war conventions these recommendations are not binding, but are only meant to be guidelines for the member States of the ILO.

1.1.3 The social security approach in the post war era

This idealistic approach was not followed in the post-war era. Although the Universal Declaration of Human Rights proclaimed in 1945 'social security' as a human right,[25] the ILO did not take up this idea. On the contrary, the worker-dominated approach of the pre-war era was developed further and served as the basis of Convention No. 102, which became the international model convention for social security regulations. The convention was prepared thoroughly and finally agreed upon by the conference delegates in 1952. It entered into force three years later on 27 April 1955. Contrary to the pre-war conventions that are based on the idea of social insurance, this post-war convention follows a broader social-security approach.[26]

The convention is to be characterised as very pragmatic. It is based on a typical Western European society in the 1950s where most of the work force is employed in industrial undertakings in stable employment relationships. The husband is the breadwinner in the family; the mother is caring for the children. Based on this model the 'standard beneficiary' is defined as a 'man with a wife and two children' who works either as a 'skilled manual employee' or as an 'ordinary adult labourer'. Benefits are calculated on this basis.

As to social security, three basic models are taken into account: systems, where prescribed classes of employees are protected against the basic risks, systems where the economically active population is protected, and systems where prescribed classes of residents are protected. The systems are expected to be constructed in a comparatively simple manner, serving exclusively the purpose of securing a more or less homogenous group against poverty in case of sickness, unemployment, invalidity, work accident, occupational disease, loss of the breadwinner, and maternity.

On the basis of this simplified model of society and social security, a very coherent system of minimum standards is built up. The contracting states receive clear prescriptions as to how the national protection systems have to be structured in order to fulfil the minimum demands. They have to protect a certain percentage of the population or of the workers, they have to grant a certain amount of money, and they have to observe certain principles regarding the administration and the adjudication of claims.

---

[25] Guy Perrin, 'The recognition of the right to social protection as a human right' 2 (1985) 10 *Labour and Society* 239-258.

[26] Albrecht Otting, 'International labour standards: A framework for social security', 2 (1993) 132 *International Labour Review* 163-171; Alec L. Parrott, 'Social security: Does the wartime dream have to become a peacetime nightmare?' 3 (1992) 131 *International Labour Review* 367-386; Guy Perrin, *supra* note 10.

Contrary to the pre-war social insurance conventions, these conventions are very flexible. They set fixed rules, but the States can choose which rules they want to apply. Even more, the States can choose the risks for which they want to legally bind themselves under Convention No. 102. The idea is to lead the States to build up comprehensive systems of social security gradually.

This model is a true mirror of the development of social security in the 1950s in Western Europe. It is based on a conception of progress typical for the industrial age. The conventions are comparatively flexible, but still offer a sound basis for the control of the contracting States' social security legislation. As the internationally agreed minimum standards set in the 1950s can be regarded as a landmark they cannot be neglected nowadays, even if the problems of the post-modern, post-industrial societies were not foreseeable in the 1950s. A minimum can be considered a minimum even if circumstances change.

Convention No. 102 has been ratified by 41 States, i.e., by a little bit less than one forth of the member States of the ILO. But only 6 out of these 41 States have ratified the Convention as a whole. Most of the States have taken advantage of the possibility to adhere only to selected parts of the Convention. The idea of a gradual acceptance of more and more parts of the convention has not been realised. With only very few exceptions the first choice of certain parts of the convention has not been changed, even if the system of social security had developed further. Six out of 178 member States accepted Convention No. 102 in full – that is not a success story.

Despite this statistical evidence, Convention No. 102 is the cornerstone of the international concept of what is an effective social security system.[27] Even States not adhering to the convention have been inspired by it. As there is no other comprehensive description of the basic elements necessary to offer a solid social security protection Convention No. 102 is quoted whenever an international harmonisation of social security protection is discussed. It contains only minimum standards and is therefore open for further developments. In order to supervise the fulfilment of the obligations imposed by the convention, the contracting parties are required to provide statistical data on the number of people insured and on the benefits they receive. Thus not only the law in the books, but also the law in action is controlled.

Convention No. 102 marks a specific point in the development of international social security standards. It is often taken as a point of reference for the concretisation of the understanding of the human right to social security. Thus Art. 12 II of the European Social Charter explicitly refers to the standards set by Convention No. 102 in order to explain what is meant by 'social security'. But that is a simplistic view as Convention No. 102 does not grant any rights, but only determines the construction of social security systems at the outset. A State already acts in compliance with the convention if protection against basic risks is offered to a part of those in need of it and not to all.

The deficiencies of Convention No. 102 are therefore quite evident. Due to its very technical nature it demands a highly developed social security administration

27 Nicolas Valticos, *Droit international du travail* (Dalloz, 1983) at 391 et seq.

collecting the relevant statistical data. The calculations based on the standard beneficiaries are very complex; there is a special training necessary in order to comply with the reporting obligations. It is quite clear that this deters countries, particularly developing countries, that already have social security administrations which struggle to comply with very basic tasks.

More importantly Convention No. 102 is fixed on the conceptual understanding of work and social security in industrial societies, neither adapted to the demands of post-industrial economies nor of developing countries. Many stereotypes underlying Convention No. 102 have proved to be not true any more. The male breadwinner-model does not coincide with reality. Provisions granting survivors' benefits only to women, not to men have been declared discriminatory on the national as well as on the international level, but they have not been changed in Convention No. 102. The assumption that only, or mostly, workers are dependent on social security protection has been falsified as well. In developing countries those working in the shadow economy as well as people running small businesses are at least as vulnerable as those employed in big enterprises. In industrialised countries stable relationships have often been replaced by new atypical forms of work. Furthermore, Convention No. 102 does not have any answers to the really important problems such as securing a stable financing of social security, coping with the ageing of the population, finding a fair balance between the interests of the older and the younger population and the pandemic of AIDS. For most of the developing countries the model offered by Convention No. 102 is nothing but illusionary. For them minimum standards would be necessary, an approach the legitimacy of which the ILO always denies as it clings to the ideal of general standards for the whole world.

1.1.4 The soft human rights oriented approach in the era of globalisation

Whereas the 1920s and 1930 as well as the 1950s and 1960s were fruitful in working out social security standards on a world-wide scale, legislative activity has stagnated in the remainder of the time. The standards set in Convention No. 102 were developed further in special conventions dedicated to certain groups of risks in the 1960s but since then the ILO has – with some minor exceptions – not returned to tackle the basic questions of social security. Only in 2002 the subject was discussed in the general conference.[28]

The positions of the member countries were so divergent that it was not even tried to reach a compromise on revising Convention No. 102 or on elaborating a new legally binding instrument. The only aim was to pass a resolution in order to give guidelines as to the actual development of the understanding of social security protection in the ILO.[29] Thus the hard legal standards of Convention No. 102

---

28 ILO, *Social security. A new consensus* (ILO, 2001); ILO, *Social security: Issues, challenges and prospects* (International Labour Conference, 89th session, 2001).

29 ILO, *Resolution and Conclusions concerning social security* (International Labour Conference, 89th Session, 2001).

are watered down in soft law. No answer as to the preferable system of social security is given.[30] Even the basic – and most controversial question – if a system based on pay-as-you-go or on capital funding is preferable is not solved. There are only vague directions as to the sustainability and the transparency of the system. Discrimination has to be prohibited; the social partners have to be involved in the decision-making process.

Thus the workers-oriented approach was abandoned in favour of a human rights-oriented approach. But even as such, social security remains excluded from the fundamental principles and rights at work as they are fixed in the Declaration of 1998.[31]

The advantage of this new soft human-rights oriented approach is that the diverging demands of the post-industrial countries on the one side and the developing countries on the other side are reconciled to a certain degree. The resolution is flexible and orientated on the key problems.

But on the other hand the new approach can be regarded as a step back as no clear legal obligations are formulated, but only vague notions that do not form a basis for any control procedure. What came out is a compromise formula without any precise contents.[32]

2. Monitoring

The ILO system of supervision has led the way for all the other monitoring bodies created after the Second World War. It has a very long-standing tradition and is based on three pillars: the regular supervision procedure by the Committee of Independent Experts, the Inter-States complaint procedure (Art. 26 of the Constitution) and the collective complaint procedure (Art. 24 of the Constitution). Whereas all these procedures are conceived as a constructive dialogue between the ILO and its member States and not as jurisdiction, controversies can also be solved on the basis of binding decisions by the International Court of Justice.

---

30 See No. 4 of the Resolution: 'There is no single right model of social security. It grows and evolves over time. There are schemes of social assistance, universal schemes, social insurance and public or private provisions. Each society must determine how best to ensure income security and access to health care. …'

31 Declaration on Fundamental Principles and Rights at Work, adopted in 1998.

32 See the critical analysis of Philip Alston, ''Core Labour Standards' and the Transformation of the International Labour Rights Regime' 3 (2004) 15 *European Journal of International Law* 457-521; see also the view of the supporters of core labour standards: Brian A. Langille, 'Core Labour Rights – The True Story (Reply to Alston)' 3 (2005) 16 *European Journal of International Law* 437-464, Francis Maupain, 'Revitalization Not Retreat: The Real Potential of the 1998 ILO Declaration for the Universal Protection of Workers' Rights' 3 (2005) 16 *European Journal of International Law* 465-479.

2.1 The inter-States complaint procedure

Complaints of non-observance by other member States may be a relevant means of pressure in politically very sensitive areas of human rights protection. For ILO supervision, such complaints are rare exceptions.[33] So far, they have not been relevant in controversies concerning social security standards. As a rule States refrain from this remedy as long as the violation of standards does not touch their own interests directly.

2.2 The collective complaint procedure

Contrary to the inter-States complaints the collective complaint procedure is actually used in practice to settle disputes on social security standards. According to the Constitution of the ILO, industrial associations of workers or employers can make representations to the International Labour Office that a member State has failed to secure the effective observance of a Convention to which it is a party. The first step in this procedure is to make the different opinions public. If deemed necessary, a Commission of Inquiry can be set up. This procedure offers the possibility to transfer controversies about social and labour law from the national to the international level.

In the field of social security this procedure has been used quite often by South American trade unions in order to protest the privatisation of the social security systems. One of the most prominent cases was the representation of the National Trade Union Coordination Council of Chile against Chile in 1985.[34] The problem was that Chile had ratified only the social insurance conventions of the 1930s that are considered to be outdated. Nevertheless these conventions had to be taken as the basis for the evaluation of the new social security system in Chile that was primarily based on obligatory savings of the employed, free choice of the insured as to the insurance company, and the private administration of the capitalised funds. The trade unions alleged, among other things, non-compliance with Art. 9 of Convention No. 35 as only the employed persons and not the employers had to pay contributions whereas Art. 9 requires contributions to the financial resources of the insurance scheme by both. The resolution of the controversy thus depended on the interpretation of the exception clause in Convention No. 35: 'Contributions from employers may be dispensed with under laws or regulations concerning schemes of national insurance not restricted in scope to employed persons.' On this basis the Committee came to the conclusion that the privatised system in Chile was not in conformity with the ILO conventions. This example shows the

33 Inter-States complaints within the ILO were for example based on Convention No. 105 and Convention No. 29; see: Nicolas Valticos and Gerard Potobsky, *International Labour Law* (Kluwer law and Taxation, 1995) at 290 et seq.

34 See: Report of the Committee set up to examine the representation submitted by the National Trade Union Co-ordination Council (CNS) of Chile under article 24 of the ILO Constitution, alleging non-observance by Chile of international labour Conventions Nos. 1, 2, 24, 29, 30, 35, 37, 38 and 111; Vol. LXXI, 1988, Series B, Supplement 1.

scarce margin of appreciation of the Commission of Inquiry in judging the compliance or non-compliance with ILO conventions. It is clearly bound by precise legal regulations.

It is worth comparing the very general comment on Mexico by the Committee on Economic, Social and Cultural Rights on the basis of the International Covenant on Economic, Social and Cultural Rights to the detailed analysis of the ILO supervision bodies. When confronted with the privatisation of social security systems in Mexico, the Committee on Economic, Social and Cultural Rights laconically states:

> The Committee is concerned about the privatisation of the social security system, which may exclude from certain benefits those not in a position to contribute to an individual pension account, such as the unemployed, underemployed, lower-paid workers and those employed in the informal sector.[35]

This example clearly shows the advantages and disadvantages of the different monitoring procedures. The procedure within the framework of the United Nations human rights protection system can single out the most important aspects without being forced to enter into a detailed legal analysis. The ILO system is bound by concrete norms and therefore has to deduce the findings from the wording of the relevant norms. It is not able to hint at central deficiencies of a social security system if there are no legal regulations on that very point in the relevant Convention. On the other hand a profound legal analysis can confer legitimacy on the conclusions reached.[36]

2.3 The report procedure

Whereas inter-State complaints and collective complaints are only exceptional measures, it is the regular supervision process based on State reports that is the backbone of the monitoring procedure and is called upon to secure the compliance of the national legislation with the international conventions in the first place. In this context, the ILO is confronted with the same problems as all the other international monitoring bodies.[37] The Committee of Experts depends on the cooperation of the member State in supplying the relevant information and in following the advice given in the conclusions and direct requests.

---

35 See: Mexico (Concluding Observations of the Committee on Economic, Social and Cultural Rights: Mexico 8/12/99 E/C.12/1Add.41, para. 19).

36 For a general overview of the different approaches in defining compliance with treaty obligations in international social law, see: Angelika Nußberger, *Sozialstandards im Völkerrecht. Eine Studie zu Entwicklung und Bedeutung der Normsetzung der Vereinten Nationen, der Internationalen Arbeitsorganisation und des Europarats zu Fragen des Sozialschutzes* (Duncker & Humblot, 2005) at 284 et seq.

37 See the different reports in: Eckart Klein (ed.), *The Monitoring System of Human Rights Treaty Obligations* (Berlin-Verl. Spitz, 1998).

But in comparison to the other human rights instruments, the supervision process in the ILO has some advantages.[38] First, the ILO office in Geneva composed of about 2.000 officials does an excellent job in preparing the annual reports for the Committee of Experts. Thus the supervision of a huge number of reports within a short period of time is not bound to be superficial but can even discuss intricate legal problems. Furthermore the ILO is, due to its tripartite structure, not exclusively dependent on the information given by the States, but obtains additional information from employers' and workers' organisations. In practice they usually provide the most pertinent information and point to the real problems in fulfilling the obligations.[39]

In the field of social security a large number of detailed problems have been discussed between the Committee of Experts and the member States. These discussions can touch upon the very basic question of what is to be understood by solidarity, but it can also dwell on problems of minor importance. In Western Europe for example the many changes introduced in order to consolidate the financial basis of the social security system are usually checked one by one. The most difficult problem is always the evaluation of the statistical data on the amount of benefits as well as the interpretation of such general clauses as 'cost-sharing shall be so designed as to avoid hardship' or 'the essential pharmaceutical supplies have to be included in the benefits in case of sickness'.

In all, the report procedure allows for a clear measurement of progress and deterioration of the social security systems in comparison to the standards set by the ILO.

3. Conclusion

Setting international standards in the field of social security is not an easy task. On one hand, even the European Community, as the most tightly bound international cooperation network, has so far refrained from harmonising social security systems. Social security is one of the few domains still more or less exclusively reserved to national regulations as it is considered dependent on many factors that are deeply rooted in national traditions. Nowadays social security is the battlefield where elections are often won or lost. Therefore this area is not really apt for international standards.

On the other hand, it is generally acknowledged that social security is a basic human right that has to be part of international human rights conventions. If it were left out, an important element in guaranteeing the preconditions for a human existence in dignity would be missing. The right to social security cannot be an empty promise, but has to be filled with concrete guarantees. No other interna-

---

38 Alfred Wisskirchen, 'Die normensetzende und normenüberwachende Tätigkeit der Internationalen Arbeitsorganisation (IAO)' 4 (2003) 34 *Zeitschrift für Arbeitsrecht* 691-733.

39 See: Ernest Alfred Landy, *The Effectiveness of International Supervision. Thirty Years of I.L.O. Experience* (Stevens & Sons oceana publications, 1966).

tional organisation but the ILO has tried so effectively to fill this gap on the international level and to explain what social security means. But the definitions given are not homogenous. They oscillate between two extremes. Either they are very technical in nature and thus mirror certain concepts realised in certain parts of the world, or they are very broad and comprehensive including all possible options. Whereas the first model offers a sound basis for legal control, the second one is too vague; it cannot be more than a non-binding guideline. On the other hand the field of application of the first model is only very restricted whereas the second one is open to all.

The process of trial and error of the standard-setting activity of the ILO shows that the idealistic approach during the war, fixed in two recommendations of the year 1944, is still the most convincing one. In view of the hardship and the sufferance caused by the World War, the basic and universal values were filtered out. The recommendations incorporated an unrealistic ideal when they were drafted - they are not even reprinted in the official collection of the 'International Labour Conventions and Recommendations' edited by the ILO - but they reflect a concept of true social solidarity that ought to be looked at today and in the future.

Social Security for Women Workers in the Informal Economy

SEWA's Social Security Programme

Shalini Sinha*

Section I: Informal Sector in India

The term informal economy broadly refers to informal arrangements of work, including home-based, casual, temporary and part-time employment, self-employment and micro-entrepreneurs. In addition, there are landless labourers and marginal and small farmers in rural areas. The main defining characteristics of the sector are the precarious nature of the work – employment is not permanent and workers are generally not covered by adequate social security. It may also imply a 'scattered' workplace and the incidence of home-based work or even acute occurrences of under-employment with more than one employer. There is often no clear employer-employee relationship and in certain work, such as home-based work and contract labour, it may be difficult to identify any employer. In most cases, the enterprises such persons work in are small and unregistered.

The term informal economy accommodates considerably diversity in workers as well as in enterprises. The door-to-door vegetable vendor, the rickshaw puller, the embroidery workers, the cobbler, the rag-picker and local tea boy are many of the informal workers whom one encounters in day-to-day life in India. There are others who less visible, work in homes or in sweatshops, including garment makers, beedi rollers, paperback makers, food processors. Neither is the informal sector an urban phenomenon; it cuts across the rural-urban divide. The landless agricultural labourer or the crafts women worker or the silkworm rearer or the forest workers are all workers from the informal sector.

The advent of globalisation in India has seen an increasing informalisation of employment, particularly home based, contract and casual labor. Coupled with this phenomenon is the complete absence of any widespread system for social security in this sector, which is alarming when we consider that the informal sector accounts for 97 per cent of the women workers. Women are concentrated in this

---

* Consultant, Self Employed Women's Association (SEWA), India. I am grateful to Mrs Renana Jhabvala for her guidance and support in writing this paper. For information on SEWA see www.sewa.org, www.sewainsurance.org and www.sewahousing.org.

low end of the spectrum, in low paying and insecure jobs; their work is insecure, irregular and often unrecognised. They balance children, home and work, and, more often than not, their income is not commensurate with their work. This paper examines the needs of the social security for this segment of workers and presents the case study of Self Employed Women's Association (SEWA) social security program.

Informal economy in India - Numbers and case studies

The informal economy is large in India, accounting for 370 million workers in 1999-2000.[1] Non-agricultural workers account for a large part of the informal sector, estimated at 134 million. The informal economy accounts for nearly 93 per cent of the total workforce and 83 per cent of the non-agricultural work force. The self-employed component is very large – nearly a half (53 per cent) of the total workforce in India is self-employed.

Women account for 32 per cent of the workforce in the informal economy in India. A total of 118 million women workers are engaged in the informal sector, constituting 97 per cent of the aggregate number of women workers. Large proportions of women workers (56 per cent) are self employed, both in rural and urban areas, 37 per cent of the women workers are employed as casual workers while only 7 per cent have regular jobs. The majority of women in the informal sector are 'own account' traders and producers or casual and sub-contract workers; relatively few are employers who hire paid workers. Even within the same trade, men and women tend to be involved in different activities or types of employment. There usually exists a relatively large gender gap in income/wages in the informal sector with women being under-represented in high-income activities and over-represented in low-income activities. There are gender gaps in education and skills, access to credit, training and information, the quality and location of business premises, the scale of business etc.

At the same time, these workers in the informal economy are extremely economically active, accounting for 63 per cent of India's GDP, 55 per cent of national savings and about 47 per cent of all exports. Their contribution to the economy is, therefore, highly significant.[2]

---

1 The statistics in this section, unless stated otherwise, have been quoted from Jeemol Unni and Uma Rani, 'Gender Informality and Poverty' (November 2003) *Seminar* 531.

2 National Accounts Statistics (NAS), 2000, Statement 76.1; B.K. Pradhan, P.K. Roy and M.R. Saluja, *The Unorganized Sector in India* (NCAER, 2000); Ghatate, *The Contribution of the Unorganized Sector in Exports,* (National Institute of Foreign Trade (NIFT), 1999).

Woman Worker In The Informal Sector – Who Is She?

Let us look at the work and lives of some women workers in the informal economy in India in order to understand what it means to be a poor woman worker in India.

Purabiben is a vegetable vendor in Ahmedabad. She lives in a crowded slum, with no sanitation facilities, where 22 houses share a tap which has water supply for only three hours in morning and Purabiben has to stand in long queues for hours in order to fetch water for her family. She is often late in reaching the wholesale market and loses out on the fresh vegetable supply. On these days, her earnings suffer – who will buy stale vegetables from her? At work, the police harass her frequently for bribes in return for protection because she has no licence and has no idea how to get one. All Purabiben wants is enough space to keep her two baskets in this vast city, to sell her goods.

Mary is 18-years old and from Kerala. Her family owns some land, but not enough to survive. Every year, Mary goes with other girls from her village with the contractor, also from her village, to the fish processing factories in Veraval.

Kalibai is from Dewas in Madhya Pradesh. She has four children and all her thoughts are concentrated on them and how to feed them and keep her house running. She and her husband do not own any land, but they get work as agricultural labourers two or three months a year and intermittently throughout the year. They live near the forests and she and her eldest children gather firewood from the forest and sell it in the village.

Chitrabai is a small farmer from Maharashtra. Although her whole family works hard on the land, the low prices for agricultural products mean that they never earn enough to survive.

These and many other women workers are employed in the informal sector, mainly as small vendors, home-based producers, wage workers and service providers. They work in back-breaking jobs, doing hard labour for long hours. Their earnings are low and irregular. Even within the informal economy, they occupy the lowest rung in terms of income, skills and social protection. They take the full responsibility for the care of the home, for the feeding of the family and for the care of the children, the elderly and the sick.

A woman worker in the informal sector lives and works under many constraints. Being a woman she would have a lower status in her wider family, meaning her family would own few assets and have few opportunities for better work, and such assets or opportunities that existed would be in for the males of the wider family and not for her. She also eats last and the least, is the last to sleep and first to wake. She would face inequality and exploitation in society and at work. Often, she may be a widow or lives alone with her children. She faces a crushing work burden of both work for income, work for subsistence, work for the household and care work of children and aged.

However, it should be recognised that the work that these women do is very much part of the national economy. Her work contributes not only to their own families but also to the development of their villages and towns and to the country as a whole. Their work contributes to the national income and to economic growth. She is the centre of the economy, whose labour and enterprise creates the wealth of the nation, and whose hard work leads to national growth. She needs security, a decent life, a share in the prosperity of the nation and the dream of a good life for her children.

Section II: Social Security for Women Workers – Identifying Needs

Child care

The women worker plays the triple role of a worker, housewife and a mother. The working mother is often bogged down by the burden of having sole responsibility for child care, which leads to the decline in her productivity as well as negative impacts on the health of both the mother and the child. The assumption that young children are taken care of in traditional family arrangements no longer holds true.

A woman worker works for long hours, often seven days a week. To reach her place of work, she often has to walk long distances by foot or travel in crowded public transport. A working mother is overworked and exhausted and often very anxious and stressed about her child's welfare.

Provision of childcare relieves the women of one of her multiple burden, creates time and space and work opportunities for women and supports her empowerment. Yet, in the absence of adequate child care facilities, a working mother has no option but to leave the child with a slightly older sibling. A large part of sibling caregivers are girl children, many of them not above the age when they no longer need intensive care and nurturing. The lack of childcare facilities also prevents the girl child from attending school and enjoying childhood.

Maternity Entitlements

The most productive years of a women's life are also the reproductive years of her life. In the absence of any provision for maternity leave, a women worker often has to leave her job to have a child. Poor health, additional medical expenses along with loss of employment make the women worker economically vulnerable during the period of childbirth, plunging her into a crisis of borrowing and high interest expenses. Often she does not take adequate rest and starts working soon after childbirth with adverse effect on her health. This repeated neglect of a women's health during pregnancy and childbirth manifests itself in a high mortality rate, anaemia and general poor health for women workers.

Health

Sickness amongst individuals or of their immediate family members may result in loss of employment and entails additional expenses in terms of medicines and/or hospitalisation. With increasing privatisation of the health care services, the woman worker is forced to shoulder the increasing financial burden in times of illness or injury. She thus has to meet these expenses by either spending her savings, borrowing from moneylenders and/or by selling or mortgaging/pledging her assets. As a result, the woman suffers reduction in her income and her savings and a simultaneous rise in interest expenses. The reduction in assets eventually leads to depletion of her income, borrowing and consequent indebtedness, thus trapping her inexorably in the vicious circle of poverty. Besides, women often put a low premium on personal health and, in a scenario where resources are scarce, the health of the children and other family members take precedence – debilitating her already fragile health and having a negative impact on her productivity as a worker. A strong body is a working woman's only capital.

Old Age

Traditionally the elderly were taken care of by the family. However, with the breaking up of the joint family, changes in employment patterns and the exodus from the rural areas, the social security needs of the elderly have become crucial. An old women worker who has no support and is totally dependent on others for survival is very vulnerable. Widowhood further adds to her vulnerability. Social security for her has many facets. Income security is only one aspect – she is often forced to work for long hours even when her age does not permit it. However, old age not only means loss or diminution of her income, it also means loss of her health and rise in the cost of medical care. A related problem is one of being lonely, helpless and dependent.

Risks and Crisis

It is usually a crisis – personal, social or natural - which drives a family into the downslide towards destitution. It could be natural contingencies like floods, droughts, cyclones; or a personal loss such as the death of husband or the family breadwinner or events such as market crash, crop failure or cattle loss through disease. Each crisis leaves the woman worker and her family weaker and more vulnerable. The main reason for such a strong negative impact is the high expenditure incurred at such times, and the lack of facilities for the poor to save for such expenditures. In the absence of micro-insurance, there is no opportunity for the worker to spread the risks over a longer period and secure coverage during times of financial risks.

Shelter based workers work from their homes, the street vendors use them to store goods or even as a place from which to sell their goods, open a petty retail shop or a small handicraft production unit. A woman worker, even if she is working from home, needs adequate lighting, enough space and hygienic environment. She needs adequate space – dry and airy – to store her finished products and raw material. She needs good health, both for herself and for her family, and adequate time away from her household chores to devote to productive work. Frequent evictions and insecurity of tenure add to the vulnerability of woman worker, both economically and emotionally. The construction of shelter and services generates income and employment and better housing and services improve people's health, productivity and well-being, particularly for women.

Section III: SEWA's Social Security Programme

Introduction to SEWA

Founded in 1972, SEWA is a trade union of women workers engaged in the informal economy. With the goals of organising women for full employment and self-reliance at the household level, SEWA organises women through its joint strategy of struggle and development. Full employment includes work and income security, food security and social security – at least health care, child care, insurance and shelter.

SEWA has a membership of over 7,00,000 today. SEWA's members are the poorest of workers in India and can be categorised into four categories:

- Street vendors.
- Home-based workers producing thousands of goods, including handicrafts, from the home.
- Small producers, i.e., own account artisans, salt farmers, small and marginal farmers.
- Manual labourers and service providers (construction workers, agricultural labourers, child care workers etc.)

SEWA's Approach to social security – economic security with social security

SEWA sees social security as an integrated concept where economic security and social security are intimately connected. Economic security is the primary means by which people are able to obtain social security. Often workers are heard saying, 'Let us earn enough income and we can take care of all our other needs'. On the other hand, social security is a means to increase and maintain the productivity of the worker, so as to increase his/her economic security. Childcare facilities can increase the hours that a woman worker can be employed and her work productivity. Food security can ensure increased productivity and a decrease in illness. Social security therefore is a means of increasing and maintaining the productivity of the worker, so as to increase his/her economic security. The provision of these elements greatly enhances the quality of work and lifestyle of the workers.

Women workers in the informal economy need economic security - a continuous flow of employment through which they can earn enough in terms of cash and kind to meet their needs. In other words they need full employment. In the informal sector, employment is a combination of self-employment, or own-account work, wage employment, casual work, part-time work and a variety of employment relations. At any one time, a poor person could be undertaking engaged different 'jobs'. For example, a small or marginal farmer would also work as a weaver; or an agricultural labourer would also have her own cattle, or a construction worker would roll bidis (cigarettes) at night. The type of work she does may also be seasonal. A salt worker may be an agricultural worker during the monsoons, or a paper picker may make kites during the kite season.

Creating employment is therefore no longer a matter of creating 'jobs', but of strengthening these workers and producers to overcome structural constraints and enter markets where they would be competitive. Often these markets, which may be labour markets, products markets or financial markets may not exist locally, and need to be built up, or institutions need to be created which would link local markets with the larger markets.

The poor need capital formation at the household level through access to financial services (savings, credit, insurance) to build up and create assets of their own (land, house, worksheds, equipment, cattle, bank balance). Asset ownership is the surest weapon to fight the vulnerability of poverty. In addition and simultaneously, the poor need social security, at least healthcare, childcare, shelter and relief, in order to combat the chronic risks faced by them and their families.

Therefore, workers in the informal sector need economic security - a continuous flow of employment through which they can earn enough in terms of cash and kind to meet their needs – and, simultaneously, social security - at least healthcare, childcare, shelter and relief - to combat the chronic risks faced by them and their families. In addition, they also need collective, organised strength to be able to actively participate in the planning, implementation and monitoring processes of the programmes meant for them.

In this paper, we will concentrate on the social security programme of SEWA. However, it is important to briefly describe SEWA's economic security programme, which includes the bank, cooperatives and the marketing linkages. SEWA Bank is a financially sound, self-reliant and profit-making cooperative bank, owned by women themselves. SEWA Bank's main goal is the capitalisation and asset creation of SEWA members to help them come out of poverty. At present there are 148,000 depositors in SEWA Bank, and the bank gives credit of about Rs 10 crores per year to over 7000 women per year, for not only developing their businesses and other economic activities, but also to pay off their old debts.

SEWA also encourages formation of producers' cooperatives and associations where women themselves are the managers, producers and owners of the cooperatives. This develops their bargaining power and managerial capacities and ushers in significant changes in their standard of living. Through the cooperatives, workers get tools and implements to manufacture their products, and exploitative contractors, middlemen and merchants are eliminated. Eventually the members become owners of their means of production.

Self-employed workers depend heavily on market systems and structures. To promote efficient and appropriate production through continuous market research and understanding of world trade market trends, SEWA set up a Trade Facilitation Centre. This Centre will help local organisations develop their own infrastructure and system to meet market demands.

Social security for SEWA members

SEWA's approach and understanding of social security has emerged from its own experience of organising social security services with and for poor women. SEWA has found that the social security services managed by poor women workers through co-operatives can become financially viable and effectively provide need-based services to the women on demand and on payment of affordable charges.

Insurance

In response to a pressing demand from its members for covering some of the risks that they face, SEWA initiated the Integrated Social Security Scheme in 1992 with coverage including life, widowhood, personal accident insurance for the member and her spouse as well as sickness benefits, maternity benefits and asset loss protection.[3] The scheme is called Vimo SEWA or SEWA Insurance. Today, SEWA offers a social insurance scheme with two packages for its members. The two packages have different maximum limits of the reimbursement amount depending upon the premium collected. A member can opt for any one of the schemes depending on her paying capacity. In addition each scheme offers limited insurance to a spouse and children on payment of an additional amount. The child medical insurance coverage has evolved out of a response to our members' demands. Now, SEWA members, with an additional premium of Rs 100, can buy medical insurance for their children, for a period of one year.

Health

One of the earliest programmes of SEWA was health, which was started in the early 1970s and pertained to health education and provision of maternity benefits. Today, SEWA Health provides a wide range of primary healthcare services. The main thrust is on providing simple, life-saving health information with a focus on disease prevention and promotion of well-being. SEWA Health has four main components: preventive healthcare, curative healthcare, training and research. The

---

3 See also: Shalini Sinha, *Strength in Solidarity, SEWA's Insurance Programme* (SEWA, 2001).

components of preventive healthcare include mental and physical health, and health awareness and education. Curative healthcare includes health centers, mobile clinics, and programmes for Tuberculosis and AIDS and occupational health. Other important goals of SEWA Health have been: (1) to build capacity among local women, especially traditional midwives (dais) so that they become the barefoot doctors of their communities; and (2) to provide services to the very poor, particularly those living in areas not otherwise served by government facilities or non-governmental organisations (NGOs).

Housing Trust and Slum Upgradation Programme

Since 1994, Shri Mahila SEWA Housing Trust, the sister organisation of SEWA has been providing housing services, both technical and financial, to women. The objective of this Trust is to improve the housing and infrastructure conditions and overall living environment of SEWA members.

There is a direct correlation between better housing and infrastructure facilities, on the one hand and increased income levels, improved health and decreasing poverty, on the other hand. The Parivartan programme, which is a slum upgradation programme, has clearly demonstrated this. The Parivartan programme transforms the environment in which women live, through provision of basic services such as water, toilets, drainage, garbage disposal, paving of roads, streetlights and general landscaping. Over 20,000 people have been availed of these services.

Childcare Programme

In 1975, SEWA started its first child care centre for vegetable vendors. Currently, 8168 children and 8100 working mothers are involved in SEWA's childcare programme. SEWA has 173 centres in Ahmedabad city and in five rural districts of Gujarat. A cooperative of the childcare workers has also been formed. In Ahmedabad, Sangini Child Care Workers' Cooperative is running centres for infants and young children. It has linked with the government ICDS programmes and the Welfare Board. In Kheda district, Shaishav Child Care Workers' Cooperatives is running centres for 0 to 6 year old children of tobacco workers and agricultural labourers.

There have been small studies to show that with access to child care, women's well being and that of their children certainly improved. Their income levels increased and the levels of everyday stress that they experience as they juggle multiple roles and responsibilities as workers, mothers and home-makers decreased. Certainly their hours of work and productivity increased. Crèches make a marked and difference to their children. Further, when these children enter primary school, and all do, the teachers there and the mothers report that they generally perform very well and are active in class. They observe that there is a noticeable difference between these crèche children and others. One can certainly see from the studies that having access to child care is a significant economic support to women living in poverty, and that it also contributes to the well-being of their young children.

Pension scheme

Owing to the highly vulnerable and economically insecure lives of most of SEWA Bank's clients, planning and saving for old age is a last priority. Their lives are carried out on a daily basis, where the prospect of saving for later years is almost considered a luxury. Lack of awareness coupled with a real lack of adequate planning and saving mechanisms for old age result in women having to work literally till they die. In 2002, the SEWA Bank launched a pension product and currently SEWA Bank has 2353 pension account holders.

Section IV: Conclusions

Lessons from SEWA's programme

An Integrated approach

As a labour union, SEWA's approach is to see the poor as workers and producers, rather than just as income-deprived or vulnerable people. The first structural issue is their place in the economy since the economic structure is closely connected with the social structure. Hence SEWA's approach has been an integrated approach, where various inputs are needed not one after the other but simultaneously.

All activities at SEWA are planned and implemented with an integrated approach. This means that every member has access to work and income security, social security services, financial services and capacity building. To achieve this, a multi-pronged approach is used for each activity. SEWA believes that by adopting a strategy of struggle and development and an integrated approach, women can and have become strong and self-reliant.

Taking ownership

For self-reliance and accountability, services should be owned, controlled and managed by people themselves. If women run their own programmes, they are not only more active participants, but they also become good negotiators for change. If women are given the right inputs, they do and can develop the capacity to run their own organisations and these organisations are far more effective in delivering services than top-down organisations. SEWA has also encouraged the formation of health cooperatives and midwives cooperatives.

Customised Services for the poor

Poor women in the informal sector need services and products designed to their needs. Experience has shown that the poor need simple, transparent and flexible collection and service delivery systems. They need handholding and service at the doorstep. They need collection mechanisms that take into account their income and expenditure patterns. Constant contact and communication are essential. Time constraints (e.g. work, domestic chores or child-care and other house work commitments) and lack of transportation to/from the service are major barriers to accessing services. For example, healthcare seeking behaviour of the women improves if the service is available to them closer to their areas and at a convenient time. Services for the workers in the informal economy should be decentralised and community based. Doorstep services such as health camps and childcare bring health, government and private providers closer to the local people, building trust and rapport. This also creates a demand from below for services that cannot be ignored.

Presence on the ground

The existence of a network of grassroot workers, and their presence in the community, is a major asset for SEWA's social security programs. SEWA's experience has shown that expansion of services can be achieved through locals (e.g. traditional midwives are trained to become barefoot doctors, local leaders become insurance promoters etc.). This form of outreach is also more affective than direct outside intervention because the locals are trusted individuals in the community; therefore their message and examples will evoke more confidence from the community. This way, strong links between the community and the organisation are provided and grounding of the organisation's activities are facilitated.

Training and capacity building

SEWA has been involved in systematic efforts at enhancing the capacity of its members to achieve greater personal and organisational development. This enables them to participate more effectively in the processes of change, and training has been an important tool for this. Besides membership education and leadership training, SEWA also conducts a host of trainings for its members – for the barefoot doctors, for the barefoot managers - to conduct insurance activities and training to run and manage their own organisations.

Social security as a fillip to organising efforts

Along with enhancing and strengthening SEWA's integrated approach, SEWA's social security has resulted in a significant boost to SEWA's organising activities. Union and cooperative organisers reported that members found this programme so useful than they encouraged other women to join SEWA and the schemes.

Linking with the government programmes

Partnership with the government is essential for ensuring that services are available for the poorest families that government services that might otherwise be inaccessible are used. SEWA links up with the government system with the primary objective of making the system accountable to the community and to the people's needs, especially those of women. The partnership with the government helps to build trust and rapport between the government officials and the community. It leads to an improvement in the services provided by the government. The partnership and the sharing save duplication of resources.

Challenges

Servicing the needs of a growing, and diverse membership

Providing services to a large and diverse clientele, with some of them located in remote and far-flung areas, is not easy. Upscaling means more staff, higher administrative costs and increased human resource development needs. The additional organisational complexity needs to be dealt with carefully.

Large capacity building needs

Experience has shown that capacity building is needed at various levels. Field workers are crucial to the success of any programme, as they are the key link between the programme and the members. However, it is also critical to train these workers to take on their new roles effectively. Mainstream policy and academics also need to be sensitised to the needs of the poor women. Growing capacity building requires resources – not just financial but also trainers and tools.

Policy action to develop suitable enabling environment – egs – Insurance, midwives, any other

Much of the upscaling efforts also requires an enabling policy environments. For example the Insurance Regulatory Authority in India needs to make certain amendments to the insurance law to facilitate a workers insurance cooperative, the municipal authority needs to change the perspective of urban policies to make space for the street vendors, the health system has to recognise the traditional midwives in the tiers of health service providers.

Upscaling and Universalising

Upscaling and universalising - of both programmes and policies - for the workers in the informal sector in a country as large and diverse as India continues to be a challenge.

Exclusion of Vulnerable Groups from Equal Access to Social Security

The Case of Asylum Seekers in the UK

Helen Bolderson*

Introduction

Asylum-seekers are amongst the most marginalised and vulnerable groups in European countries. While awaiting the outcome of a claim that they have made for formal recognition of refugee status they may be at risk of being excluded from welfare and social security support in the country to which they have migrated/fled (the 'receiving country'). In this paper we examine the nature of this risk, using illustrative material from United Kingdom (UK) policies, and examine how policies that deprive asylum seekers of social security or reduce its value to them sit side by side with rights enshrined in international conventions.

1. Rights for Asylum Seekers in International Conventions

1.1 Protective Rights

Asylum seekers' rights include the right, conferred by the Universal Declaration of Human Rights (UDHR, 1948), to 'seek and enjoy' asylum but there is no right to asylum itself.[1] A right to protection is conferred by the UN Convention Relating to the Status of Refugees 1951 (the Refugee Convention) and its Protocol of 1967. With some exceptions it forbids the return (or *refoulement)* of refugees from the receiving country to 'the frontiers of territories where [their] life or freedom would

* Dr. Helen Bolderson was Reader in Social Policy at Brunel University. She has thirty years' experience as a researcher in the field of social policy and has published widely.
My thanks to Professor Lydia Morris, University of Essex, UK, and Dr Caroline Sawyer, Oxford Brookes University, UK, for helpful comments on a draft of this paper.

1 Gina Clayton, *Textbook on Immigration and Asylum Law* (Oxford University Press, 2004) at 364.

be threatened on account of [their] race, religion, nationality, membership of a particular social group or political opinion'.[2]

Note that the language of the Refugee Convention is in terms of 'refugees' and a refugee is stated to be a person who 'owing to a well-founded fear of being persecuted for reasons of race, religion, nationality, membership of a particular social group or political opinion, is outside the country of his nationality and is unable, or owing to such fear, is unwilling to avail himself of the protection of that country; or who, not having a nationality and being outside the country of his former habitual residence, is unable, or, owing to such fear, is unwilling to avail himself of the protection of that country…'.[3]

Although the language refers to refugees it has been accepted that, in relation to *non-refoulement* it includes, and applies to, those who are on the territory of a receiving country and are claiming asylum. The United Nations High Commissioner for Refugees (UNHCR) was given legal opinion in 2001 that *non-refoulement* was not limited to those formally recognised as refugees since the Convention did not define a 'refugee' as someone formally recognised as such.[4] This confirms an earlier UNHCR statement that 'a person is a refugee within the meaning of the 1951 Convention as soon as he fulfils the criteria contained in the definition. This would necessarily occur prior to the time at which his refugee status is formally determined. Recognition of his refugee status does not therefore make him a refugee but declares him to be one. He does not become a refugee because of recognition, but is recognised because he is a refugee'.[5] On this view, and in relation to the application of Article 33(1) of the Convention, therefore, an asylum seeker is presumed to be a refugee.[6]

1.2 Socio-economic Rights

Articles 21-24 of the Refugee Convention are concerned with socio-economic rights. They stipulate that elementary education, public relief, labour legislation and social security (the latter 'subject to any appropriate arrangements for the maintenance of acquired rights')[7] should be made available to 'lawful refugees' and on a par (i.e. accorded 'the same treatment as is accorded to nationals')[8] with that provided for the receiving country's nationals. Housing and education above elementary level should be 'as favourable as possible' but in any event not less

---

2 Article 33(1).

3 Article 1A(2) Refugee Convention.

4 Elihu Lauterpacht and Deniel Bethlehem, The Scope and Content of the Principle of 'Non-Refoulement': Opinion (UNHCR, 2001) para. 90.

5 UNHCR, Handbook on Procedures and Criteria for Determining Refugee Status under the 1951 Convention and the 1967 Protocol relating to the Status of Refugees (UNHCR, 1992) para. 28.

6 The Refugee Convention confers other protective rights including the right not to be penalised for illegal entry but the attendant issues are not discussed here.

7 Article 24(1)(ii).

8 Article 22.

than 'those accorded to aliens generally in the same circumstances'.[9] The recipients of these rights are referred to as 'refugees' for elementary education, public relief, and as refugees 'lawfully staying' for purposes of housing, labour legislation, and social security. The use of the term 'lawfully staying' may seem curious given that the Convention by implication recognises that many refuges are illegal entrants.[10] It arose in the drafting of the Convention out of a compromise between the French delegate who required the insertion of a residency condition for access to benefits and the delegate from the USA who felt that the French terms describing residency were too restrictive. Eventually the term 'lawfully staying' was adopted to cover 'any refugee who, with the authorisation of the authorities, is in the territory of a contracting State otherwise than purely temporarily'.[11] 'Purely temporary' was to denote a momentary visit to a country e.g. that of a performing artist. However, as we shall see, in the examples from UK domestic policies, the term 'refugee', in the transposition of these rights, has been confined to those with recognised official refugee status, and their extension to 'asylum seekers' (a term not used in the drafting of the Convention) has been problematical.

1.3 Universal Human Rights

The Refugee Convention is the tailor made source of rights for refugees.[12] Several other instruments of international law also forbid *refoulement* directly or indirectly, of which, in the UK context, the European Convention on Human Rights (ECHR) is the most important.[13] The ECHR has universal application to members of the states that have ratified it and, broadly speaking, confers 'thin rights' in the form of providing negative freedoms as distinct from 'thick' rights stipulating the provisions of concrete measures.[14] Articles 3 and 8 have particular relevance to refugees/asylum seekers in prohibiting torture and inhuman or degrading treatment or punishment (Article 3) and interference with private and family life (Article 8).

---

9 Article 21.

10 Article 31.

11 The Refugee Convention 1951: The Traveaux Preparatoire Analysed with a Commentary by the late Dr Paul Weis, (1995) 7 *Cambridge International Documentary Series* 378.

12 There are many criticisms of the Convention, for example, that it is too narrow, but these are not central to the discussion here.

13 Convention for the Protection of Human Rights and Fundamental Freedoms, 1950, as amended by Protocols Nos. 3, 5, 8 and 11. Other instruments, not in all cases fully recognised by the UK, are discussed in: Dallal Stevens, *UK Asylum Law and Policy: Historical and Contemporary Perspectives* (Sweet and Maxwell, 2004) para. 426.

14 'Thick' and 'thin' rights are responses to concepts of 'thin' and 'thick' needs discussed in: Glenn Drover and Patrick Kerans, *New Approaches to Welfare Theory* (Edward Elgar, 2003). 'Thin' needs are abstract, objective and universal and 'thick' needs are cultural and particular.

1.4 Regard and Disregard of Convention Rights to Welfare

Despite the provisions in the Refugee Convention, social security benefits have been withheld from asylum seekers in the UK since 1996. This was achieved by two means: first, by the withdrawal of benefits from particular sections of asylum seekers, who were made ineligible in 1996 and in 2002; and second, by the introduction, in 1999, of a highly conditional parallel welfare ('support') system for all asylum seekers which allowed no access to any of the UK's mainstream benefits.

We give a summary of these policies and the legal challenges to them in Section 2, and in the Conclusion suggest two underlying problems that may help to explain the disregard of the socio-economic Convention rights. The first is definitional. As outlined above, the Convention does not at any stage speak of 'asylum seekers' but only of 'refugees': are asylum seekers by definition 'presumptive refugees'? The second concerns the derivation of socio-economic rights: can it be argued, especially in relation to public relief, that they stem exclusively from social transactions within the nation-state and that it is therefore a matter of domestic decision to whom they should extend? We return to these definitional and theoretical issues in the Conclusion.

2. Destitute Asylum Seekers in the UK

The UK had a relatively good track record of accepting refugees over many centuries, although not always in great numbers or willingly, and has paid heed to the Refugee Convention's criteria since its ratification. However, until 1993, neither its asylum policies nor its social security arrangements for asylum seekers were securely based in legislation.[15] The practice, if not the law, was to treat asylum seekers as one of a group of 'persons from abroad' who could claim and receive 'urgent payments' the value of which was 90% of the assistance benefits provided generally. This practice was codified after 1993 when the Refugee Convention was incorporated into UK primary legislation.[16] Social Security Regulations made

[15] Until 1993 the policies were contained in non-statutory Home Office Immigration Rules and in rather uncertain, although statutory, social security arrangements that allowed urgent assistance payments to be made to some categories of 'persons from abroad' (the Income Support (General) Regulations 1987 Regs. 21 and 70). Persons from abroad were taken to include asylum seekers but the latter were not specified in law as a special group to whom payments could be made until 1993 (the Income Support (General) Amendment No. 3 Regulation, Reg. 2).

[16] Asylum and Immigration Appeals Act 1993 S. 1 and 2 (the extent to which the inclusion of Convention obligations in primary legislation amounts to 'incorporation' was the subject of conflicting interpretations in the British Courts until 2004 when the Convention was judged to be clearly incorporated into domestic law (*R v Immigration Officer at Prague Airport and another, ex p Europeans Roma Rights Centre and others,* [2004] UKHL)).

in 1993 thereafter specifically included asylum seekers as a group to whom urgent payments to the value of 90% could be paid.

2.1 1996 - Withdrawal of Benefits from 'In-country' Applicants

The first phase of benefit withdrawal occurred in 1996 when the benefits described above were withdrawn from those asylum seekers, who at the time formed 70 % of the total, who had not applied for asylum immediately on arrival but had made a claim for asylum later on (referred to as 'in-country' applicants). Those who applied immediately ('port' applicants) were still entitled to claim urgent payments but these were no longer to be paid during an appeal against an asylum decision. In addition to losing income support all asylum seekers also lost other means tested benefits (housing benefit and council tax benefit) and non-contributory benefits (family credit, disability working allowance, attendance allowance, disability living allowance, severe disablement allowance, and invalid care allowance).[17]

The withdrawal of benefits was introduced by means of subsidiary legislation[18] and agreed in Parliament by a small minority despite contrary advice from many quarters, notably the Government's own Advisory Committee.[19] One set of concerns related to the irrelevance of the location and timing of an asylum application to a person's credibility as a 'genuine' asylum seeker.[20]

The Regulations quickly ran into difficulties. They were challenged in judicial review relating to a woman who had not claimed asylum when arriving on the Eurostar at the port of entry, and was not thereby classed as a 'port' claimant, although she had travelled straight to the Home Office immigration centre.

The claimants argued that the Regulations were 'inconsistent and in conflict with the internationally recognised rights of refugees' but the case was dismissed in the Divisional Court on the grounds that the Refugee Convention did not require countries to extend any particular form of positive support to refugees or asylum seekers and that withdrawal of benefit did not amount to constructive deportation (which would be in breach of the Convention). Moreover the Court judged that the Refugee Convention was not incorporated into law and could not limit the powers of the Secretary of State for Social Security who was entitled to

---

17 However, most of the non-contributory benefits were, even for nationals, subject to a 26-week prior residence condition and therefore not accessible to new arrivals.

18 The Social Security (Persons Abroad) Miscellaneous Amendment Regulations 1996.

19 The Social Security (Persons from Abroad) Miscellaneous Amendments Regulations 1996, Report by the Social Security Advisory Committee, Cm 3062, HMSO, 1996.

20 House of Commons, Social Security Committee, First Report, Session 1995-6, *Benefits for Asylum Seekers*, 1/3 HMSO, January 1996. Evidence from Immigration Law Practitioner Association (ILPA) Annex A to Appendix 12; Child Poverty Action Group, Appendix 6, Part 2, 3.

make savings in the social security budget and that the withdrawal of benefits was merely contingent on this.[21]

The case went to appeal in June 21, 1996.[22] It was once again judged that the Secretary of State for Social Security had not exceeded his powers and the Court did not accept that Article 24 of the Refugee Convention 'positively obliged signatories to provide benefits before being designated as refugees' thus concurring with the legal advice that had been given to the Home Office.[23]

However the Appeal Court Judge (Simon Brown LJ) added, 'that is not to say that up to that point their fundamental needs can properly be ignored' and the Court agreed with the appellants that the curtailment of benefit meant that access to refugee-determining procedures, including appeals, was made so difficult that the rights of asylum seekers to a proper consideration of their claim was jeopardised. It decided that the Regulations were *ultra vires* on the grounds that they 'contemplate a life so destitute that no civilised country can tolerate'.[24] It was not necessary to invoke the European Convention on Human Rights: 'So basic are the human rights here at issue, that it cannot be necessary to resort to the Convention for Protection of Human Rights and Fundamental Freedoms ... to take note of their violation'.[25] Instead, the judgement rested on a case in English Common Law of 1803, viz: 'As to there being no obligation for maintaining poor foreigners before the statutes ascertaining the different methods of acquiring settlements, the law of humanity, which is anterior to all positive laws, obliges to afford the relief to save them from starving'.[26] Brown LJ ended his judgement in the Appeal Court as follows:

> I ... regard the 1996 regulations now in force as so uncompromisingly draconian in effect that they must indeed be held *ultra vires*. I would found my decision not on the narrow ground of constructive *refoulement* envisaged by the UNHCR and rejected by the Divisional Court, but rather on the wider ground that rights necessarily implicit in the 1993 Act are now inevitably being overborne. Parliament cannot have intended a significant number of genuine asylum seekers to be impaled on the horns of so intolerable a dilemma ....[27]

He nevertheless observed that there is no obligation on states under the Refugee Convention to provide benefits to asylum seekers that are equivalent to the rights enjoyed by nationals. Thus:

---

21 *R v Secretary of State for Social Security, ex p. Joint Council for the Welfare of Immigrants* (QBD) Queen's Bench Division, 26 March 1996. Summary: Scoular J 'Case Analysis', 4 (1997) 2 Journal of Social Security Law 87.

22 *R v Secretary of State for Social Security, ex p. Joint Council for the Welfare of Immigrants; R v Secretary of State for Social Security, ex p. B* [1996] 4 All ER 385.

23 Scoular, *supra* note 21, at 88.

24 *R v Secretary of State for Social Security, ex p. Joint Council for the Welfare of Immigrants, supra* note 22, Brown LJ at 401.

25 *Ibid.*

26 Lord Ellenborough, CJ in *R v Eastbourne (Inhabitants)* (1803) 4 East 103 at 107, 102 ER 769 at 770 cited in *ibid.*

27 Brown L J at 402, *ibid.*

> If and when [refugee] status is recognised, refugees become entitled under Art 24 to benefit rights equivalent to nationals. Not for one moment would I suggest that prior to that time their rights are remotely the same; only that some provisions should be made … many European countries provide benefits in kind by way of refugee hostels and meal vouchers … urgent needs payments could be made at significantly lower rate than the 90% hitherto paid … certain categories of claim (perhaps, as suggested, in-country claims brought more than four or six weeks post arrival) could be processed under the 'without foundation procedure'. All that will doubtless be for consideration.[28]

Three features of this judgment are worth noting. First, it was not accepted that asylum seekers have the same rights as formally recognised refugees. Second, a precedent established in domestic common law rather than a right conferred by an international legal instrument was used to justify the conclusion that the policy was intolerable in a civilised society (it should be noted however that the UK's Human Rights Act 1998 which obliged it to comply with the ECHR was not in existence at the time). Third, it challenged the appropriateness of using subsidiary legislation to introduce measures of great import and raised a question about how so 'draconian' a measure could have been the intent of Parliament.

The Court's rulings that the Regulations were *ultra vires* had the effect of reinstating benefits to asylum seekers for a short period from June 21 to July 24. However, the Government quickly reintroduced the measures into primary legislation, enacted on July 24.[29] That Act also made asylum seekers ineligible for local authority housing accommodation and homelessness provisions.

One of the consequences of benefit withdrawal was that it shut one door but opened another for those affected by the policy. People who now had no claim to social security turned to provisions under legislation of 1948 that gave powers to local authorities to provide care. Local authorities challenged the resultant impositions at law but were unsuccessful. They had to continue to provide accommodation, food and other essential provisions in kind, but not cash, for those categorised as in-country claimants who were without their own resources. In compensation they could recover part of the associated costs via a grant from central government (at this stage from the Department of Health) but it was insufficient and they remained out of pocket.

2.2 1999: Abandonment of Mainstream Benefits for Asylum Seekers

This unsatisfactory situation led to a major change in 1999 when the Immigration and Asylum Act (IAA) was passed. Responsibility for support was removed from local authorities and a new, centralised system, run by the Home Office, was instituted. From now on asylum seekers were not allowed to access any mainstream social security benefits (exceptions were made for unaccompanied children). The Home Office alone became responsible for providing subsistence to destitute asy-

[28] *Ibid.*

[29] The Asylum and Immigration Act 1996 Section 11 and Schedule 1.

lum seekers who became subject to provisions in the form of vouchers and a small amount of cash, and/or accommodation, together said to be equivalent to 90% of mainstream benefits. This time alternative doors to support were slammed shut.[30]

These measures constituted a parallel and disadvantageous welfare system run by the National Asylum Support Service (NASS) in the Home Office. Asylum seekers were no longer categorised as 'port' or 'in-country' applicants: all were eligible to apply for NASS support if they were destitute, but the criteria used to determine whether they fitted into this category were rigorous and it was not mandatory for NASS to provide the service. There was no clear 'right' to support even in the case of a person who met the destitution criteria, a situation later remedied as a result of the European Reception Directive, one of four Directives developed in the process of harmonising asylum policies in Europe, which stipulates that support should be mandatory.[31] The system instituted in the UK in 1999 can be summarised as being more akin to Britain's residual Poor Law of the nineteenth century than to its contemporary form of social security. For example, in contrast to definitions of need used in current income-related mainstream social security benefits, cars or other vehicles, goods, and land, were taken into account and jewellery worth over £1,000 had to be declared.[32]

The Government's view was that the benefits under the new asylum support system were comparable in value to the benefits asylum seekers would have received under mainstream social security and housing benefits since, in addition to vouchers and cash, accommodation and some benefits in kind were provided. Campaigners argued that vouchers and cash amounted to less than 70% of the potential mainstream cash benefits since these carried family premiums that were not included in the calculations. It was difficult to see how benefits that were below subsistence level and a service that was residual and conditional allowed asylum seekers to be 'accorded the same treatment as nationals'. UNHCR favoured the granting of full benefit entitlement to all asylum seekers, arguing that they fell within the provisions of Articles 23 and 24 of the Convention, but nevertheless endorsed the UK support system because benefits denied to an asylum seeker were paid retrospectively if and when refugee status was granted. However, since then the backdating of benefits has been abolished and UNHCR has expressed unease about the UK support system.[33]

The Immigration and Asylum Act came into force in April 2000 but it proved extremely difficult to deliver vouchers and/or accommodation. A flow of reports and criticisms made clear that, contrary to the Governments wishes, centralisation had produced complexity rather than a properly managed and controlled system or a reduction in the numbers applying for asylum. At the same time, the low level

30 For a period asylum seekers could still take work after 6 months of waiting for their asylum determination but this possibility too was cut off in July 2002.

31 Council Directive 2003/9/EC 27 January 2003: The Reception Conditions Directive OJ L31 6.2.03, at 18.

32 The Asylum Support Regulations SI 2000 No. 704 2000 6 (5) and Application Form attached, Note 8.

33 Asylum and Immigration (Treatment of Claimants etc.) Bill, 2004: Briefing on Proposed Amendments 12 and 13 for the House of Lords Committee.

and uncertainty of support caused great distress.[34] Vouchers had to be abandoned in April 2002 and replaced with cash and less than two years later further major policy changes were announced.

However, it is worth noting that in the post 2000 period, after the Human Rights Act came into force in the UK, and before the implementation of new policies (below) in 2003, there appear to have been relatively few challenges to the support system through the Courts on grounds of breaches of refugee or human rights Conventions. Despite the rigorous conditions attached to the receipt of support, there was no category of asylum seeker that was deliberately made destitute as in 1996, and, with some limitations, refusal of support was subject to appeal to Home Office Asylum Support Adjudicators who could decide in the claimant's favour or return the decision for reconsideration on grounds of inadequate evidence.

2.3 Refusal of Support to 'Late' Claimants

In February 2002 major proposals were outlined for changing support in the direction of a managed system of induction, accommodation, reporting and removal centres, and the phasing out of vouchers.[35] They were enacted in the Nationality, Immigration and Asylum Act, 2002 (NIAA), which also contained a further measure (introduced late in the parliamentary process) that involved a return to the 1996 policy of distinguishing between port and in country applicants and withdrawing support to the latter. Section 55 of the NIAA prohibited the provision of asylum support services to asylum seekers whose claims to asylum had not been made as 'soon as reasonably practicable after the person's arrival in the UK'.[36] Certain categories were exempt including families with dependent children (under 18), and those with special needs beyond needs arising out of destitution.

Two aspects of the measures in Section 55 are of particular interest to our subject matter. First, there was no definition in the Act of 'as soon as practicable'. The Home Office's Guidelines[37] did not guard against officials' interpretation of this phrase, which came to mean 'immediately on arrival' or at least 'within 24 hours'. For many asylum seekers it was impossible to claim asylum immediately, given the circumstances under which they had arrived and the complexities, superficialities and delays of the formalities that had to be undergone to make an asylum claim. The target group for deterrence by means of Section 55 was not described by reference to the circumstances or situations of its members. Instead, an

---

34 There were many critical reports including those from, or connected with, the Government, for example, Audit Commission, *Another Country: Implementing Dispersal under Immigration and Asylum Act* 1999 (Audit Commission, June 2000); Home Office, *Report of the Operational Reviews of the Voucher and Dispersal Schemes* (October 2001).

35 Home Office, *Secure Borders, Safe Haven: Integration with Diversity in Modern Britain*, CM 5387, (The Stationery Office Limited, February 2002).

36 Nationality Immigration and Asylum Act Section 55(3)(b).

37 NASS Policy Bulletin 75 - Section 55 (Late Claims) 2002 Act Guidance.

irrelevant administrative cut-off point (time) had been constructed to define a category of non-genuine asylum seekers.

A second important aspect of Section 55 was its subsection 5(a) which stated 'this section shall not prevent the exercise of a power by the Secretary of State to the extent necessary for the purpose of avoiding a breach of a person's Convention rights (within the meaning of the Human Rights Act 1998)'. By the time of the introduction of Section 55 the ECHR had been incorporated into UK legislation. The avoidance of its breach was on the face of the Act, and any destitution arising from lack of asylum support, could be considered in the light of its Article 3 (prohibition of torture and inhuman or degrading treatment or punishment). Its inclusion in the Act meant that the Courts could invoke the ECHR as a limitation on the support withdrawal policy without appearing to question the supremacy of Parliament.

Section 55 became operational in January 2003 and by November 2003 had the following result according to a senior judge:

> A major flow into the courts of asylum seekers denied benefit or housing under the new system and now without food or shelter and frequently ill .... To rescue them, judges of the administrative court have made 800 emergency orders for interim payment of benefit. Every week about 60 more orders are having to be made. It is thanks to the safety net of the Human Rights Act [incorporating the ECHR] ... and perhaps also to the judiciary's unwillingness to pass by on the other side that these people are not starving on the streets.[38]

The Asylum Support Adjudication System that had been instituted in 1999 allowing an internal but independent appeal did not extend to Section 55. Challenges to negative decisions under Section 55 therefore took the form of judicial review proceedings. In an early test case in February 2003[39] six asylum seekers sought judicial review of a negative support decision and the Court ruled that there was a breach of Article 6 of the ECHR (right to a fair trial) since there was no appeal system other than through judicial review. It considered that the support determination procedures were inadequate; and that 'a real risk' of destitution would engage Article 3. The Court allowed the applications but the Home Office appealed the rulings. The Appeal Court agreed with the earlier judgement relating to Article 6, but took the view that improved initial decision-making combined with access to judicial review would satisfy Article 6, with the result that procedural changes were subsequently made (which included, later, a lengthening of the period within which a person could apply for asylum to 72 hours). However, the Appeal Court disagreed with the suggestion that a 'risk' of destitution engaged Article 3.[40]

---

38 Sir Stephen Sedley, Lecture delivered to Legal Action Group, cited in House of Commons Home Affairs Committee, *Asylum Applications*, Second Report of Session 2003-2004 Vol. I, HC 218-I (House of Lords, 26 January 2004) para. 194.

39 *R (on the application of Q) v Secretary of State for the Home Department [2003] EWHC 195.*

40 *R (on the application of Q) v Secretary of State for the Home Department* [2003] EWCA Civ 364.

A further test case in the High Court ruled that three applicants succeeded in their case on the grounds of Article 3 of ECHR although this did not mean that inevitably all challenges to negative decisions could activate Article 3.[41] This judgement was overturned when the Home Office appealed against it in relation to one of the three asylum seekers on the grounds that he had had access to food and some shelter (in an airport). In this instance the Court ruled that a person would have to be reduced to begging for food or shelter before Article 3 of ECHR could be engaged.[42]

We can see that the Courts had difficulties in determining the threshold that would have to be met for circumstances to amount to 'destitution'; and whether being 'at risk' or 'on the verge' of destitution would in themselves engage Article 3. The rulings resulted in negative decisions about individuals being overturned and in the institutional determination procedures being revised but the policy was not ruled unlawful until May 2004 when the Court of Appeal decided that the scale of the problem of destitution amongst asylum seekers was such that the Secretary of State had a positive obligation to take general action to avoid breaches of Article 3.[43] Practical considerations about the large number of asylum seekers waiting in the aisles to have their cases heard in the courts carried a great deal of weight leading the Court to take into view the collective, as well as the individual, impact of government policy.[44]

The effect of the judgement was held by the Government to be that support should not be refused under Section 55 unless it can be shown positively that a person has alternative sources of income.[45] Since people are not in any case eligible for support if they have other means, this amounts to saying that the Section 55 policy cannot function.

The Home Secretary appealed against this decision to the House of Lords but lost the case in November 2005.[46] A recurring Opinion in this case (the *Limbuela* case) was that since the legislation (Nationality Immigration and Asylum Act 2002) contained both S 55 (1) which excluded asylums seekers from support, and S 55 (5) (a) which said that there must not be a breach of Convention rights, it could not be the case that Parliament had willed that the policy should deprive asylum seekers of their human rights[47]. The sub-sections are, however, contradictory and a policy analysis view would suggest that the problems of reconciling

---

41 *R (on the application of T) v Secretary of State for the Home Department* [2003] EWHC 1941.

42 *R (on the application of T) v Secretary of State of the Home Department* [2003] EWCA Civ 1285.

43 *R (on the application of Limbuela) v Secretary of State of the Home Department* [2004] EWCA Civ 540.

44 Laura Dubinsky and Joseph Middleton, 'Public Law Update' 25 June 2004 *New Law Journal*.

45 Home Office Policy Bulletin 75-Section 55 (late Claim) 2002 Act.

46 *R (Limbuela) v. Secretary of State for the Home Department* [2005] UKHL 66.

47 *Ibid.*, House of Lords, Opinions of the Lords of Appeal for Judgment in the Cause paras. 73, 75.

them was consciously left to the front-line decision makers, as tends to be the case with legislation that is either vague or multi-value based.[48]

Further opinion was that while it was not the function of Art. 3 to prescribe a minimum standard of welfare support for those in need, the situation was quite different 'if a statutory regime is imposed on an individual, or on a class to which the individual belongs, barring that individual from basic social security and other state benefits to which he or she would, were not at statutory regime, be entitled'.[49] It was also held that the state's exclusion of asylum seekers from support when they are destitute amounted to a positive action against asylum seekers and therefore constituted 'treatment' within the meaning of Art 3. Whether the treatment was 'inhuman and degrading' would depend on whether the severity of the entire package of restriction and deprivation surrounding asylum seekers reached the level of severity established in the European Court's case-law in Pretty[50] but would also take account of the relativity of the assessment which would depend on the circumstances of the case.[51]

In dismissing the Home Secretary's appeal the Law Lords therefore confirmed the Appeal Court's judgment that the destitution as a result of S.55 was so severe as to engage Art 3 of the ECHR. Meanwhile, however, the European Reception Directive that allows Member States to refuse support when the asylum claim is not made as soon as 'reasonably practical'[52] became operative in February 2005.

Conclusion

The policies described above were introduced in response to a rising number of asylum applications in the UK between 1988 and 2002. Numbers rose from 3,998 in 1988 to 11,640 in 1989, and continued rising, with some temporary dips, to 84,130 in 2002.[53] Compared with the number of people seeking asylum in countries just across the border from those they had fled, the flow of asylum seekers to Europe was small. In the UK, asylum applicants, despite the rise in numbers, still formed only a small proportion of the total number of immigrants, and a very small proportion (0.19%)[54] of the total population even at the peak period of applications in 2002. However, fears about growth in absolute numbers of asylum

[48] See social policy and political science policy-making and implementation literature e.g. Helen Bolderson `Ambiguity and Obscurity in Policy-Making for Social Security' 10 (1982) 3 *Policy and Politics* 289-301.

[49] *Limbuela, Opinions, supra* note 47, Lord Scott of Foscote, paras. 67, 68.

[50] *Pretty v United Kingdom* 35 EHRR, 1,33, para.52.

[51] *Limbuela, Opinions, supra* note 47, Lord Hope of Craighead, para. 54.

[52] Council Directive, *supra* note 31, Article 16(2).

[53] House of Commons, Debate, Vol. 193, c. 28W, 17.6.91; Home Office, *Control of Immigration: Statistics United Kingdom 2003*, (Command Paper) 6363, at 10. Figures relate to principal applicants.

[54] UNHCR, Asylum Applications Lodged in Industrialised Countries: Levels and Trends, 2000-2002,' (Population Data Unit, UNHCR, 2003) at 4.

seekers, their composition, the validity of their claims, and the increase in people-trafficking, were amongst factors that created the political imperative to stem what appeared to be a tide, and formed justifications for the politics of deterrence adopted in the UK by both Conservative and Labour Governments.

The socio-economic rights written into the Refugee Convention appear to have had little effect in preventing the benefit exclusions and reductions to which asylum seekers were subjected. There are a number of possible reasons of general interest (i.e. not particular to the UK's stance in relation to the Refugee Convention or the ECHR). The first relates to uncertainty about the nature and genesis of the rights concerned. On one view, socio-economic rights are seen as claims on particular governments rather than on the world at large: they reside morally in communitarian ideals and in practice depend on the relative ability of states to provide them. The value of their inclusion in international conventions lies chiefly in their assertion of desired standards. An opposing view is that socio-economic rights are driven by the needs of individuals as human beings *per se* and are therefore not different from other human rights. A compromise position might agree that socio-economic rights are intended to meet universal needs, but that the nature and implementation of the measures that make those rights operative respond to the needs of defined target groups: welfare arrangements, especially social security, are allocated with reference to categories of beneficiaries.[55]

A second reason for the apparent lack of influence of the Refugee Convention on the construction and implementation of asylum support policies may stem from the Refugee Convention's comparative lack of an enforcement structure notwithstanding UNHCR's important oversight, and the lack of judicial processes that may allow individual rights of petition to an international court. In this situation national determination systems cannot be challenged at international level.[56]

A third reason, connected with the first, lies in the different constructions put on the term 'asylum seeker'. The definition of the target groups for welfare support measures is crucial. On one construction they are presumptive 'Convention' refugees, that is, they are seeking and awaiting the conferment of refugee status under the Convention, which also protects them from being treated as 'illegal' on account of clandestine entry.[57] As shown in the discussion above [58] the drafters of the Refugee Convention considered a person to be a refugee prior to formal recognition as such and eligible, therefore, as a refugee, for welfare support measures under Articles 21-24.

---

55 Discussion of the positions taken by Cranston (1967a, 1967b, 1973); Walzer (1983); Gewirth (1978:1982) Plant (1980) can be found in: Peter Jones, *Rights: Issues in Political Theory* (Macmillan, 1994).

56 Colin Harvey, 'Dissident Voices: Refugees, Human Rights and Asylum in Europe' 3 (2000) 9 *Social and Legal Studies,* 367-396.

57 Refugee Convention, Article 31 states 'the Contracting State shall not impose penalties on account of their illegal entry or presence, on refugees who, coming directly from a territory where their life or freedom was threatened under Article 1...provided they present themselves without delay and show good cause for their illegal entry'.

58 Above, p. 2.

This is not the case on another construction where the term 'asylum seeker' also describes people who have left their country of origin or residence under circumstances - civil war, famine, natural disaster, lack of livelihood - that do not merit the Convention's narrow (if widely open to interpretation) criteria for qualifying as a refugee and as a result of which they are not seen to have lost the protection of their own country. They may be legal or illegal entrants, or overstayers, and make a claim for asylum. Because of the conditions prevailing in their countries they may not be 'returnable' for humanitarian or diplomatic reasons but within this construction of the 'asylum seeker' they are not the presumptive refugees to whom the Refugee Convention measures for welfare support apply.

The asylum seeker so constructed features in UK legislation and in the European Reception Directive where he or she 'shall mean a third country national or a stateless person who has made an application for asylum in respect of which final decision has not yet been taken'.[59] It is a minimalist definition that has the virtue of encompassing a broad range of people, but without a clearer description of the person, including his or her likely needs and circumstances, it leaves a large space for the introduction of populist formulations of asylum seekers as illegal and undesirable immigrants. As Goodwin-Gill points out, this makes it useful to States who thus gain more leeway in the treatment of asylum seekers.[60]

The term 'immigrant' is itself unclear: strictly speaking it refers to migrants who settle permanently but more popularly it has a wider usage which includes people who enter the country legally for various periods and have a status conferred by a category that is related to purpose: they hold an employment permit, visa or student permit, or come for the purpose of family reunion. By contrast, persons without such status (who are 'third country nationals', 'stateless persons' 'claimants' for asylum) can be made the subjects of deterrent policies. In default of definitions that enable the allocation of specific rights, they can be made to meet the descriptions that the policy purpose requires, without regard to evidence or circumstance or justice.

The limiting features of the Refugee Convention described above are not shared by the ECHR, which seeks to ensure negative freedoms, allows individual petition to an international court, and, in the nature of universal human rights, does not require definition of its target group. However the interpretation of its Articles, in a democratic national context, is difficult as the deliberations in the cases described in this paper and the following summary indicate. Thus

> There is a spectrum of treatment which would engage Art 3. At one end of the spectrum is state-authorised violence: the paradigm case of violation of Art 3. At the other end of the spectrum are executive decisions in the exercise of lawful pol-

---

[59] Council Directive, *supra* note 31, Article 2(c). Nationality, Immigration and Asylum Act 2002, S. 18 (1).

[60] Goodwin-Gill sees the reclassification of refugees as 'displaced persons, illegal immigrants, economic migrants… etc.' as a means by which states assert 'greater freedom of action' (given that none can claim the freedom to return a refugee to persecution): Guy Goodwin-Gill, *The Refugee in International Law* (Clarendon Press, 1996).

icy objective with such severe consequences for individuals that the Court would be bound to limit the State's right to implement the policy on Art 3 grounds.[61]

The UK's failure to regard the rights of asylum seekers in relation to welfare and social security provisions can be seen in terms of political expediency at a time of growing demands made by asylum seekers on European countries. At a more enduring level of explanation there are the problems of using international conventions to secure socio-economic rights and the uncertainties, as yet, in the interpretation of human rights law and its transposition. More fundamentally, the reluctance to extend citizens' and residents' welfare rights to strangers are tensions arising from conflicting policy paradigms which, on the one hand, derive social security and welfare rights from solidaristic transactions within nation states[62] and, on the other, from theories that view national boundaries as merely functional and see the basis of welfare in the universality of human rights[63] thus attaching benefit rights to the individual.

These different worldviews affect not only who shall have rights to social security benefits and where they can be called in, but also choices between open or closed immigration policies and between equal or unequal treatment of outsiders. Two halfway positions give food for thought. Walzer,[64] a leading exponent of communitarian political theory, nevertheless stresses that newcomers to states must be treated as members. Hathaway,[65] a foremost authority on asylum, is willing to acknowledge 'the importance of boundedness to the viability of genuine community in the extant political context' but demands that constraints on freedom of international movement must be fully justified. The same might be said to apply to any constraints on equal access to benefits.

61 Laura Dubinsky and Joseph Middleton, *supra* note 44.

62 Alasdair Macintyre, *After Virtue: a Study in Moral Theory* (Duckworth, 1985); Bhikhu Parekh, 'Three Theories of Immigration', in Sarah Spencer (ed.), *Strangers and Citizens* (Oram Press, 1993).

63 Alan Gewirth, *Human Rights: Essays on Justification and Applications* (University of Chicago Press, 1982); Raymond Plant, 'Free Lunches Don't Nourish: Reflections on Entitlement and Citizenship', in Glenn Drover and Patrick Kerans, *supra* note 14; Robert Goodin, 'What is so Special about our Fellow Countrymen?', 98 (July 1988) *Ethics* 663-686; Thomas Baldwin, 'The Territorial State', in Gross Hyman and Ross Harrison (eds.), *Jurisprudence: Cambridge Essays* (Cambridge University Press, 1992).

64 Michael Walzer, *Spheres of Justice* (Martin Robertson, 1983).

65 James Hathaway, 'Three Critical Questions about the Study of Immigration Control', in Cornelius A. Wayne et al. (eds.) *Controlling Immigration: a global perspective* (Stanford University Press, 1994) at 49.

Social Security Systems and the Neo-Liberal Challenge

Peter Bakvis*

1. Introduction

In the half-century since the International Labour Organisation adopted its Social Security Convention,[1] social security systems have been under considerable strain in the face of phenomena such as the rapid growth of the so-called informal economy, especially in developing countries, and ageing populations in industrialised countries. Well over half of the world's workers do not enjoy any formal coverage for old-age security, which is the specific type of programme that this paper considers.

Numerous questions have been raised as to whether some models for reform that have been put forward with the purported aim of addressing weaknesses in State-run old-age pensions systems will actually bring about needed improvements to the systems. This paper focuses on two such examples of structural reform that have received considerable attention: (i) the proposal of US president George W. Bush, launched shortly after his November 2004 re-election, to partially privatise the US Social Security system and (ii) the World Bank's approach to pension reform in developing and transition countries over the past fifteen years. The paper examines whether the two approaches on reforming pensions systems meet the standards affirmed during the ILO's most recent discussions on the theme of social security, or whether they are in fact driven by motives largely unrelated with objectives of improving and expanding social security.

* Peter Bakvis is the director of the Washington office of the International Confederation of Free Trade Unions (ICFTU) and the associated Global Union Federations.

1 International Labour Organization, *Social Security (Minimum Standards) Convention - C102* (ILO, 1952).

2. Points of consensus on social security

While expressions of highly conflicting points of view have characterised recent debates on the future of social security both within countries and internationally, the ILO was able to reach consensus on several important points after a two-week discussion that took place at the 2001 International Labour Conference. The tripartite plenary session of the ILO's general conference adopted a resolution on social security that indicated agreement on a number of issues, including the following[2]:

- Adequate social security should be seen as an instrument for economic as well as social development since it is an investment in people
- There is no single right model of social security, but the State has a priority role in the facilitation, promotion and extension of coverage of social security
- Social security is not available to a majority of the world's people and the highest priority must be given to the extension of social security to those who are not covered
- Policies must aim at integrating the informal economy into the formal economy
- Social security systems must not only provide equal treatment for men and women but also ensure equitable outcomes for women
- Concerning pensions systems, the ageing of the population has just as real an impact on advance-funded as on pay-as-you-go systems
- Systems of individual savings accounts, where the risk is borne by the individual, should not weaken solidarity systems which spread risks throughout the whole of the system's membership
- Statutory pension schemes must guarantee adequate benefits and ensure national solidarity
- Initiatives to establish or extend social security require social dialogue, including the development of policy options to address any financial imbalance

The two specific examples considered in this paper are analysed taking into account the above criteria for reform enunciated in the ILO's 2001 resolution.

3. President Bush's plan for partial privatisation of US Social Security

The old-age pension system in the United States known as Social Security was established in 1935 as a statutory government-run system for all American workers. It consists of a pay-as-you-go retirement system financed by contributions from employers and workers and also provides benefits for dependents and the disabled.

---

2 International Labour Organization, *Social Security: A New Consensus* (ILO, 2001).

Compared to many pay-as-you-go pensions schemes throughout the world, the US system is in relatively solid financial shape and will require only fairly minor changes in contributions or benefits to remain self-financing. According to the US Congressional Budget Office, if nothing in the current Social Security regime is changed, the system's 'trust fund' has sufficient accumulated revenues to ensure payment of full benefits until 2052. At that point, the system would still be able to pay 80 per cent of promised benefits.[3] Nevertheless, President Bush began questioning the long-term solvency of the system early during his first mandate beginning in 2001 and also during the 2004 presidential election campaign.

However, it was only during a press conference held two days after his November 2004 re-election that Bush announced that changes to the Social Security system would be a centrepiece of domestic reform initiatives undertaken by his second administration. During his February 2005 State of the Union address, Bush declared that the Social Security system was 'headed toward bankruptcy' and proposed that younger workers should be able to place part of their contributions in private retirement accounts for which they would make individual investment decisions. A few weeks later, the White House released the details of the Bush proposal.[4] 'Younger workers', defined as all those born in 1950 or later, would be allowed to place up to one-third of the contributions normally made on their behalf into Social Security in personal accounts which would be invested in stocks and bonds according to choices made by the worker. The savings and interest accumulated in the account would be available to the worker upon retirement.

Numerous experts spoke out, either in favour or against the plan, and contributed to voluminous media coverage of the proposal. President Bush himself contributed to the coverage by undertaking an extensive speaking tour during the first half of 2005 to promote his plan for partial privatisation of Social Security. However he managed to garner little support for the proposal. The AARP retirees' association and the AFL-CIO trade union federation expressed their strong opposition to the privatisation plan, as did several members of the US Congress, which would have to adopt legislation to make changes to the system. In July 2005, congressional leaders of the president's own Republican Party decided to postpone consideration of Social Security reform, a day after the Wall Street Journal published the results of a public opinion poll which showed that only 33 per cent of Americans supported private accounts whereas 57 per cent were opposed.[5] The Republican chairman of the Senate Finance Committee later stated that the US Congress was unlikely to tackle Social Security reform before 2009, that is, not before President Bush's departure from office.[6]

The main points raised by critics were that the privatisation plan would reduce benefits for many retirees and potentially increase poverty among the elderly, and would cause a substantial rise in the federal government's deficit as Social Secu-

3 'Partisan Social Security claims questioned', (27 February 2005) *Washington Post.*

4 George W. Bush, *Strengthening Social Security for the 21st Century* (Washington, February 2005).

5 'Delay to Social Security reform', (15 July 2005) *Financial Times.*

6 'Whatever happened to reform?', (31 January 2006) *San Francisco Chronicle.*

rity contributions were diverted into private accounts.[7] In addition, the AFL-CIO noted that the massive borrowing necessary to finance private accounts would drive up interest rates and reduce the value of bond holdings in existing pension funds, and also the equity holdings if the higher interest rates were to precipitate an economic slowdown.[8]

While proponents and opponents have differed as to whether the system really is 'headed toward bankruptcy' and on the levels of risk and extra administrative costs associated with the privatised accounts, it is notable that there has been no disagreement on some substantial points.[9] One point of consensus is that the creation of private accounts would not improve the system's solvency; in fact, there is agreement that the diversion of part of the system's contributions out of the trust fund would worsen the situation. In later speeches on the issue, Bush seemed to have accepted this consensus since he no longer spoke of his plan as a means of preventing the system from going bankrupt, but rather as a way for younger workers to protect part of their contributions by putting them in a safe place before the system 'goes bust'. While there is disagreement among experts as to whether those who opt for private accounts are more or less likely to see their retirement income increase, both sides agree that there will be losers as well as winners.[10]

Since even the proponents of partial privatisation of Social Security no longer claimed that their plan would prevent the insolvency of the system that they predicted, one must look elsewhere for the motives behind the plan. An obvious beneficiary would be the financial services industry, which would administer investments in stocks and bonds estimated at around $100 billion a year. However, given that these will be small, relatively low-fee accounts, there is some doubt as to how much profit brokerage firms would actually obtain from the accounts, especially in the initial period.[11]

More certain motives can be identified among those proponents who see privatisation of Social Security as a privileged tool for achieving certain ideological or political transformations. Some, including a staff economist with the President's Commission to Strengthen Social Security, Jeffrey Brown, have seen the creation of private accounts as a key building block of George W. Bush's 'Ownership So-

---

7 Some may be surprised to find the International Monetary Fund among those expressing warnings about the fiscal implications of the Bush plan: 'The Administration proposal to permit younger workers to divert a portion of their Social Security contributions into personal retirement accounts … would also imply a significant increase in federal deficits and debt in coming decades …' (International Monetary Fund, *2005 Article IV Consultation with the United States of America: Concluding Statement of the IMF Mission* (International Monetary Fund, May 2005) at 6).

8 AFL-CIO Center for Working Capital, *The Negative Impact of Social Security Privatization on Defined Benefit Pension Funds* (Washington, March 2005).

9 See for example the opinion articles of seven Social Security experts published under the heading 'A new act for Social Security' (23 January 2005) *Washington Post.*

10 'Whichever way we go, some get left behind', (13 March 2005) *Washington Post.*

11 'Unions muffle Wall Street support of private accounts', (8 March 2005) *Washington Post.*

ciety', since the accounts 'would extend to all workers the benefits of asset ownership' and thus their stake in the private enterprise system.[12]

Related to this motive is that of proponents who see the proposal as a way to reduce Americans' expectations that the government has a responsibility in assuring senior citizens' financial well-being. Thus, the White House's director of strategic initiatives was quoted as stressing in a memo sent to Republican Party activists that the Bush plan deserved support because it would operate a shift 'away from dependency on government and toward giving greater power and responsibility to individuals'.[13] A long-time proponent of Social Security privatisation, Michel Tanner of the Cato Institute, spoke more explicitly about how the initiative would help to bury the Welfare State: 'We're changing fundamentally the relationship of people to their government … [It would be] the biggest shift since the New Deal'.[14]

4. The World Bank's involvement in pension reforms

Starting in the mid-1980s, the World Bank has offered technical and financial support for pension reforms in more than 80 developing and transition countries. In 1994 the Bank published a policy paper, Averting the Old-Age Crisis, which enunciated its overall approach on pensions. The principal theme of the policy was the affirmation that partial privatisation of pensions systems would protect pensions against the effects of ageing populations, extend coverage to unprotected workers and contribute to the country's financial development and economic growth.[15]

The specific model for pension reform that the World Bank put forward in Averting the Old-Age Crisis was called the 'three-pillar' model. The Bank recommended that countries reduce the scope of the pay-as-you-go public pension system (the 'first pillar'); that they create a second 'foundation pillar' consisting of mandatory defined-contribution privately managed pension funds, following the example of the pioneering pension privatisation carried out in Pinochet-era Chile in 1981; and that they encourage (for example through tax incentives) voluntary retirement savings composing the 'third pillar'.[16]

The three-pillar model constituted the template for World Bank-sponsored reforms in a number of countries, but the Bank particularly concentrated its efforts on middle-income countries that already had comprehensive public pensions schemes, most notably in Latin America and in Central and Eastern Europe. The Bank paid scant attention to lower-income countries that offered little or no old-age security protection. The Bank gave its priority to encouraging the former

---

12 'Why personal accounts are a real benefit' (23 January 2005) *Washington Post.*

13 'A bit of social engineering in disguise' (23 January 2005) *Washington Post.*

14 *Ibid.*

15 World Bank, *Averting the Old-Age Crisis: Policies to Protect the Old and Promote Growth* (Oxford University Press, 1994).

16 *Ibid.*

group of countries to scale down the public system and devoted most of its technical and financial assistance to helping countries establish a system of private accounts, into which part of pension contributions would be diverted.

A few years after the World Bank claimed to have discovered the recipe for 'Averting the Old-Age Crisis' and extending coverage to the unprotected, it had become obvious to many analysts that not only had the Bank not achieved the objectives it had set for itself, but it had created some new problems. Trade unions in several countries, most notably in Latin America and in Central and Eastern Europe, were among the first to point out these problems.

In April 2001 the International Confederation of Free Trade Unions (ICFTU) and its Global Unions partners summarised the labour movement's objections in a statement in which they criticised the World Bank for its policy of encouraging governments to reduce or dismantle public pension plans: the World Bank's 'haste to scale back or dismantle public pension schemes is particularly troublesome in view of the high level of corruption and administrative costs associated with the privatised "multi-pillar" schemes. ... Instead, the Bank must accept fully the need to promote comprehensive public pension schemes that can provide the equitable basis for old-age protection that all people desire and need'.[17]

Eventually, the failures of the Bank's approach on pension reforms became recognised by no less an authority than the World Bank itself, in a paper dealing with the reform experience of Latin America prepared by the Latin America and Caribbean regional division of the Bank. Given that Latin America is the region that has experienced the longest period of Bank involvement in pension reforms, this report is of particular significance.[18]

The findings of the Bank's report, *Keeping the Promise of Old Age Income Security in Latin America*, confirmed earlier assessments made by trade unions and others critical of the Bank's approach on pension reforms. Among the most important failures is no doubt the fact that one of the primary goals of the reforms – extending pension coverage to the unprotected – had not been met. The Bank's report found that 'pension coverage remains low and unequally shared among income groups in Latin America' and 'are perhaps the most revealing sign of the need to re-examine design issues surrounding the multi-pillar model'[19]. The report also confirmed complaints that high administrative costs for the privatised pillars, as compared to the public schemes, had severely reduced pensioners' income: the private accounts 'are faced with steep commissions that reduce the accumulated balances drastically'.[20]

A further important criticism made by trade unions and others of the World Bank-sponsored pension reforms relates to the fact that women have suffered a greater loss of benefits than have men. *Keeping the Promise* agrees with this cri-

---

17 ICFTU, TUAC & ITS, *Statement by the ICFTU, TUAC and the ITS to the Spring 2001 Meetings of the IMF and World Bank* (Washington, April 2001).

18 Indermit S. Gill, Truman Packard and Juan Yermo, *Keeping the Promise of Social Security in Latin America* (World Bank, November 2003).

19 *Ibid.*, at 69 & 6.

20 *Ibid.*, at 111.

tique, noting that 'women earn lower returns from the new systems relative to men' in most of the Latin American countries where the reforms took place.[21]
Another important objective that the World Bank announced in *Averting the Old-Age Crisis* for supporting pension privatisation concerned the expected beneficial financial impact. It was predicted that the development of private pension funds would, on the one hand, stimulate the development of capital markets and overall economic growth, and on the other hand, reduce the burden of the pension system for the State.

Keeping the Promise found that both predictions had been vastly over-stated in the case of Latin America. In almost all of the countries where a second-pillar reform of privatised pensions took place, 'the main beneficiary has been the government debt market', with most of the funds used to buy government bonds.[22] Thus the State continues to finance a nominally private scheme, while allowing private administrators to offer reduced benefits in exchange for generous fees. Even where there may be some evidence, notably in Chile, of privatised pensions having contributed to the growth in debt and equities markets, *Keeping the Promise* observes that a similar expansion of the capital market took place in Brazil, which did not privatise its pension scheme. The Bank's report concludes that 'financial sector development can take place effectively in the absence of pension privatisation'.[23]

As to the expectation that privatisation would reduce the fiscal burden to the State of old-age security, many analysts have pointed out that privatisation in fact usually increases costs to the government over a certain period because, while part of workers' contributions are diverted into private funds, the State continues to make payments to current and even new retirees. As well as assuming past obligations, in many countries the government provides minimum pensions to those who otherwise would be destitute, and the failure of private accounts to provide adequate pensions often means that the costs of minimum pension provisions have become substantial.

The World Bank has euphemistically called these costs of privatisation 'transition costs', in the expectation that they would whither away as the private plans matured. In the case of Chile, the costs to the State of the almost fully privatised pension regime have continued to grow and in 2005, 24 years after pensions were privatised, the so-called transition costs absorbed more than a quarter of the national budget, almost as much as spending for education and health care combined.[24] On the basis of the experience with privatisation in several countries, the Bank's report on pension reform in Latin America observes that 'fiscal sustainability is far from assured. ... Further, pension reforms can create new implicit and explicit liabilities ... [and] can produce severe cash-flow problems ... and hence seriously constrain public sector liquidity'.[25]

---

21 *Ibid.*, at 71.

22 *Ibid.*, at 67.

23 *Ibid.*, at 212-213.

24 'Chile's retirees find shortfall in private plan', (27 January 2005) *New York Times*.

25 Indermit S. Gill, Truman Packard and Juan Yermo, *supra* note 17, at 42.

5. A revised World Bank approach?

More than a year after the World Bank's Latin America and Caribbean regional division released its report criticising various aspects of the Bank's approach on pension reform, the Bank's social protection unit, responsible for overall pension policy, produced its own report. *Old-Age Income Support in the Twenty-First Century*[26] constitutes the Bank's first comprehensive revised policy paper on pensions since it issued *Averting the Old-Age Crisis* in 1994. Many of the optimistic claims made in the 1994 report about the gains to be reaped from privatising pensions are absent from the new report, and it also contains criticisms (it would be more accurate to speak of self-criticism, but the Bank's report does not go as far as admitting past error) of the previously sacrosanct three-pillar model. Thus, *Old-Age Income Support in the Twenty-First Century*:

- No longer claims, as the Bank previously did, that private accounts systems provide better protection for an ageing workforce than pay-as-you-go systems
- Admits that private accounts pay out benefits that are volatile and unpredictable, and, as compared to public systems, have high administrative costs which 'significantly reduce the workers' benefits from the new system'[27]
- Admits that the three-pillar reforms have failed to extend pension coverage; in fact, 'coverage has stagnated at low levels and has become the single most important concern of policy makers'[28]
- Emphasises the need for social dialogue, particularly with trade unions, on pension reform options,[29] a position that constitutes a radical change from as recently as 2001, when the Bank's lead pensions expert told an international trade union delegation that 'unions have nothing useful to say on pension reform'

While the World Bank's policy paper does announce a more flexible approach by asserting the need for 'careful consideration of benefits and costs' before privatising,[30] it is clear that the creation of a second pillar of mandatory private accounts remains the preferred default option. In a key passage, after asserting that the particular context of pension reform varies widely from country to country, *Old-Age Income Support in the Twenty-First Century* states that the Bank's approach 'seeks to use the experience of mandated individual retirement-savings systems as a baseline or starting point for analysis of the outcomes of a proposed reform'.[31] Since the Bank is not speaking of laboratory experiments but rather of 'real-world experience', it is obvious that the Bank intends to continue pushing countries to

---

26 Robert Holzmann and Richard Hinz, *Old-Age Income Support in the Twenty-First Century: An International Perspective on Pension Systems and Reform* (World Bank, 2005).

27 *Ibid.*, at 201.

28 *Ibid.*

29 *Ibid.*, at 29.

30 *Ibid.*, at 15.

31 *Ibid.*, at 77.

put in place second-pillar private accounts, even if the pretext is that they should only serve as a 'benchmark'.[32]

The Bank's policy document implies that countries should set up the complex bureaucracy for administering millions of mandatory private investment accounts only to create an instrument for measuring the performance of the public pension system. This seems about as plausible as suggesting that a city should build an expensive network of automobile expressways not to carry significant traffic, but just to measure whether it could get people around the city as effectively as the existing subway system. In actuality on a country-level, the World Bank has pressured governments that have taken the plunge and invested in the establishment of second pillars to subsequently increase the contributions to the private accounts, and to decrease those to the public system, in order to make the private system more viable. This was the Bank's policy in 2004 in Bulgaria, a country that had adopted a three-pillar system in 2000 but had left the mandatory second-pillar contributions at a level that the Bank considered too low.[33]

In a revealing passage about what Bank officials intend to do in practice, as opposed to what declared policy may be, the Bank's new pensions policy document states that 'most Bank staff see the potential economic benefits of a multi-pillar pension scheme with a major second (mandated) or voluntary (third) funded pillar ...',[34] even though the same document includes numerous expressions of caution that the expected benefits of second pillar reforms may not exist. Moreover, recent World Bank country assistance strategies continue to promote classic three-pillar pension reforms as the only option that the Bank will support.[35]

Criticism of the World Bank's approach to pension reform made by trade unions and others found additional support in an exhaustive report published in February 2006 by the Bank's own Independent Evaluation Group (IEG), a unit that operates independently of World Bank management and reports directly to the board of executive directors. After analysing more than 200 pension reform loans granted by the Bank between 1984 and 2005, the IEG found that the Bank's financial support was heavily skewed in favour of privatised pillars and that it continued to promote pension privatisation even after 2000, when the failures of the approach were becoming obvious, in some low-income Latin American countries where the financial sector was completely unprepared.[36] The IEG also concluded that, contrary to the Bank's rhetoric about prioritising expansion of social security to those who had no coverage, this issue was mostly ignored in the Bank's reforms. In particular, the report noted that 'little support was provided to expanding old-age benefits to workers in the informal economy'.[37]

32 *Ibid.*

33 Interview with World Bank country team, Sofia, 20 October 2004.

34 *Ibid.*, at 66.

35 See, for example, World Bank, *Country Assistance Strategy for Serbia and Montenegro* (World Bank, November 2004) at 14.

36 Independent Evaluation Group-World Bank, *Pension Reforms and the Development of Pension Systems: An Evaluation of World Bank Assistance* (Washington, 2006) at 12-13 & 23-24.

37 *Ibid.*, at 12.

In summary, the World Bank's own recent analyses have confirmed the criticisms made earlier by trade unions and others, that second-pillar reforms have proved to be inefficient, costly, reinforcing of inequality, unsuccessful in extending coverage, and have put considerable strain on public finances. Despite this, the model continues to be the Bank's preferred approach. The one 'economic' argument in favour of privatisation that still gets some degree of credit in *Old-Age Income Support in the Twenty-First Century* is the supposed role that the private accounts play in contributing to capital market development.[38] This raises the question of why the cost of developing capital markets should be imposed on workers and retirees by forcing them to give up part of their pension benefits to inefficient private-sector administrators. Unfortunately the Bank does not even pose the question, much less offer a rationale, of why retirees, rather than some other sector of society, should be obliged to make this sacrifice to help the financial services industry develop.

A second motive for pushing pension privatisation despite the inherent inefficiencies associated with the option might be found in the use of pension reform as an instrument for imposing reductions in other government expenditures. As noted, privatisation has the effect of diverting part of pension contributions into private accounts, even though the obligation to pay out benefits from the public system continues.

In a manner similar to that of conservative politicians in the United States who have promoted tax cuts in order to squeeze public finances and oblige the government to curb 'wasteful' or 'harmful' spending – although the usual end result is less money for big-budget items such as schools that can hardly be considered wasteful –, World Bank officials have pushed governments to partially privatise pensions through second-pillar reforms and then later pressured them to reduce expenditures for other public services in order to pay for the cost of reform. For example, in 2004 the IMF and World Bank signed on to a joint report addressed to the authorities of Nicaragua which stated that 'the government will need to rationalise its expenditures to make room for the costs of pension reform'.[39] The operational premise of the international financial institutions in making such policy recommendations is that a smaller and weaker State is necessarily a better State.

---

38 We noted above that the World Bank's study *Keeping the Promise of Old Age Income Security in Latin America* does not fully share this positive assessment. The Bank's IEG went even further in expressing doubt about the positive impact of pension privatisation and concluded that 'most capital markets have not developed significantly as a result of multi-pillar pension reform …' (Independent Evaluation Group-World Bank, *Pension Reforms and the Development of Pension Systems: An Evaluation of World Bank Assistance* (Washington, 2006) at 36).

39 IMF and World Bank, *Nicaragua: Joint Staff Assessment of the Poverty Reduction Strategy Paper, Second Progress Report* (Washington, January 2004) at 11.

6. Conclusion: Pension systems should not be held captive by reformers pushing unrelated goals

Although there are differences in the approaches taken by the Bush administration in the United States and by the World Bank in developing and transition countries as regards the reform of public pensions systems,[40] they have one important feature in common: in both cases pension (or Social Security) reform is not promoted with the primary objective of improving the system for its beneficiaries. Neither type of reform meets any of the criteria for social security reform enunciated by the ILO in its consensus resolution of 2001, such as expanding coverage, incorporating the informal economy into the formal economy, ensuring equitable outcomes for women, strengthening solidarity systems, and ensuring adequate benefits.

In both cases examined here, the aim is to remake pension systems in order to achieve goals that are essentially unrelated to the intended beneficiaries of pensions. Our analysis has shown that these goals appear to be related to financial market development and to diminishing and redefining the role of the State in society in conformity with a neo-liberal ideology.

While pensions systems around the world do face important challenges, a starting point for establishing a new system or reforming an existing one must be that any changes should be designed so as to improve the system for workers and retirees, not to prioritise unrelated goals. Policy makers would do well to refer to the ILO's 2001 consensus on social security for establishing the goals and parameters on which the process of reform in their country could be based.

---

40 The most important difference is that the World Bank's model entails putting part of contributions into *mandatory* private accounts, while the Bush plan would make private accounts voluntary, at least for now. However the World Bank sees an identity in the approach. When the Bank officially launched *Old-Age Income Support in the Twenty-First Century*, the first line of the Bank's communiqué declared that the new policy was addressed, among others, to 'policy makers in the United States … [who] grapple with the long-term affordability of their pensions systems' (World Bank News Release No. 2005/456/HD, 24 May 2005).

Evaluating Reforms in Social Security Protection

Warren R. McGillivray*

1. Introduction

A renowned social security expert once said that social security was like a car which had only one gear – forward. Social security could not reverse direction due to the real or perceived social and economic dislocations which would occur, and the risk of political suicide for those who moved into reverse gear. In this paper, reforms of social insurance (i.e. contributory) schemes which provide cash transfers are considered.[1] The evolution of social security since World War II is briefly traced. Why it has become necessary to reform some social security programmes is indicated, and the principal types of reforms along with specific examples are illustrated. How reforms have been carried out – the political economy of social security reform – is not dealt with in this paper. Given the long-term impact of many reforms, their evaluation soon after implementation can only be tentative. While a particular reform may be regarded by some as a shift into reverse, others will consider it a means of enabling the social protection programme to continue to move forward. At the end of this chapter a brief list of references which deal in depth with issues raised in this article is provided.

2. Social Security since World War II

The years of recovery and economic growth following World War II were a time of development and expansion of social protection. The landmark ILO Social Security (Minimum Standards) Convention 1952 (No. 102) provided a framework

---

* Policy Associate, Caledon Institute of Social Policy. Formerly Chief, Studies and Operations Branch, International Social Security Association (ISSA). The views in this paper are those of the author and do not necessarily reflect those of the Caledon Institute or the ISSA.

1 Tax-financed universal benefit schemes and means- or income-tested social assistance benefits and services provided under social security health care schemes are not considered in this paper.

and guidelines for national social security schemes. This comprehensive instrument identified nine social security branches: medical care; short-term benefits (sickness, maternity, unemployment, family and employment injury benefits[2]); and long-term benefits (old-age, invalidity, and survivors benefits). This Convention became the basis for ILO advice to policymakers in developing countries and the establishment of social security schemes there.

In the 1970s, in the industrialised countries economic conditions (e.g. the 'oil shocks') led to a period of consolidation of the gains in social protection which had been made in the previous 25 years. It became clear that lower rates of economic growth would not permit unlimited expansion of social protection: the schemes had to take into account not only social security needs, but greater attention had to be paid to the national economies in which they operated. For example, in the USA the 1983 President's Commission proposed long-term reforms which were designed to put the old-age, invalidity and survivors pensions system back on a sound financial footing. In Chile, the failure of multiple social security schemes led to the introduction in 1981 of a new system of providing pensions which would have a major impact on public pension schemes elsewhere in the following decades.

After 1990 the transition countries which had followed the Soviet system of state budget financed social security had to reform their social security protection schemes. In 1994, a World Bank publication promoted the adoption of pension systems based on the Chilean model. Adaptations of this model have been implemented in a number of Latin American countries and some countries in Central and Eastern Europe and the former Soviet Union. Elsewhere, financial and demographic realities have led countries to re-examine their public pension and other social security schemes to assess whether they are meeting their objectives and whether they are financially sustainable. Are schemes meeting the needs of workers in the face of current and likely future labour market conditions – part-time, casual, teleworking and clandestine employment, homework, increasing female participation in the labour market? This has led to consideration of targeting benefits by expanding welfare or assistance benefits based on means- or asset-tests. In both industrialised and developing countries, attention is also focused on extending social security protection to persons who are not covered by the existing schemes.

3. Social Security Reform Issues

Governments have an implicit – and sometimes explicit – obligation to organise systems of social protection for the persons for whom they are responsible, and to ensure that the schemes are properly governed. At the same time, participants in the schemes – workers and employers – have an obligation to abide by the condi-

[2] Permanent incapacity employment injury benefits are similar to long-term benefits.

tions of the social security schemes. If either of these conditions is unfulfilled, the social security scheme will fail.

Social security schemes paying cash benefits are transfers of resources from active workers to inactive beneficiaries at the time the benefits are paid. The amounts paid, which beneficiaries convert into goods and services that they consume, are equal to consumption (and investment) that workers forego. The goods and services that workers and beneficiaries share must almost all be produced by workers at the time benefits are paid.

Whatever the statutory basis or the implicit obligation of governments to provide social security protection may be, the transfer of resources from active workers to beneficiaries is a political issue. Equity must be preserved both within and between generations, but equity is subject to different interpretations. For example, in pension schemes, the principle of intergenerational equity – scheme participants in each generation should pay roughly the same share of their disposable incomes in contributions in order to receive pensions at comparable replacement rates after they retire – is open to diverse interpretations.

The mutual obligations of governments and participants do not preclude the government from changing conditions of a social security scheme, notably the amount of the benefit.[3] This is clearly so for tax-financed universal or social assistance benefits. It is sometimes argued that contributions to social insurance schemes are like premiums paid to an insurance company, and hence changes should not be possible. But commercial insurance (e.g. automobile, fire) policies are normally renewable annually at terms and premiums agreed by the policyholder and the insurer, and the sum insured under a life insurance policy is adjusted if an insurer faces insolvency or becomes insolvent. In any event, reforms to contributory public pension schemes normally respect the rights to benefits which participants have acquired at the time of a reform.[4]

Inevitably reforms produce 'winners' and 'losers', and the latter object strenuously and penalise those who have enacted them. This is inevitable, but the issue is ensuring that the social security scheme meets its objectives and can continue to operate in a sustainable manner. Indeed, political leaders willing to take a longer perspective than the next election should be rewarded, not penalised.

Reforms are often necessary to correct abuses of a scheme. Abuses (not necessarily outright fraud) often arise due to the benefit formula of a scheme. For ex-

3 This is central to the controversy over whether (and, if so, how) the liability for future benefits of a defined benefit public pension scheme (the scheme's 'implicit debt') should appear in countries' national accounts. Aside from methodological questions over how it should be calculated, the implicit debt can be altered by future reforms to the scheme which the government may introduce. Hence the implicit debt of a public pension scheme is quite different from sovereign debt (i.e. bonds) of a country. The implicit debt only becomes explicit when a public defined benefit scheme is wound up and the government assumes the liability for pensions due under the scheme. This leads to the transition cost when a defined benefit public scheme is replaced by a defined contribution scheme.

4 Participants may be given the choice of remaining in the former scheme or opting for the reformed scheme.

ample, if the benefit in a pension scheme is based on the final five years average contributory earnings of a participant, the participant (generally along with his/her employer) can contrive to artificially inflate his/her final earnings. Or, if a pension scheme has a benefit formula such as 30% of pensionable earnings after 15 years of contributions and 1% of pensionable earnings for every year of contributions thereafter, a participant (again with his/her employer) can contrive to contribute to the scheme for only 15 years. Before operations were computerised, administrative constraints meant that benefit formulas had to be simple, and scheme designers sometimes neglected the propensity of individuals to act in what they perceived to be their own enlightened self-interest (even when this was illegal).

Social security is recognised as a necessary component of a well-organised market economy, and globalisation has resulted in new and renewed challenges to social security. For example, high social security contributions are criticised for being a 'tax on jobs' since they increase labour costs and thereby reduce national competitiveness and employment. In the short run, reducing contribution rates would reduce labour costs. But since employers pass most of the burden of contributions down to workers in the form of lower wages and to consumers in higher prices, a reduction would not have a long-run impact. The challenges have led to a re-examination of all aspects of social protection. Many national social security programmes evolved independently, and their relationship to each other and to the labour market is being analysed and the programmes rationalised. For example, in the years just prior to retirement age there is often interaction between unemployment insurance, sickness benefit, invalidity benefit and early retirement pensions.

The package of social security benefits should encourage workers to be more productive. The relationship between social security and the labour market raises fundamental questions: Does social security encourage people to engage in the formal economy? Do sickness benefits encourage prolonged absences from work? Do unemployment benefits delay people's return to the labour market? Do benefits (e.g. early retirement pensions) encourage people to leave the labour force? Does the scheme treat males and females equally?

4. Reforms

Reforms of social security schemes are undertaken:

1. to ensure that the schemes meet their objectives;
2. to remove perverse incentives and abuses which:
   - have undesirable labour market and social implications,
   - increase the cost of the schemes; and
3. to ensure the sustainability of the schemes.

Social security reforms are usually unpopular, and there is an extensive literature on how the reform process proceeds through proposals, dissemination, promotion, discussion and finally implementation.[5]

4.1 Short-term Benefits

Short-term social security benefits (sickness, maternity, unemployment, family and employment injury benefits) are normally financed on a pay-as-you-go (PAYG) basis, that is, in a contributory scheme the annual income of the scheme is equal to its annual outgo in benefits and administration expenses. Here, the PAYG system is a manifestation of intra-generational solidarity.

In short-term benefit schemes, the effect of reforms on the annual frequency and average duration of claims soon becomes evident. From a technical point of view, whether a reform to short-term benefit scheme meets the requirements mentioned above can be assessed after a relatively short period, and it is not uncommon for there to be a subsequent reform to correct unexpected or unintended results of the original reform. Persons covered by the scheme will also quickly ascertain whether they are winners or losers as a result of a reform.

4.1.1 Sickness Benefit

For several years there has been great concern in **Sweden** over the extent of absences from work due to sickness. Between 1997 and 2002, the number of days during which sickness insurance benefits were paid nearly doubled, and the number of sickness cases lasting over 30 days increased substantially. During this period efforts were being made to reduce the open unemployment rate, and as the unemployment rate declined, the days lost due to sickness increased. In 2002 the government set the objective of reducing the level of absences due to sickness by half by 2008.

The National Social Insurance Board 2002 Annual Report asks 'To what extent changed living habits and attitudes and greater demands with regard to family life and recreational activity have raised the inclination and need to take sick leave?' It notes that it is probably reasonable to assume that attitudes to taking sick leave have changed as absence due to sickness has increased during the period 1997–2002, and that these changes must have occurred not only among those absent from work due to sickness but also among doctors, employers, colleagues, insurance office staff etc., i.e. all the groups who are involved in sick leave.

Action to reduce absences due to sickness focused on improving co-operation among the various actors – improved doctors' certificates, information and education of the medical profession, strengthening of the industrial health service and influencing societal attitudes and values. It was necessary to review the sickness, disability and unemployment benefit provisions together. In 2003 disability insur-

---

5 See, for example, Katharina Müller, *The Political Economy of Pension Reform in Central-Eastern Europe* (Edward Elgar Publishing, 1999).

ance was modified to include an 'activity benefit' for persons under age 30, while older persons receive a sickness benefit. From January 2005 a system of co-financing sickness benefit was introduced with the objective of reducing long-term absences of employees due to sickness by making it financially advantageous for employers to take preventive measures and enhance rehabilitation and reemployment possibilities. Employers' responsibility for paying employees' full sick pay for the first three weeks of absence due to sickness was reduced to two weeks, and employers were made responsible for paying 15% of the sick pay costs indefinitely after the first two weeks. The employer's obligation ceases if the sick employee receives rehabilitation pay from the social insurance scheme or returns to work on at least a half-time basis.

4.1.2 Unemployment Insurance

Unemployment is different from other risks insured by social security schemes since unemployment is an economic, not a physical or demographic, risk. Unemployment insurance schemes are designed to provide income replacement to workers during periods of frictional (short-term) unemployment. Income replacement due to widespread structural unemployment is normally beyond the scope of the schemes. Unemployment insurance schemes typically run surpluses during periods of strong economic growth when the level of employment is high and deficits during recessions. The effect of an unemployment insurance reform depends greatly on the phase of the economic cycle when it is introduced, hence the effect of a reform may not be evident as quickly as are the effects of reforms to other short-term benefits.

In **Germany**, the 2005 Hartz IV reform of unemployment assistance and social assistance has had an immediate statistical effect.[6] It will take some time to ascertain whether this major reform which seeks to strengthen individual responsibility and lower transfers to unemployed persons who are capable of work achieves the objectives of increasing employment and maintaining the financial sustainability of the system.

4.2 Long-term Benefits – Pensions

In a defined benefit (DB) pension scheme, the benefit is typically related to earnings and years of service of a participant. In contrast to benefits for short-term contingencies, pensions are long-term obligations characterised by increasing annual expenditures. Each year new persons qualify for pensions, and new pensions are greater than those in payment due to higher earnings on which the pensions are based and in immature schemes due to longer periods of service. In addition, existing pensions are increased to take into account inflation. Added to this automatic escalation is the effect of increasing life expectancy at older ages. Conse-

6 This effect is obscured by the adoption of ILO definitions of employment for statistical purposes.

quently, using a PAYG financial system to finance pensions results in steadily increasing annual expenditures relative to earnings subject to contributions, and thus for many years annual increases in the contribution rate. In order to try to maintain both intergenerational solidarity and equity, contribution rates which are higher than the PAYG rate can be used to build up reserves to finance public DB pension schemes (e.g. in Canada, Japan and the USA).

The state provides an implicit (and sometimes explicit) guarantee of the benefits promised under a public DB pension scheme which it has enacted. The perennity of the scheme is founded on the scheme's statutory authority to collect contributions and the state's capacity to level taxes.

Unlike short-term benefit schemes, the effect of reforms to pension schemes is evident only after several generations. It can thus be more difficult to identify winners and losers at the time of a reform, and there are opportunities for obfuscation. For example, if future reforms of a DB scheme are thought to be likely to reduce pensions, participants can be induced to give up a DB scheme in favour of uncertain but possibly higher pensions from a funded defined contribution (DC) savings scheme. With respect to pension reform in Canada, Battle writes '[opponents] said government should forget about fixing the Canada Pension Plan and instead replace it with some form of mandatory … retirement savings plan. The scrap-the-CPP faction was able to advance the cause by exploiting the fears and ignorance of the Canadian people, who have little understanding of the purposes, workings and advantages of the CPP and are highly susceptible to fear-mongering about its future in a time of cutbacks to social programs and lack of confidence in governments generally.'[7] In the end, Battle observes 'The extremist option of abolishing the CPP was never on the political table …'.[8]

Reforms to public DB pension schemes are parametric where the conditions and parameters of the scheme are modified, or structural where the DB scheme is wound-up and replaced by an entirely different scheme.

4.2.1 Parametric Reforms

The alternatives for modifications to DB schemes are limited. Thompson provides a disaggregation of the retirement burden which identifies where changes can be made to public pension schemes to reduce the burden of retirement pensions.[9]

---

7 Ken Battle, 'Sustaining Public Pensions in Canada: A Tale of Two Reforms' in Noriyuki Takayama (ed.), *Taste of Pie: Searching for Better Pension Provisions in Developed Countries* (Maruzen Co., 2003) 37-91.

8 Battle notes 'Even if the federal government wanted to take the enormous political risk and contend with the incredible transition problems of winding down a 30-year-old program that has promised many billions of dollars worth of pensions to the entire Canadian workforce which pays into the plan, it probably would not be able to do so because of opposition from at least some of the provinces' (two-thirds of which, with two-thirds of the total population, must approve any change to the CPP). *Ibid.*

9 From Lawrence Thompson, *Older and wiser: the economics of public pensions* (Urban Institute Press, 1998), if Y = total income, C = aggregate consumption, C_p = aggregate

From Thompson, there are three basic parametric changes to public DB schemes which can be made in order to maintain the financial sustainability of the schemes. These are:

- increase the contribution rate;
- cut pensions (for example, by reducing the benefit accrual rate or pension adjustments to take into account inflation); and
- reduce the number of pensioners (for example, by raising the retirement age or modifying conditions for receiving a pension).

Examples of selected parametric reforms in several OECD countries are summarised in the following paragraphs.

The Social Security programme in the **USA** replaces about 40 percent of the wages of a full-career average-wage contributor.[10] In 1983 the retirement age was increased from 65 to 67. Persons born in 1937 or earlier maintained the retirement age of 65, with gradual increases in the retirement age so that the age 67 retirement age applies to persons born in 1960 and later. Hence, in 1983 those persons aged 46 or older were unaffected by the change, and those persons who would be fully affected were age 23 or younger.

In **Germany**, 1992 reforms raised pension age to 65 by 2004. The 2002 Riester reforms introduced changes in the pension indexation formula and subsidies to encourage the development of occupational and voluntary private pension schemes. The contribution rate to the public scheme is to be kept below 20% until 2020, and thereafter below 22% to 2030. From 2005 a 'sustainability factor' which links pensions to economic and demographic developments operates whereby annual pension adjustments will be reduced if the ratio of pensioners to contributors rises. It is intended that the gross standard pension level, 52% in 2005, not fall below 46% in 2020 and 43% in 2030.[11] The minimum early retirement age will gradually be raised from 60 to 63 by 2008.

---

consumption of retired persons, n = total population, and p = number of retired persons (pensioners), then:
Number of retirement pensioners/Total population = p/n;
Average consumption of retired persons = Cp/p;
Average consumption of total population = C/n;
Retired persons living standards ratio =
Average retiree consumption/Average total consumption = (Cp/p) / (C/n);
hence the Retirement Burden = Cp/Y = C/Y * p/n * [(Cp/p) / (C/n)].

[10] In Canada, Ireland, Japan, the United Kingdom and the USA the public schemes are supplemented by occupational schemes which cover around one-half of employed persons.

[11] The gross standard pension level (redefined following changes in income tax legislation in 2004) is based on the pension (net of health and long-term care contributions) payable to a contributor who contributed for 45 years at the average earnings level each year. Under the former definition of the standard pension level, the replacement rate was expected to fall from 70 per cent of average net earnings to 67 per cent over the period 2011 to 2030.

The **Canada** Pension Plan (CPP) replaces 25 per cent of the wages of a full-career average-wage contributor. Along with the Old Age Security programme which covers residents, the total replacement rate is in the order of 40 per cent. Canada gradually raised the contribution rate to the CPP from 5.85 to 9.9 per cent of contributory earnings over six years from 1998. The reserves which build-up under this partial funding system are invested by the CPP Investment Board, a body which was set up to operate at arms' length from government and be accountable to the public and governments. New CPP pensions were slightly reduced by modifying the way in which earnings from previous years are adjusted to reflect current earnings when calculating the amount of retirement pensions.

With effect from 2004, in **Austria** the accrual rate for calculating pensions is gradually reduced from 2 per cent per year to 1.78 per cent starting in 2009. The period for averaging revalued earnings for the calculation of pensions is gradually lengthened from the highest paid 15 years to 40 years by 2028. Provision for retirement before age 65 (females age 60) after 35 years service is being phased out by 2017. The female retirement age is gradually raised to age 65 between 2019 and 2034.

In **Japan**, demographic and economic circumstances have led to reforms to the public DB pension schemes since 1980 which apply all three basic types of parametric changes. In 1994 retirement age was raised (gradually) from 60 to 65, and indexation of pensions was based on net wage increases.[12] Reforms enacted in 2004 gradually increase the contribution rate to Employees' Pension Insurance from the 13.58 per cent of covered wages to 18.3 per cent in 2017, and raise the State subsidy to the National Pension Programme which covers residents from one-third to one-half of the cost in 2009. Demographic factors which take into account declining numbers of contributors and increasing longevity of pensioners will reduce the current replacement rate from both schemes of about 60 per cent of net income for a full-career contributor to around 50 per cent by 2023. During this period the real value of pensions in payment will be reduced by applying a demographic factor which lowers the indexation of pensions.

Sweden spearheaded 'notional defined contribution' (NDC) pensions, a system which has characteristics of both DB and DC schemes. In a NDC scheme, contributions are accumulated in individual accounts just as in a funded DC scheme, but the contributions are used to pay current pensions on a PAYG basis. The notional accounts are revalued annually according to the rate of increase in average earnings. At retirement, the balance in an individual's notional account is converted into a pension taking into account the life expectancy of the cohort retiring at that time.

4.2.2 Structural Reforms

Parametric modifications to public DB schemes are contentious, and it is difficult to reach a consensus on acceptable changes. Battle has suggested that some para-

[12] This measure had been taken in Germany in 1992.

metric reforms are 'social policy by stealth' whereby arcane and complex technical changes are made which few participants recognise or understand.[13]

The public may indeed be more readily persuaded to accept a major structural reform such as the introduction of a funded DC savings scheme, especially if the reform is simple and the proposed scheme is portrayed as providing superior benefits. But, the effect of reforms to public pension schemes cannot be known for many years; hence those responsible are wary of the risks and uncertainty of DC schemes, since if the expectations of participants in DC schemes are not met, it is the government which will ultimately be responsible for their income support after they retire.

Beginning in the 1990s, in Latin America and in the transition countries of Central and Eastern Europe, major structural (or paradigmatic) reforms have been made to public pension schemes. In the transition countries reforms of public pensions and other social protection measures were necessary as the countries moved from centrally planned to market economies. In these countries, the reform movement coincided with a period when traditional DB schemes were being seriously challenged and an alternative approach involving DC savings schemes was being promoted.

By the 1980s, in a number of Latin American countries their DB schemes were failing to deliver the promised pensions. In some countries, the schemes were victims of macro-economic mismanagement which led to currency devaluations and inflation which depleted the schemes' reserves. Sometimes, political interference and mismanagement of the schemes contributed to depletion of the reserves and to a widespread loss of confidence in the schemes. In addition, pension reform was necessary due to a multitude of other problems: multiple, inequitable schemes covering different sectors of the population (but rarely the poor); a weak relationship between contributions and benefits; a decline in the ratio of contributors to beneficiaries (partly due to widespread contribution evasion); excessive administration costs; low efficiency. Governments had failed in their responsibility to organise social security protection for their populations.

Countries which have opted for major structural reforms of their old-age benefit schemes have generally introduced privately managed funded DC individual accounts schemes based on adaptations of the 1981 Chilean model. In these schemes, contributions are paid into a participant's individual account which is credited with interest annually. The amount in the account is converted into periodic payments when a participant retires. As well as correcting the deficiencies noted above, the DC schemes are expected to alleviate distortions in labour markets, and confer economic advantages such as possibly increasing national savings (and thereby economic growth) and developing national capital markets. There is a vast literature which analyses the pros and cons of this arrangement for providing retirement protection.

Privately managed DC individual account schemes are to a considerable extent an ideological reaction to failures of governments to operate the previous DB schemes properly. The new schemes empower participants – whether they want to

---

[13] Ken Battle, *supra* note 7, at 37-91.

be empowered or not, or have the capacity to take informed decisions – to take greater responsibility for their own retirement protection. They seek to isolate 'political risk', the potential pernicious influence of a government over the public pension scheme, except for the government's role as a stern regulator of the private account managers. But, in modern states governments are expected to be responsible for organising appropriate social protection for their populations; hence it is unrealistic to expect governments to cede social protection of retired persons to private pension managers.

In DC schemes, the investment risk is borne entirely by participants. Unlike DB schemes, the pension under a DC scheme is not predictable, and whether it will be adequate depends on participants' individual earnings patterns and the future rates of return on investments. Consequently, structural reforms which have been implemented have generally involved setting up tiers of pension protection: a first tier DB scheme with a DC individual accounts scheme as a second tier.[14] A third tier, individual savings, is often encouraged by tax concessions. Minimum pensions can also be introduced.

5. Conclusion

Reforms of social security schemes, in particular public pension schemes, have largely focused on stabilising or reducing future expenditures in order to make the schemes sustainable. But the distributional consequences of reforms are important, and it is necessary to pay attention to the objectives of benefit adequacy and equity, and the overall economic well-being of retirees. If these objectives are not met, governments risk being called upon by future expanding aged populations to supplement their pensions from general tax revenues. Political survival provides strong encouragement for governments to respond to the demands of their retired populations.

In democracies, reforms to public schemes must secure the support of an informed electorate. This adaptability is a strength of public pension schemes. But parametric reforms are regarded in some quarters as a manifestation of 'political risk', the repudiation or default of public pension promises. In countries where civil society has a strong influence on public policy, political risk is not considered to be so malign, and in these countries parametric reforms have been implemented gradually after prolonged debate to reach a national consensus. Seeking parametric changes does involve another form of political risk – the risk that despite a manifest need for reform of the public scheme, since individual losses are readily identified and resisted, the body politic is unable to reach a consensus on an acceptable reform, thereby resulting in a 'reform deadlock'.

Reform of a particular social security scheme should take into account the whole gamut of social transfers in a country. It is desirable that social security re-

---

14 For example, in Estonia, Hungary, Latvia, Poland, the Russian Federation, Sweden and Uruguay.

forms be simple, but few reforms (especially parametric reforms of public pension schemes) meet this criterion. A complicated reform may be socially and economically superior, but it will not be well understood and it will be suspected by those it is designed to benefit. A balance must be struck between complexity and simplicity. In some countries there has been a sequence of sometimes contradictory reforms extending over several years which undermine the credibility of the scheme and sap public confidence in it.

In industrialised countries, despite frequent dire warnings of public pensions crises in the popular press, there has been little support for massive structural reforms of their public pension systems. In countries where a structural reform has been implemented, major changes are usually phased in over long periods so that the generation approaching retirement is little affected. The full impact of the structural reform will be felt by subsequent generations which are unaware or insouciant of the possible implications of the reform or unable to express their opinions.

In the end, social insurance schemes prescribe how consumption of goods and services is to be shared between worker contributors and inactive beneficiaries. Reforms to public pension schemes are necessary to take into account social, economic and demographic conditions, notably projected declines in the size of the labour force relative to pensioners. Just as beneficiaries shared in the improving living standards which resulted from post-war expansion of national economies, they must also bear their share of possible future declines in living standards.

References

Nicholas Barr, *The economics of the welfare state*, 3rd ed. (Oxford University Press, 1998).

Nicholas Barr, 'Reforming pensions: Myths, truths and policy choices' 2 (2000) 55 *International Social Security Review* 3-36.

Roger Beattie; Warren McGillivray, 'A risky strategy: Reflections on the World Bank Report: Averting the old age crisis' 3-4 (1995) 48 *International Social Security Review* 5-22.

Colin Gillion; John Turner; Clive Bailey (eds.), *Social security pensions: Development and reform* (ILO, 2000).

International Labour Organization, *Social Security (Minimum Standards) Convention, 1952 (No.102)* (ILO, 1952).

International Labour Organization, *World Labour Report: Income security and social protection in a changing world* (ILO, 2000).

Warren McGillivray, 'Contribution evasion: Implications for social security pension schemes', 4 (2001) 54 *International Social Security Review* 3-22.

Warren McGillivray, 'Ten Years of Public Pensions Reform', in Noriyuki Takayama (ed.), *Taste of Pie: Searching for Better Pension Provisions in Developed Countries* (Maruzen Co, 2003) 401-417.

Organisation for Economic Co-operation and Development, *Reforming Public Pensions: Sharing the experiences of transition and OECD countries* (OECD, 2004).

Pensions Commission, *Pensions Challenges and Choices: The First Report of the Pensions Commission* (The Stationery Office, 2004).

www.pensionscommission.org.uk/publications/2004/annrep/index.asp.

National Social Insurance Board, *Social Insurance Annual Report, Budget Year 2002* (Stockholm, 2003).

Noriyuki Takayama, 'The Balance Sheet of Social Security Pensions in Japan' in *The Balance Sheet of Social Security Pensions*, Proceedings No. 6, Institute of Economic Research.

World Bank, *Averting the Old Age Crisis: Policies to Protect the Old and Promote Growth* (Oxford University Press, 1994).

Summary of Discussion

Alexia Bierweiler*

Session 1: Opening: Human Rights and Social Security

The first session was opened by presentations on the topics 'Current Challenges in the Field of Social Security' by *Emmanuel Reynaud*, 'The Human Right to Social Security: Some Challenges' by *Eibe Riedel*, and 'The Right to Social Security and Implications for Law, Policy and Practice' by *Malcolm Langford*.

In the discussion the first issue addressed was the differentiation between the human rights approach, implying that everybody has a right to social security, and the statistical approach taken by the ILO, which requires, as a first step, that a certain percentage of specified population groups need to be protected against the social risks accepted under the ILO Convention No. 102 such as sickness, unemployment or old-age which may be followed later by universal coverage. A participant held that the human rights approach is rather idealistic, since it is impossible to guarantee social security to every single person in the world at once, whereas the statistical approach could be seen as more realistic and pragmatic. Another participant pointed out that the Committee on Economic, Social and Cultural Rights (CESCR) usually does not take into consideration statistical figures, but rather looks at every single state in a country-by-country approach in order to avoid a 'ranking list' of member states. The advantage of setting benchmarks by the states themselves was stressed, as that is not only a way of dealing with social security issues, but also a way of achieving progressive realisation in this field.

A representative of the ILO emphasised that ILO Convention No. 102 of 1952 - which only deals with social security benefits - needs to be seen as the technical part of the Declaration of Philadelphia, i.e. the ideal the ILO wants to achieve. He remarked that this ideal was reaffirmed in the Conclusion of the International Labour Conference in 2001. By drafting Convention No. 102, the ILO strove for a minimum level of protection, which it considered to be the only thing that could be achieved regarding social security under the given circumstances, even though the Convention excludes a substantive part of the overall population. This had been seen as the socio-economic reality in 1952. However, since the International

* Senior Research Assistant at Mannheim University. I would like to thank Malcolm Langford for his support in editing this report.

Labour Conference in 2001, the ILO has taken the comprehensive approach to social security, and in its Conclusion it addressed social insurance, social assistance and private schemes to support this approach. Additionally, the outcome of the Conclusion was to reaffirm the Declaration of Philadelphia and the ILO Convention No. 102 as relevant instruments. Although the task of finding ways to implement the right to social security will require further steps, the inspiration given by the International Labour Conference and its Conclusion in 2001 might help to achieve this target, and this can be considered as the point where the statistical and the human rights approaches converge.

A participant remarked that one needs to keep in mind that only 6 out of 41 member states have ratified the ILO Convention No. 102 in its entirety. Nevertheless it was admitted that it still might be better to rely on a convention with lower ratification rates providing social security at least for some parts of the member states' population than not to have a convention on social security at all. However, the comprehensive approach taken by the Charter of Fundamental Rights of the European Union is to be preferred. One participant remarked in this context that the low ratification rate of ILO Convention No. 102 does not necessarily mean that it has exerted little influence on social security. However, the question of its practical effect remained open.

The issue of social assistance and art. 9 ICESCR was then addressed. Whereas one participant was concerned that the inclusion of social assistance might lead to a duplicative general comments on the issue – one comment on art. 9 and one on art. 11 ICESCR, which also covers social aid - another participant underlined the pragmatic advantages of dealing with social assistance in the context of art. 9 ICESCR. A State party report on art. 11 ICESCR does not allow for focused questions on social assistance, as art. 11 already comprises a huge range of issues. The CESCR has made short remarks on social assistance under art. 11 but this issue is not properly dealt with by the Committee in its practice, which has decided to focus on other problems under this article. Furthermore, sometimes a distinction between social security benefits and social assistance seems difficult, if not impossible. Therefore, art. 9 is the better 'place' to deal with social assistance. The participant pointed out that the CESCR is not obliged to follow the ILO approach of differentiating between social security and social assistance. In any case, the ILO has widened its concept in the last few years. Furthermore, it can be argued that art. 9 was originally intended by the drafters to cover both income-related and publicly financed aspects of social security. Although embedding social assistance in art. 9 ICESCR might still be considered an academically open question, from a practical point of view, it appears useful to do so, since this would allow to deal with social security and social assistance as one issue.

Another participant held that one should not focus on social insurance and social assistance only, but rather concentrate on the outcomes for the inhabitants of the member states. In response, it was noted that the Committee, is interested though in the situation of individuals rather than the average situation in a country.

The importance of avoiding a narrow approach to social security, for example, by concentrating on the poor only, was highlighted. This was underlined by a quotation saying that 'focusing on the poor is a poor scheme'. Social security needs to encompass society as a whole. A wide focus is needed, for example looking at income replacement, poverty relieving measures and the World Bank's 'zero pillar'.

Regarding privatisation of social security schemes, it was mentioned that this triggers the states' obligation 'to protect', although states might dislike this fact. The decisive point is not whether social security is granted by a public scheme, a private scheme or Public Private Partnership (PPP), but its impact on the living conditions of individuals, since we start from the recipients point of view.

The position of women in social security systems was taken up, particularly since the CESCR has focussed on women's rights and gender equality in its General Comments. In any General Comment on the Right to Social Security, one participant called for specific emphasis on the role and rights of women. In this context, it was important that women are not seen and treated as a vulnerable and marginalised group only. Fighting discrimination against women requires a treatment that differs from that of other marginalised groups. The importance of women's independence in the field of social security was pointed out, as some aspects of traditional social security schemes might push them into greater dependence. For example, if women are not entitled to their own social security benefits because of the higher income of their spouses. There is a need to eliminate these forms of discrimination in existing family models. Additionally, a participant drew attention to the fact that women might be part of a vulnerable group such as the Roma, raising the issue of double-discrimination.

Session 2: Comparative Perspectives on Social Security Rights

The second round of discussion was opened by the Chairperson after the presentations on the topics 'Latin America and Eastern Europe' by *Katharina Müller*, and 'Enhancing Accountability for the Basic Needs of the Poor: The Judicial Enforcement of Social Security Rights in South Africa' by *Sandra Liebenberg*.

Since South Africa social security policy and its implications can be shaped by the court, questions were raised regarding the work of the Constitutional Court of South Africa. For example, how was the bottom line for non-contributory benefits defined since the existence of a bottom line makes this a topic of human rights? In response, it was said that unfortunately this question remained open, as the Constitutional Court of South Africa has refused to define such a bottom line in its jurisprudence. The discussion also focused on the definition of the term 'most vulnerable groups' and whether the jurisprudence of the Constitutional Court of South Africa provides a possible definition for this term. It was stated by one participant that the Court only concentrates on the question whether a group is in desperate need. Therefore, to date neither an abstract definition nor categories of marginalised groups exist in South Africa.

Another concern was how to reconcile social protection with non-discrimination. In this context a participant, once more, drew attention to the role of women and emphasised that in reality women still receive lower wages, and as a result receive lower pensions. This issue has been addressed in Eastern countries, and several of these countries, i.e. Poland, changed their wage system in order to guarantee more equality.

Due to the difficulties in guaranteeing equal pensions, as illustrated above, the advantage of non-contributory pensions systems was pointed out, and several participants gave examples of countries that paid pensions on a non-contributory basis. For example, Brazil provides pensions in rural areas of 87 dollars a month from the age of 60 for men, and from the age of 58 for women. It is a tax-financed system without means testing. Bolivia, however, only pays 225 dollars a year in cash from the age of 65. Those unconditional grants had somewhat controversial impact in rural areas since the 225 dollars were given to pensioners in one instalment and was often spent immediately.

Participants also addressed the importance of unisex retirement ages, which are necessary to solve the problems caused by the different life expectancies of men and women. Attention was raised to the fact that unisex lines already exist in some developing countries and that the Court in South Africa is likely to shortly strike down the legislated differential retirement ages of women (60) and men (65).

Session 3: ILO and the Right to Social Security

This session dealt with the topics 'The ILO and the Right to Social Security' presented by *Germán López Morales* and 'Evaluating the ILO's Approach to Standard-Setting and Monitoring' presented by *Angelika Nußberger*.

One main objective of this session was to focus on links between the ILO and CESCR, although both institutions have their very own history and culture.

With regard to *Nußberger*'s historical taxonomy, one participant asked for clarification of the idealistic approach – the approach to social security taken by the ILO during World War II. In response, it was emphasised that this era was not only influenced by the Declaration of Philadelphia, but also by Recommendations 67 and 69 adopted in 1944, dealing with Income Security and Medical Care. These documents represented a novelty at the time, as they established the principle of universality in a coherent and codified form and were comprehensive as to coverage of persons and contingencies. An idealistic vision was reflected in concrete principles and put on paper. Even from today's perspective these recommendations cannot be seen as outdated. For example, even self-employed people could be included as a risk group, where this is possible without producing too high costs.

One participant was concerned about how to reconcile the approach to social security taken by the ILO with the human right to social security. How much of the ILO's work, especially since 2001, could be translated into a General Comment? Taking the branches covered by the ILO Convention No. 102, these have to be seen as examples only. The most difficult question might probably be – disregarding details – to what extent precise guidelines should be brought into a General Comment and what amount of detail should be left to the state parties.

One participant stated that the different approaches taken by CESCR and ILO are caused by the differences between the treaty bodies. While the ILO can access almost 200 conventions and recommendations, the CESCR has to rely on only one broad and comprehensive instrument. If a state ratifies one of the ILO conventions, the ILO starts a dialogue with this specific state on a specific subject, whereas the CESCR entertains dialogues with 151 states about all economic, social and cultural rights and about achieving higher standards regarding those rights. In order to bring all states that have not yet ratified ILO Convention No. 102 into a dialogue with the ILO and to deal with their reasons for not ratifying, a resolution was adopted in 2002. With this legally non-binding resolution (soft law approach) one tries to get states to ratify the legally binding ILO Convention No. 102 (hard law approach), which implies ending up with a legally binding convention by using soft law.

A representative of the ILO emphasised that a certain level of social security cannot be seen to be excluded from fundamental human rights, i.e., improving basic needs situations cannot be the sole aim. With regard to human rights lawyers and their focus on law, policy and strategy, the importance of having a source of inspiration such as the Declaration of Philadelphia was pointed out. Using law, policy and strategy is the focus and starting point of the ILO when dealing with social security, and the representatives were delighted to hear that human rights lawyers are taking this direction as well.

Next, a participant proposed to take an 'experimental approach'. The ILO Convention No. 102 should be viewed from an historical point of view. Additional emphasis was put on the practical effect of the Declaration of 1998, which intended to encourage states to ratify more ILO Conventions, and turned out to be very successful.

Another argument for considering ILO Convention No. 102 as a good starting point is art. 12 of the European Social Charter (ESC). Sub-paragraph 2 of the provision explicitly refers to the ILO Convention No. 102, and the European Committee of Social Rights therefore takes this Convention as a basis for its work on social security.

In this context, a participant argued that the European Committee of Social Rights tends to make very broad statements but the majority of complaints refer to specific violations of individuals. So the general statements of this Committee might not really be helpful and the question therefore arises as what can and should be done from a human rights perspective, particularly as it impacts the national level. Another participant noted that the collective complaint procedure under the European Social Charter has so far not concentrated on the most important social security issues, which are coverage or exclusion of certain groups, inequality and discrimination.

Next, a participant wondered about the impact of the debate in the European Union on the need for flexibility and security on the work of the CESCR and ILO. It was countered by others that the discussion in Europe only touches a small part of the global problem and is therefore - in a broader or global context - only a very minor or even unimportant problem.

It was questioned whether there was a fear of moving away from the ILO Convention No. 102 and taking a human rights oriented approach, as exemplified by the International Labour Conference in 2001. A representative of the ILO emphasised that ILO Convention No. 102 might still be considered as the starting point of the approach taken by the ILO in 2001. The attempt at the International Labour Conference was to recognise some of the current issues and to deal with them in a resolution rather than in a new convention. A clear statement about the role of the states seemed to be of particular importance. Consequently, the approach taken at the Conference included a primary role for the state, defining and setting standards and, moreover, addressing social security in the context of an ageing population. Although there was an extended debate within the working group, a formal position on privatisation or financing systems was not taken. But privatisation has been strongly criticised. Even though the World Bank still pushes the idea of prefunded schemes, it has realised that demographic changes influence every system. At the International Labour Conference in 2001, doubts occurred about the compatibility of private pension schemes with ILO Convention No. 102, as private pension schemes are based on the idea of general capitalisation: They are set according to the level of previous earnings without considering the foreseeability of what future pensioners will be able to accumulate as private savings. Therefore, the importance of the states' responsibility regarding private pension schemes and minimum guarantees had to be stressed.

The session was closed by ILO representatives, who addressed the issue of technical co-operation and noted that despite different approaches taken by the ILO and the CESCR, they are increasingly moving in the same direction, especially by using law, policy and strategy as their focus and starting point.

Session 4: Protection of Marginalised and Vulnerable Groups

After the presentations on the topics 'SEWA's Social Security Programme for Women Workers in the Informal Sector in India' by *Shalini Sinha* and 'Equal Access to Social Security in the European Countries: Case of Asylum Seekers' by *Helen Bolderson*, the Chairperson opened the discussion by pointing out the additional challenge the issue of asylum seekers might pose when drafting a General Comment on the right to social security. He also highlighted some problems that exist in the Refugee Convention.

The first question was whether the United Kingdom ratified the ILO Convention No. 118 of 1962, the Equality of Treatment (Social Security) Convention, which covers stateless persons and refugees.[1] The question remained unanswered, as the focus in the specific case of the asylum seekers was on the importance for

1 Convention No. 118 is not ratified by the UK to this date.

individuals to be able to file complaints to a Court such as the European Court on Human Rights, where individual complaints are possible and enforcement procedures do exist, which unfortunately is not the case to a significant extent at the ILO. However, the importance of asking the State to justify its actions regarding equal treatment in the field of social security, as done by this ILO-Convention, remains and cannot be substituted by becoming a party to other human rights treaties.

Another issue discussed was whether assistance to asylum seekers should be lower than social assistance of residents or if there is a social security minimum in the sense of art. 9 ICESCR. The participants agreed that the minimum paid to asylum-seekers should be as much as residents and nationals would get, plus housing benefits. Regarding the UK, the government should re-establish the standard that existed before 1996, although it can be complimented on providing several non-contributory benefits for individuals staying in the UK for a certain amount of time.

Strong interest was shown in the work of the Self Employed Women's Association (SEWA) and in the prominent role women play in India. One participant asked what would be a possible motivation for informal workers to enter the formal sector. Another participant wondered whether SEWA is receiving subsidies or whether they insure the social security risks by themselves. Subsidies should not be viewed negatively, though it would be easier to transfer the system built up by SEWA if it does not rely on subsidies.

Attention was also drawn to the target set by SEWA to achieve full employment, income security and social security. The question was if this should be achieved with the help of the government. Another concern was if SEWA also addresses the issue of maternity rights, as those had not been dealt with in the presentation. In addition, a participant requested an illustration of the term 'integrated approach' by SEWA. Furthermore, SEWA was asked for its minimum demand on the state to implement micro-insurance-scheme welfare boards.

Addressing the questions of the participants, it was emphasised that the informal economy in India is growing fast, which increases the importance of extending social security systems. Welfare boards and working in this area can be named as examples in this context. However, SEWA is critical of these institutions since they discriminate against women; specific needs of women are not addressed. Furthermore, the health systems introduced by the government are dysfunctional as subsidies help the rich rather than the poor. Yet, SEWA does not work only by itself, the connection to the government is particularly important, particularly at the local level where access to government schemes for individuals has to be provided. At the same time the government must be enabled to reach the poor. There have been cases in which the government realised its important role in satisfying basic needs, but was not able to access poorer groups. Childcare in SEWA, for example, is linked to the state childcare system in order to help the state system reach local areas that were not reached before. In this context communication between politicians and the 'grass-root level' was strongly encouraged. The second national labour commission took a big step forward by creating a prototype system, in which social security is given to every individual. However, the government changed before this system could be implemented. With regard to maternity needs, the India Maternity Act includes only employed women. Therefore, SEWA created a 'micro-insurance' program dealing with maternity needs of women that are unemployed or employed in the informal sector. It was also noted that while SEWA undertakes significant capacity building, the importance of 'hand holding' should not be underestimated, given the difficulty of explaining and advancing security systems. Research in the area of social security is also an integral part of SEWA.

Another participant raised the issue of protection of assets that the self-employed rely upon for earning income. In such cases, there is no strong distinction between labour and capital. In response, a member of the ILO recommended focusing not only on the ILO Convention No. 102, but also the Declaration of Philadelphia, which takes a wide approach and is the central part of the ILO system for dealing with social security. While there has been a discussion between economists and the World Bank about the sustainability of micro insurance schemes, which was questioned, it was pointed out that this system is supported by the ILO. Nevertheless, in the case of SEWA, the linkage to the government is of extreme importance as the concept of micro-insurance might not have been accepted without subsidies.

This session was closed by some deliberations on a possible Draft General Comment on art. 9. A participant wondered whether a draft should give a definition on social security and whether it should refer to the work of the ILO. It was proposed to utilise the Declaration of Philadelphia for a definition, as ILO Convention No. 102 is only a technical instrument applying this definition. Taking a comprehensive approach from a human rights perspective, participants emphasised the importance of linking the right to social security to other rights, such as the right to housing and the right to water. Furthermore, not only the state but also other institutions were considered to be important in giving access to social security schemes and benefits. Therefore, the question whether those actors need to be recognised in a General Comment should be considered carefully when drafting a General Comment on art. 9.

Session 5: Social Security Models

The presentation by *Peter Bakvis* on the topic 'Social Security Models and the Neo-Liberal Challenge' was followed by a comment from *Warren McGillivray*.

The commentator first addressed the proposed privatisation of social security pensions in the USA. In particular, he felt that the scheme was problematic since the administration would be very expensive as people pay contributions into their accounts every single month. Furthermore, billions of dollars will go into the financial market and participants would see huge amounts of money in their accounts, but these assets would probably decline in value as soon as large numbers of people retire and start selling their assets.

The next issue was the low number of ratifications of the ILO Convention No. 102. From the commentator's point of view, the low number of ratifications should not be overemphasised. Emphasis should rather be placed on the fact that ILO Convention No. 102 provides important guidelines for all states. The Convention was adopted in the 1950s and, following the *Zeitgeist* of that decade, provides for a uniform standard for all countries, which makes it inappropriate for the labour forces in many developing countries today. Addressing the defined benefit schemes mentioned in the previous presentation, the commentator stated that the failure of many schemes in developing countries was due to massive macroeconomic mismanagement. Failures in health care and education can also be cited as examples. It was impossible for social security systems to function under such conditions. In the 1960s, the Bismarckian social security system was transplanted into developing countries which were expected to have formal employment at the levels of industrialised countries by the end of the century. However, most developing states have not reached these levels and, consequently, a different social security system is needed.

ILO Convention No. 102 has come under strong criticism for a number of reasons. Nevertheless, considering the replacement rate of 40 per cent which it specifies, and the problems faced by many western countries, for example Germany, with their much higher replacement rates, one has to admit that while ILO Convention No. 102 might be old, it is not outdated, and can even be a useful guide for developed countries. Moreover, it might be a useful source for a General Comment on art. 9 ICESCR.

The ensuing discussion in this session mainly dealt with the role ILO Convention No. 102, the World Bank's three pillar approach and its recent developments, and the role the Bismarckian social security system should play in the drafting process of a General Comment on social security. In addition, the importance of policy coherence was emphasised.

The positive and negative aspects of ILO Convention No. 102 were initially discussed. A representative of the ILO confirmed that the ILO Convention No. 102 is extremely useful in daily work. As an example, Jordan is about to ratify the ILO Convention No. 102 and is consequently reforming its system. One should also pay attention to the fact that the ILO is trying to complement the ILO Convention No. 102 with the Recommendation of 2001. In the case of Mexico, for example, an agreement with the ILO was reached to analyse the situation in Mexico first and then make proposals for necessary reforms.

A participant wondered what kind of replacement rate could be considered appropriate, as ILO Convention No. 102 seems to be complicated on this issue. This was rejected by an ILO representative who argued that regardless of whatever opinion one might have concerning the precise replacement rate of the ILO Convention No. 102, one has to admit that very thorough technical work has been done. Although ILO Convention No. 102 provides a retirement pension minimum replacement rate of 40 per cent, Germany was criticised for falling below the rate of 45 per cent. Additionally, the replacement rate might be a problem in low-income countries.

In this context, another participant drew attention to the fact that many isolated pensioners starve in Germany as their pensions do not suffice for them to be taken care of properly, especially in cases of dependency. Therefore, this is not only a problem which developing countries have to face. The situation might be even better in those countries, as family bonds are generally closer.

A participant remarked that – besides all criticism regarding ILO Convention No. 102 – it should not be forgotten that the ILO's philosophy is progressive and that gradual implementation is foreseen which is necessary to achieve full coverage.

Addressing the presentation 'Social Security Models and the Neo-Liberal Challenge', a participant asked for further clarification of the key theses at the end of the presentation, which described reforms needed to improve the system. A second question was what concrete steps should be taken in the presenter's opinion and whether he had an idea who the winners of the Bush plan might be. With regard to the situation immediately before Roosevelt's 'New Deal', the question arose as to whether it is an option to revert to this situation or if one should rather find a new way in terms of investing in bonds and shares. Another question concerned the possible consequences of employees contributing to the pension scheme without the prospect of receiving a pension themselves, which leads to the question whether non-contributory or tax-financed systems might be the only way of financing social security systems. Underlining the importance of tripartism, the participant was curious to learn about the experience of the ILO with regard to ILO Convention No. 102 and possible recommendations for drafting a General Comment. Finally the issue of alternatives to the Bismarckian approach was addressed.

In response, it was said that old age poverty in the United States is also a problem of winners and losers in the financial market. According to analyses of the bond market, people tend to sell their assets at the same time, which puts a strain on the market.

The biggest concern is that pensioners might lose by investing in their accounts. It was underlined that such a kind of old-age poverty would not be acceptable anymore in the United States. If people invest unwisely and lose their savings, the State will have to step in and finally the population in general will be the biggest loser. A return to the New Deal was not considered realistic; the participant rather expected the State to accept that people fall into poverty. In his eyes the opinion of the US administration was that people realise the existence of risks as a libertarian consequence and, therefore, will act rationally and invest safely.

The same participant added that while tax-based contributions work in many countries, strong tax incentives for voluntary savings could be a good proposition in this context. Trade unions might also feel comfortable with tax-based systems. As it is already a challenge to enunciate basic principles, one needs to face the concern that coverage might not match ILO Convention No. 102. The development in Slovenia can be viewed as a positive example. It considered the World Bank's proposals too costly and decided to introduce a third pillar, consisting of voluntary savings with tax incentives. This result was influenced by strong trade unions which refused to accept privatisation. Nowadays, it is the healthiest of the transition countries. With regard to countries such as ex-Yugoslavia, which are facing a lack of contributions but view a more effective working administration as a major priority, the World Bank should step in and provide long-term loans.

Dealing with the issue of financing social security systems, a participant drew attention to the fact that we live in a situation of a 'demographic time bomb'. In this context the concern was addressed that in European countries people are not willing to pay contributions due to the fact that people were forced into compulsory social security systems. Additionally, emphasis was put on the universal means-tested and tax-financed social assistance scheme in the UK which provides for benefits if pensions are too low and do not even reach the subsistence level. It was also said that a similar system can be found in Chile where a minimum guarantee for existence is given. For those falling under this level, means-tested benefits are provided. Moreover, a guarantee of income supplement exists in other countries as well. It might be a good idea for countries without such a minimum guarantee to establish one.

The next point of discussion was the role of the World Bank and the issue of policy coherence, particularly with regard to the work of the ILO. One participant called to mind that the social protection department of the World Bank basically takes care of pensions. Interaction between different departments does not occur, as they do not provide for a uniform system. In contrast to the organisation of the World Bank a lot of interaction between the different branches of the ILO takes place. Because of the questionable success of the three-pillar model, the World Bank is more open to other approaches and for dialogues with other institutions today. Although co-operation with the World Bank might be easier, problems arise when trying to define uniform values for the ILO and the World Bank. It was suggested to wait for a coming report on the work and impact of the World Bank. It could raise awareness of the importance of social as well as economic development.

With regard to the three-pillar model of the World Bank, opinions varied. Some thought it ambiguous since the key issue is the size of the pillars and the creation of a well-functioning social security system while others found the three-pillar approach interesting. It might overcome some of the problems, as it is a public scheme where the market comes in. Interest was also shown in the Singapore model - a system operated completely via the financial market - and the tendency in China of moving away from the Bismarckian system towards a more individualised system. Others strongly criticised the World Bank's three-pillar approach as it has not proven to work in practice. Indeed some states would prefer to move away from this approach but as this is not possible, one has to deal with it.

The discussion then focused on the change of the World Bank in official discourse. Meetings with the World Bank now take place, where its approach is discussed and suggestions for changes are made. A specific World Bank pension model no longer exists. The World Bank seems to be open to new approaches, which is revealed by discussions about a five-pillar system consisting of the 'three-pillar' model, a 'zero-pillar' with tax-financed social assistance and a 'fifth pillar' addressing the issue of co-operation. It was observed that the World Bank's pension reforms have not achieved the objectives, but instead sometimes created new problems. The need to change the World Bank's policy with regard to social security was affirmed by many participants.

While the importance from an ideological point of view of having one standard for all countries is crucial it was questioned whether such an approach was realisable. The transfer of the Bismarckian model to developing countries was the wrong starting point, but the same applied for the World Bank's approach. Therefore, one has to look very closely at whether approaches are operable for all countries. It is of major importance to refrain from 'giving one remedy for all', especially since the International Labour Conference in 2001 emphasised that more than just one model exists.

With regard to the failure of the Bismarckian model in developing countries, the question was brought up why it took more than 40 years to realise that the model was not working. This was denied, but it was conceded that perhaps until the end of the 1970s, people were confident that it would work eventually, but then structural adjustment programmes and stagflation began. Eventually, in the 1980s some countries started to change their social security systems.

Stressing that there are different ways of shaping social security systems, the participation-model used by the ILO was introduced. This means that the ILO works closely with countries trying to develop a system which is able to satisfy the needs of a particular country. This participation model is supported by the Recommendation of 2001, which clearly states that ILO Convention No. 102 does not promote a specific model and stresses the flexibility of ILO Convention No. 102. Another reason for its flexibility is the tripartite structure of the ILO. Therefore the ILO is extremely strong in its articulation of relevant principles, but flexible in their implementation.

Some final considerations were made about the influence of this session on a General Comment on the right to social security. Regarding the question as to whether the CESCR should provide one particular model or rather take the ILO approach of not providing any specific model, the majority of the participants believed that one model for all countries cannot work, as each state is different and has its own needs. Nevertheless emphasis was put on the fact that social security needs to comprise social assistance, social insurance, and private or public schemes. With regard to social security systems, a list of principles such as adequacy, security of pensions, transparency, efficient management and participation of social partners seemed to be of particular importance. Concerning the question of whether the government should be responsible for contribution collection, it was emphasised that although neo-liberals are diminishing the role of the state, it is important to realise that the role of the state is to guarantee, regulate and to administer its social security scheme.

Session 6: Non-Retrogression and Right to Social Security

The Chair person introduced the session 'Non-retrogression and Right to Social Security' by quoting par. 32 of the General Comment on the Right to Health which contains the presumption against non-retrogression in the field of economic, social and cultural rights.[2] The presentation on the topic 'Evaluating Reforms in Social Security Protections' by *Warren McGillivray* was followed by a comment on the topic 'Judicial Review of Retrogression in Social Security Rights' by *Malcolm Langford*.

Langford enumerated some of the most pressing issues noting that there was a tendency to concentrate on the average or general need of people for social security instead of looking at how reforms will deal with those who cannot make significant or any contributions, their impact on women and families and whether the reform will entrench discrimination.

He noted that it is difficult for courts to deal with all these issues in the context of potentially retrogressive reforms and in some countries independent parliamentary committees were established to review such proposals, e.g., in Finland. But courts still had a role to play in setting the parameters for reform and ensuring the protection of social rights for the most vulnerable and often under-represented groups. The most difficult issue is how the judiciary should deal with the issue of resources but he noted his research which showed how a number of courts had taken a nuanced and flexible approach to the issue of resources in human rights cases and essentially deployed four criteria - the seriousness of the violation, the strength of the relevant legal obligation of the state, the complicity of the government in the violation and the potential cost to the state – in determining to what degree they would interfere with the government's decision.

In the context of non-retrogression, one possible approach that could be taken by the courts is to concentrate on guaranteeing a minimum level of social security. This would assure that retrogressive steps do not lead to social security benefits falling below a level essential for survival. Another approach is legal certainty where a court recognises that decisions are made on the basis of expected benefits. For example, if family or maternity benefits are curtailed, then individuals and families must be given reasonable time to adjust to a new social reality since they may have made decisions on starting or expanding a family on the basis of available social security. In this context the commentator referred to a case where the Hungarian court stopped a social security reform on the basis of legal certainty. He also pointed out the importance of a transparent decision-making process and

[2] The paragraph reads: 'As with all other rights in the Covenant, there is a strong presumption that retrogressive measures taken in relation to the right to health are not permissible. If any deliberately retrogressive measures are taken, the State party has the burden of proving that they have been introduced after the most careful consideration of all alternatives and that they are duly justified by reference to the totality of the rights provided for in the Covenant in the context of the full use of the State party's maximum available resources'.

access to documents, another two areas where courts could potentially assist affected parties confront potentially harmful reforms.

The relevance of discrimination with regard to retrogressive measures was also emphasised. This was underlined with a decision of a Canadian court which dealt with a discriminatory reduction of social security benefits for people under the age of 30. Nevertheless, the slight majority of the court dismissed the case. Another important issue, which should be included into the court's considerations, is the duration of cut-backs, i.e. whether they are permanent or temporary. Additionally the commentator considered justification of retrogressive measures as an issue of particular importance. He pointed out that cutbacks might be justified, e.g. by a lack of resources or by the principle of burden sharing, but in other cases reforms may not meet the reasonableness standard.

Furthermore, he drew attention to the fact that social security systems were not introduced in 'boom years', as it was often maintained. Social security systems were often introduced in a time of crisis.

In the discussion, retrogression was classified as a difficult issue. The question of time was seen as important, particularly concerning pension systems, where regulations are made at one point of time, but might not even apply in the future. Emphasis was placed on the importance of gradual changes, and participants confirmed that the political key issue was the ageing of the population. Although some reforms might be simple others might be very complicated. For example, the major reform by Margaret Thatcher was mentioned, which had far-reaching and firstly unnoticed implications in the 1980s, almost destroyed the whole system. Therefore, small reforms might have far reaching implications, as well.

Concerning the issue of permanent or temporary reforms, a participant remarked that it is necessary to find a system that can persist for a longer period. Too many reforms can also destroy confidence, but confidence of the beneficiaries is essential for an effective social security system.

The question of non-retrogression and distribution was then addressed. A major difficulty in dealing with the issue of non-retrogression is that through a reduction of a country's standards, a higher level of equality might be reached. It is also questionable which priorities should be set and how they can be balanced. Governments should at least be forced to justify differentiation between groups and to create a plan of action for excluded groups. Concerning non-retrogression it is remarkable that according to Equador's constitution the money spent on health care has to grow with the GDP, which make it impossible to move backwards.

Next, the problem of limits of democracy was brought up. A participant claimed that judges are working on the basis of legal certainty. They are not held responsible for their judgments, whereas the government is. Another participant disagreed and took the view that the government of the day is not held responsible, either, because the next government will pick up the pieces. Regarding the issue of democracy and responsibility of governments, it was stressed that governments have to deal with growing numbers of pensioners voting and therefore can be held responsible for their decisions, including reforms of the pension systems.

In this context it was pointed out that although democracy is based on majority rule, vulnerable groups regarding social security are – at least in most cases – in the minority, and therefore a constitutional duty of protection exists. It was criticised that most countries adopt the World Bank's policy as their own, and consequently the needs of vulnerable groups are not sufficiently taken into account.

In relation to availability of resources, it is sometimes hard to grasp the logic of the defence. While no resources seem to be available at all, governments suddenly procure resources for other issues, e.g., the cases like the Asian tsunami, Germany, was able to provide millions of euros. But it was countered that in the case of the tsunami or other emergency cases one has to outlay funds only on one occasion, whereas a decision of a country to spend more on social security is a commitment for a long period of time.

The progressive improvement clause in Art. 12(3) European Social Charter was subsequently brought up. The system has to be steadily improved, and therefore includes a principle of non-retrogression. However, the principle of equality must also be taken into account. The European Committee of Social Rights has developed criteria to help to deal with the situation of retrogression. In some cases, states even refrained from regression because of their obligations under art. 12. The question remained open if the principle of progressive realisation still applies, even if a state meets the target set in art. 12(2) ESC (three out of nine pillars).

Another participant wondered how one can connect the political and legal approaches. If individuals claim a right to social security before a court how far-reaching could decisions possibly be? In this context it was stressed that generally courts are very cautious, but still try to set standards. Another participant added that in the UK it is difficult for judges to intervene in politics. In the decision concerning asylum seekers in the UK, for example, where judges stated that measures taken by the government were unlawful, the government decided to proceed against this ruling. The reasoning of the judge in this decision is interesting. About 800 cases already existed on this issue, so the judge held that the issues raised in the case affected not only a few individuals, but many persons, which gives the case a particular importance. In this case, the number of asylum seekers living on the streets was submitted to the court and this helped influence the outcome of the case. Although decisions like these are unusual for judges in Great Britain, they were obliged to take note of UK's obligations under art. 3 of the European Convention on Human Rights. Another participant suggested leaving policy choices to the parliament and to limit the discretion of judges to a test of reasonableness. One needs to trust that democracy is going to bring a satisfying result at some point in the future. Stressing the existence of a bottom line for each right, it was questioned by one participant whether a human rights treaty body should only concentrate on the bottom line or if it needs to focus on other standards as well.

Session 7: Debate: Defining and Implementing the Right to Social Security

The final debate was accentuated by the so-called 'hidden agenda' of this workshop: the drafting of the General Comment on the right to social security. There was consensus on the importance of adopting a General Comment and the ensuing discussion suggested both aspects for inclusion as well as possible risks and unintended side effects that need to be taken into account:

The idea of human dignity, as it is a part of every human right and creates their inalienable nature, had to be considered as a starting point. Human dignity is the 'core' of social security, and defines a minimum level that has to be guaranteed and respected. Mere charity is not acceptable.

A General Comment should highlight the indivisibility of all human rights, and the interrelationship and interdependency of the right to social security and other rights. Emphasis was placed on the principles of non-discrimination, justice, equity and equality.

Access to social security for marginalised and vulnerable groups, including migrants, was considered to be of particular importance. One has to take women's greater need for social security benefits into account, particularly health care and maternity benefits, but also old-age benefits due to the higher life expectancy of women.

It was generally agreed that a comprehensive approach to the definition of social security should be taken, whereby it would include social assistance. The General Comment should take an individually based approach, but also strengthen solidarity. Collaboration with the ILO was suggested as ILO Convention No. 102 can serve as an inspiration for the drafting of a General Comment.

It was noted that more than one social security model exists, which means that there is significant scope for different policy choices. It was suggested that a country-by-country approach should be adopted, where the impact of the model is analysed across the various sectors, especially marginalised and disadvantaged groups, and short, medium and long term effects are taken into consideration. Concerning progressive realisation and retrogressive steps, it was suggested that the burden of proof should be shifted to the state to demonstrate that their actions are consistent with the right to social security. In cases of privatisation, States have to be held responsible rather than relieved from their obligations.

Democracy was seen as important with regard to the implementation of social security through 'law, policy and strategies'. Transparency, accountability, proper administration, credibility and a coherent social security system are essential for the sustainable realisation of the right. The variety of cultural backgrounds and differences in family structures throughout the world also calls for a flexible approach when implementing this right. There is a need to offer people appropriate choices.

Problems might arise for poor countries who lack the means to fulfil the minimum content. Nevertheless, even those countries have to stop interfering with the right to social security.

Although justiciability of social rights is often questioned, participants confirmed that certain aspects of the right have to be, and are, justiciable. The inclusion of obligations for non-state actors though is considered as very problematic for states to accept.

Finally, it was conceded that problems remain, such as a definition of the right to social security and its normative content. Nevertheless, the '–ilities', such as affordability, accessibility, accountability, quality, equality etc, non-retrogression, the core content, the capacity of states, minimum standards, indicators and benchmarks, possible violations and the responsibility of the States have to be addressed in a General Comment on the right to social security.

Annex: List of Participants

Erfried Adam, Director, Friedrich Ebert Foundation, Geneva, Switzerland

Valentin Aichele, Legal Advisor, German Institute for Human Rights, Berlin

Peter Bakvis, Director, ICFTU / Global Unions, Washington Office, USA

Jochen von Bernstorff, Desk Officer Human Rights Division, German Federal Foreign Office, Berlin

Heiner Bielefeldt, Director, German Institute for Human Rights, Berlin

Alexia Bierweiler, Senior Research Assistant, University of Mannheim

Helen Bolderson, Former Reader in Social Policy, School of Universal Studies, Brunel University, Uxbridge, England

Wolfgang Heller, Director, International Labour Organization, Berlin

Malcolm Langford, Senior Legal Officer, Centre on Housing Rights & Evictions

Wieland Lehnert, Assessor, Legal Trainee

Sandra Liebenberg, Professor of Law, University of Stellenbosch, South Africa

Germán López Morales, Co-ordinator, Social Security Team, International Labour Standards Department, ILO, Geneva, Switzerland

Warren R. McGillivray, Policy Associate, Caledon Institute of Social Policy, Ferney-Voltaire, France

Katharina Müller, Economist, German Development Institute, Bonn

Angelika Nußberger, Professor of Law, University of Cologne, and member of the ILO Committee of Experts

Sabrina Regent, Legal Counsellor, Social Security Policy and Development Branch, International Labour Organization, Geneva, Switzerland

Emmanuel Reynaud, Senior adviser on the Informal Economy, Social Protection Sector, at the International Labour Office (ILO) in Geneva

Eibe Riedel, Professor of Comparative Public Law, European and International Law and Director, Institute of Medical Law, Public Health and Bioethics, University of Mannheim, and member of UN Committee on Economic, Social and Cultural Rights

Hanna Beate Schöpp-Schilling, Member of the UN Committee on the Elimination of Discrimination against Women (CEDAW)

Frauke L. Seidensticker, Deputy Director, German Institute for Human Rights, Berlin

Shalini Sinha, Self Employed Women's Association, Ahmedabad, India

Printing: Krips bv, Meppel
Binding: Stürtz, Würzburg